Fifteen Days in Paris

For Jerry
Hope you enjoy
exploring Paris with me
Jen xx :)

Hi Jenny,

Hope you enjoy exploring Paris with me.

Love, Mom

FIFTEEN DAYS IN PARIS

AND FIFTEEN YEARS TO WRITE ABOUT THEM

JON DAVEY

First published in Great Britain in 2025 by 526 Press,
52/6 Bath Street, Edinburgh EH15 1HF

Copyright © Jon Davey 2025
Photographs © Jon Davey 1976, 2010, 2011, 2012, 2013, 2015, 2020, 2022
Illustrations © Tom Morgan-Jones 2025
Foreword © Paul Lambie 2025

Jon Davey has asserted his right under the
Copyright, Designs and Patents Act 1988 to be
identified as the author of this work.

A CIP catalogue record for this book
is available from the British Library.

ISBN 978-1-0684279-0-9
EBOOK ISBN 978-1-0684279-1-6

Typeset in 11.5 / 13.5 pt Minion Pro by 526 Press
Printed and bound by The Amadeus Press

Contents

Foreword by Paul Lambie	ix
Introduction	1
A note about the photographs	7
Samedi 24 avril / 2010	11
Dimanche 25 avril / 2011	25
Lundi 26 avril / 2012	55
Mardi 27 avril / 2013	77
Mercredi 28 avril / 2014	107
Jeudi 29 avril / 2015	123
Vendredi 30 avril / 2016	145
Samedi 1 mai / 2017	159
Dimanche 2 mai / 2018	173
Lundi 3 mai / 2019	183
Mardi 4 mai / 2020	199
Mercredi 5 mai / 2021	231
Jeudi 6 mai / 2022	243
Vendredi 7 mai / 2023	259
Samedi 8 mai / 2024	273
Acknowledgements	285
List of photographs	287
Sources	291

For Mum, who loved France

Foreword

Jon and I share a love of the French word 'flâneur' – an aimless urban saunterer. It's possible 'aimless' is misleading. A flâneur's aimlessness is purposeful and so might be, despite their best intentions, an aim. A flâneur sallies out on the sort of sortie that couldn't be described as exploration on account of a definitive lack of a plan. The flâneur walks without defined intent, to amble through an urban landscape. Were they roaming by hill and glen they might be considered a rambler.

I'm rambling. Jon and I like the word flâneur, is the point.

I came out this morning for an aimless wander, with a flâneurial lack of intent, vaguely supposing I'd eventually find a coffee shop in which to sit and read the latter half of Jon's book about Paris and perhaps start writing this foreword. Maybe Jon's book is a book about struggling to write about Paris. A foreword that starts with a reflection about writing a foreword to a book about writing a book seems apposite.

Jon's book is also about the unique but complexly interconnected worlds we construct for ourselves through observation and experience.

Maybe this is a book about taking artistic risks? Have I tacked on a question mark for fear that an assertion or statement might be 'wrong'? You definitely won't read the same book I read. It's unlikely you'll read the first half alone in a wee cottage in a quiet fishing village on the Moray Firth and then the second half in

Staple, a raucous hipster bakery coffee house in Westgate, Kent, beside a counter stacked high with croissants and pain au chocolat. This is where my flâneuring led. The coffee is excellent.

Portishead 'Roads' plays through the coffee shop's ceiling speakers. On my laptop, on the table in front of me, Jon describes Avenue, Pont, Rue and I'm listening to 'Roads'. Portishead's 1994 *Dummy* is a near-perfect work of art. Jon questions the reality of perfection and I get his reluctance but this album settles like a weighted blanket on me and I feel complete and protected beneath its perfect harmonics. Avenues, bridges, roads.

The City of Light seems to have that comforting effect on Jon. His fifteen days have embedded a multidimensional mental meta map of the city's streets that he appears to be able to open and unfold across space and time at will. Sometimes it appears to happen against his will: Paris asserting itself into or over his Edinburgh life.

The ways that Paris calls out to him, calls him back and up and forward from unexpected places speaks to me of the relationship a person has with the world when their mind and all their senses are alive to the myriad overlapping ripples of consequence that wriggle outward from every act of artistic creativity. Jon sees art everywhere. He explores Paris like a detective looking for clues to solve a crime he's not even sure has been committed.

A woman in the queue of this Kent bakery, waiting patiently for coffee and croissants, has a Stravaig branded dryrobe. I'm five hundred miles from my seaside Edinburgh home in the Englandest of Englands and here's a Scots word I recognise. I know the Glasgow restaurant bar Stravaigin quite well, but I realise I don't know what the word means or why it would be relevant to the wild-swimming set. I pause my reading, google, and discover that 'stravaig' has almost the exact same meaning as 'flâneur' and in *Fifteen Days in Paris*, on my laptop screen beside the coffee that led me to Staple, obscured temporarily by the Google search results, Jon's just been wandering 'flâneur-like' along the Boulevard Beaumarchais.

This happens all too often. Coincidences. Alignments. Serendipity.

I find that the people I like to talk to call as I need to talk to them most. Or a neighbour will drop round with spare spices that they'd not use before the expiration date and could I use them? And then those spices are called for by a recipe in a cookbook I'd lifted off the shelf only because the spill from a hastily watered spider plant threatened to soak its spine.

Sometimes the déjà vu is 8k.

At any time I feel my life exists as a complex venn diagram of interlocking experiences.

Jon finds Parisian connections where he's left them, in places he's built for the purpose of reminding himself that his self and his story exist: annual reminders on Blip, recurring sporting fixtures, books and maps on his office shelf. But Paris won't be contained or controlled. Jon's Paris is an incurable virus that has taken hold of his imagination, forcing its host to replicate its DNA in a forever repeating fractal landscape of photography, art, music, friendships and love.

OR, Jon was just letting his mind wander while he put off writing this book.

I'm glad he didn't put it off for ever. I'm grateful for a tour of Jon's beloved city and for an introduction to artists, musicians and films I might never have otherwise encountered. *Emily in Paris* notwithstanding.

As you read, I'd encourage you to take Jon's approach, let your mind wander, get lost in his Paris, and see where you end up. I feel certain you'll enjoy travelling with him.

Paul Lambie
Edinburgh, March 2025

Introduction

The writer Geoff Dyer says that when he sits down to start a new book he writes a note for himself that reads, 'Write the book that only you could write.' Its purpose is to encourage him away from the doubt that can sneak in when you know that your book is a bit different. Odd. Misshapen. I only came across Geoff's tactic a few months ago, but I wish I'd known it earlier because I feel it has both liberated me and clarified things. Liberated in the sense of giving me the freedom, in the face of so much writing about Paris, to still produce my own book. And clarified in the sense of showing me how to go about it, writing about myself and about Paris as I explore each through the lens of the other.

Twenty years ago I'd been working in IT for twenty years. I'd started out writing computer code for the Scottish & Newcastle brewery and then moved to a bank. Married but without kids, I felt there had to be something more to the next twenty years than just waiting for my pension – so I quit. When colleagues asked what I was going to do, I said I was looking for something more creative. On my leaving card most people wished me luck in my search but one message said, 'See you back here in six months.' I laughed, but also wondered if that said more about them than me.

After a mid-life gap year I ended up studying photography at the then Stevenson College in Edinburgh, first on a six-month NQ and then on a two-year HND (Higher National Diploma). We were told there might be a trip to Paris later in the course. The college had to apply to the European Commission's Leonardo da Vinci programme for the funding every year, so it wasn't guaranteed.

I was one of forty HND students, divided into two classes. Most were in their twenties, although there were a few middle-aged ones like me, and even a couple of people in their sixties. Having made the decision to return to education, maybe we wanted to wring as much as we could out of the time and the college facilities. I and some of the other older students often stayed on after formal lectures were over to work in the studio or the darkroom when many of our younger peers had left. That said, one of the things I enjoyed most about the course was collaborating with other students of all ages. I remember one particular assignment in the studio working with Trish and Liz, one twenty years younger than me and the other twenty years older. There was also a big Eastern European cohort in the class and I became good friends with great people from Poland, Czechia, Slovakia and Latvia.

Our Paris trip was confirmed early in our second year, but by the time it came round I found I hadn't prepared for it at all. Looking back, I'm not quite sure why this was. Maybe it was just that I was busy doing coursework or maybe I didn't think it was important. I'm not what I would call well-travelled, but I'd been to several European countries, to North Africa and Mexico, and indeed to Paris, so maybe I just thought I'd take it in my stride. We knew we'd have to take photographs in Paris that would count towards a documentary project, but the idea I'd had wasn't working out. In any case, the net result was that I arrived in Paris with no agenda and my fifteen days there were allowed to unspool as they might. Later, though, I found my mind kept going back to the trip – kept wanting to find patterns and meaning and depth in the seemingly random routes I'd taken around the city. I'd been a longtime fan of Georges Perec and French cinema, but when I discovered the Paris-inspired writing of Ernest Hemingway, Walter Benjamin, Éric Hazan, Baudelaire and others, I found a new, retrospective context for my Parisian experiences.

The idea for a book came to me when I got back, but it wasn't in this form. Initially I wanted to make a book of photos. However, something else happened around that time too. In Paris, my friend Anita had told me about the photo-blogging platform Blipfoto. Blip's thing is that you post a photo every day, adding text if you want. Almost immediately I discovered that I wanted to write about things as well as photographing them, which kind of steered me away from doing a photo book about Paris, and towards . . . something else. At this time of writing my unbroken streak on Blip runs to more than five thousand days. An early slogan for the site was 'Save Your Life' – and I have. I can look through my Blip archive and see what I was doing and thinking on just about any day in the past fifteen years. It's less random than social media and *much* more reliable than my memory. I used my Blips to write about my progress with this book, or lack of it, and have asked for and received advice and help from the brilliant worldwide community of Blippers. In many ways this book wouldn't, and couldn't, have been written without Blipfoto.

As the realisation that I wanted to write about Paris and its meaning in my life more generally grew, so did my doubts. You might be familiar with the term 'imposter complex'? If not, let me just explain that it's something that can happen when low self-confidence creates the belief that you don't really belong in a particular field. It can happen in nine-to-five work but it's common in open-ended creative contexts where the success conditions aren't clear and being surrounded by gatekeepers can mess with how you judge your own work. For me, it just meant I couldn't get going. I'd start but then freeze up. In their book *Art & Fear* (yeah, I've read them all), David Bayles and Ted Orland describe how so many artists face doubts about their abilities.

Doubts which can stop them in their tracks, or even make them quit altogether. I didn't quit but I was very stuck for a very long time, until I came across another adage that showed a way forward: 'Make the problem the subject.'

Making the problem the subject gave me the third of the three strands that make up this book. The first strand is an account of my time in Paris in 2010, the fifteen days of the trip I took with my college classmates. You'll find as you go through that the days in the first week have more detail in them than the days in the second week. I suspect this is because, over several attempts to write about the trip, every time I was full of confidence and enthusiasm for the project at the start but by the second week doubts had crept in. I always had a good idea of where I went, though, so the maps of my wanderings that accompany the individual days are accurate.

The second strand is about a theme that I've come to believe is central to my personality and how I view the world: connection. Since childhood I've been drawn to seeing patterns in things and to find comfort and security in how everything knits together. I don't have an official diagnosis of any neuroatypicalness, but I've done some reading and some online tests and I'm comfortable in saying that there is an element of this in me. So the pattern created by spotting Paris popping up in my world since I was there has created its own narrative.

The third strand is the story of this book. How it began, how it changed, how it languished, how it was resurrected. When I decided to turn the spotlight on that element of the process, rather than hiding it, I thought that as well as helping me to get this damn thing across the finishing line, I might also help someone else who wants to make something and just can't seem to do it. I hope so anyway.

Introduction

A note about the photographs

Late in the process of creating this book I realised fully the implications of French privacy laws around the publication of photographs. Although there are other, competing rights, such as to the freedom of expression and public information, the 'droit d'image' gives everyone in France exclusive rights to their image and any commercial use that might be made of it. It's generally believed this doesn't cover people who are incidental to an image, who are not isolated as the main subject, but several of my favourite photos taken in Paris were candid shots of recognisable individuals. I took the decision, therefore, to leave them out and not run the risk of legal action.

In the images I have used, I've blurred some faces that, while not isolated as the main subject, might still be a little too clear. The pictures of people that remain are those of fellow students who were on the trip with me and who are happy to be included.

Copyright restrictions on using photographs of works of art for commercial purposes occasionally means I can only describe what I photographed, rather than show it.

Fifteen Days in Paris

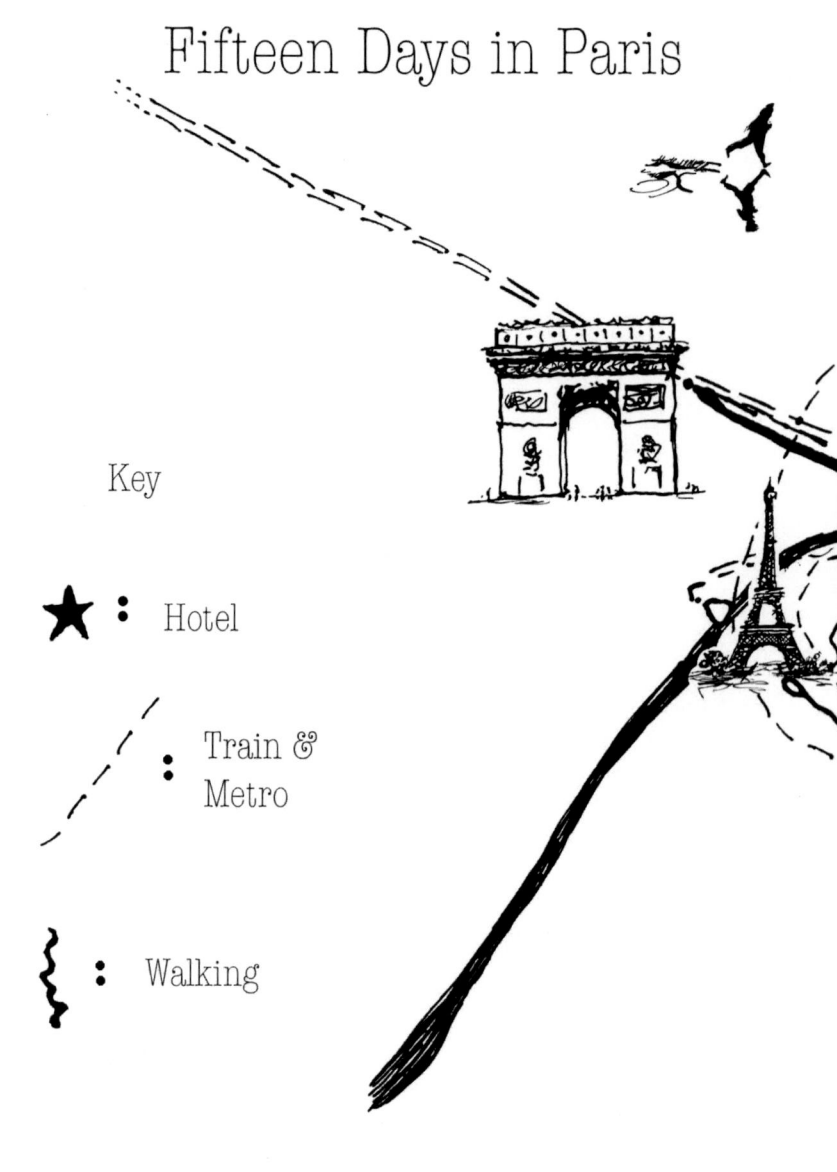

Key

★ : Hotel

⋮ : Train & Metro

〰 : Walking

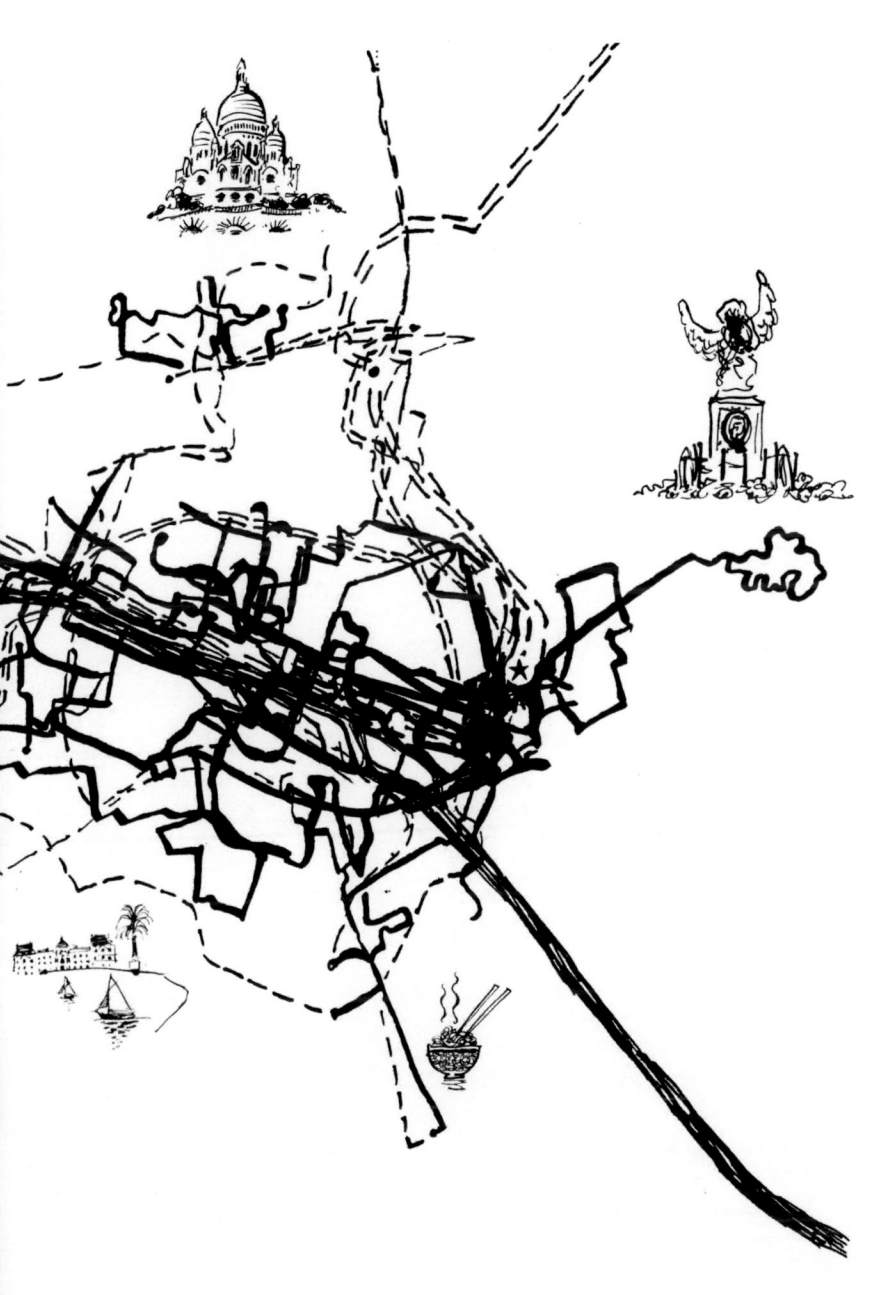

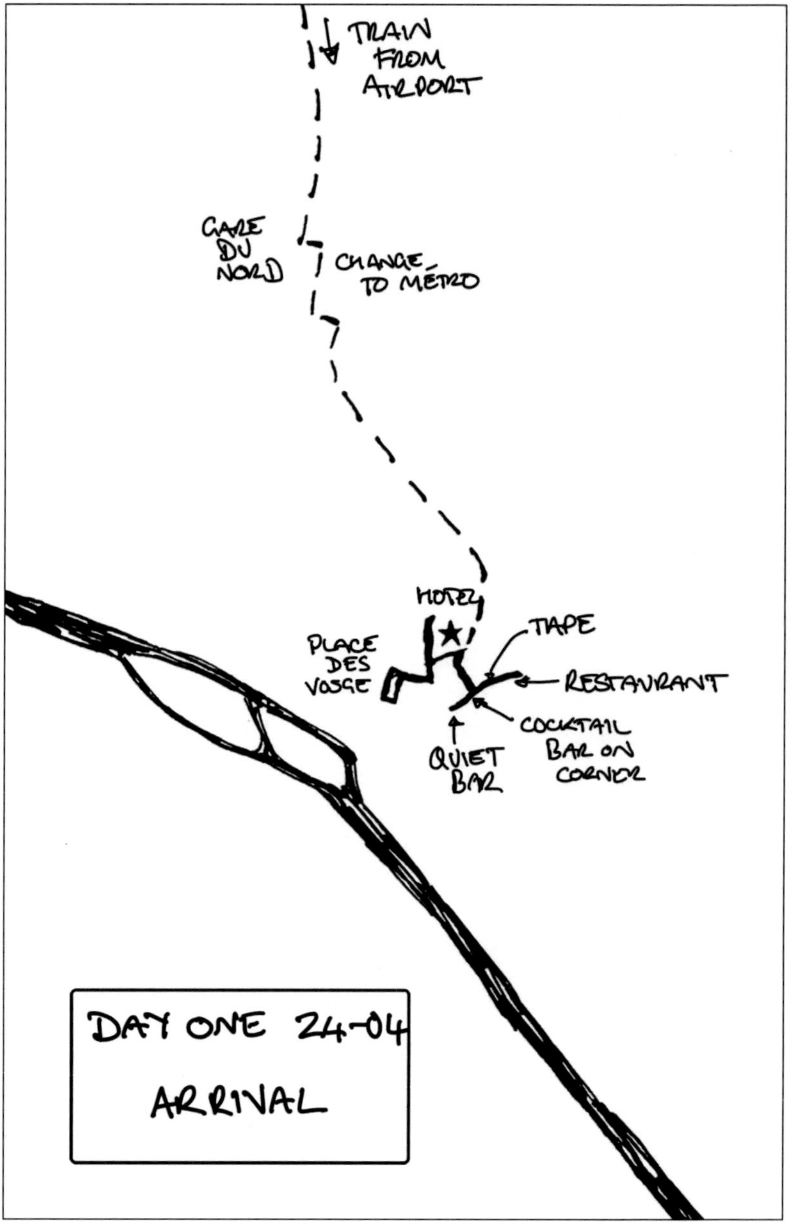
TRAIN FROM AIRPORT
GARE DU NORD
CHANGE TO MÉTRO
HOTEL
PLACE DES VOSGE
TAPE
RESTAURANT
COCKTAIL BAR ON CORNER
QUIET BAR
DAY ONE 24-04
ARRIVAL

Samedi 24 avril / 2010

We walked out of the shady narrow street into the bright open space of the Place des Vosges. The park in the middle of the square was packed. Over to one side, a violinist was playing, their music on a stand in front of them. There were circles of young people in bright summer clothes sitting on the grass at the centre of the park, eating, drinking and listening to music. One group was playing cards. There were families too, the adults sitting talking and young children running around, shouting and laughing. Under the shade of neatly trimmed small trees around the edges of the park, and more cautiously dressed, as if expecting the sun to go in at any moment, older people sat on benches. Some were in the midst of animated conversations while others were reading or watching the activity in front of them. So this was Paris! A world away from the dreary and chilly Edinburgh we had left that morning.

The prospect of a trip to Paris had been mentioned right at the beginning of our studies, in autumn 2008, and well over a year later here we were.

The college had prepared us with a weekly conversational French class. Nothing too ambitious but enough to be able to ask for directions, understand the reply, and to say 'I am a photography student from Edinburgh, please can I take your photograph?' The coursework element was a documentary module and three of us who shared an interest in football decided we should attempt a football-related project. We'd already succeeded in getting into top-level events in Edinburgh for photojournalism sports assignments, so we aimed high and decided we'd try and get behind-the-scenes access to the top football team in Paris – Paris Saint-Germain. We found someone to translate our email request, sent it off and waited for a response.

And waited.

Today it seems unsurprising that such a massive club didn't respond, but back then they didn't have Qatari money behind them and were in something of a crisis. They'd only just avoided relegation a couple of years earlier and had problems with a notoriously violent section of their support. Perhaps that was the reason we didn't get a reply. Even if our request had reached the right person in the club's media office, maybe they'd decided the last thing they wanted was three foreign student photographers hanging about. More likely, even a chaotic PSG just got too many requests like ours.

So we needed a Plan B. But weirdly, considering the size of the city, and the success of the national team in recent decades, Paris doesn't have a strong tradition of elite football. PSG itself was only founded in 1970 and as we looked around for alternatives there was a surprising lack of other teams. London has a dozen professional teams, with five in the Premier League back in 2010. Even Edinburgh has two teams who spend most of their time in the top Scottish division. It seemed strange to us that Paris only had room for one big team. At any rate, the best option seemed to be Red Star Football Club, even if they were down in the fourth tier of French football. They had a much longer history than PSG, having been founded by the same Jules Rimet who instigated the first World Cup and after whom the original trophy was named. They also had a strong connection with leftwing activism, which was a further point in their favour. But they too didn't reply to emails from three Edinburgh-based students.

We were just beginning to think the unthinkable – that we might have to start considering other, non-sporting options – when the volcano in Iceland with the long name erupted again (it had done it in the 1820s too). Which may sound like a non-sequitur but the ash cloud from Eyjafjallajökull spread east and south and led to the closure of airspace first over the UK and then over much of the rest of Europe too. The Saturday before our planned departure there were no flights operating and the whole trip hung in the balance.

The college decided that if there were no flights then we couldn't get there and the visit was therefore cancelled. I had always felt it was a bit too good to be true – a paid-for fortnight in Paris just to take photographs – so now here was the universe righting itself again.

Messages flew around between us students as we discussed what might be done. Could the college be persuaded to let us go by train instead, or even hire our own coach, always assuming we could find one at such short notice? We didn't hold out much hope, and moaned a bit about it online, but there seemed to be nothing that would sway the college authorities. They'd made their decision. So instead of working out a Plan B for our documentary project in Paris, it would have to be Plan C for a project at home in Edinburgh, just like the other students who'd been unable to make the Paris trip. I came up with ways to take advantage of the unexpected time to advance my other coursework, now that I wasn't going to have to leave it behind for two weeks.

Which is what I was thinking about the next morning when word came through that the decision had been reversed and the trip was back on, assuming flight restrictions, at that point fully lifted, weren't reimposed before Saturday morning.

So, it was all happening again.

Unless it wasn't.

There was still that proviso, that the trip depended on airspace remaining open.

Which is all to say that I really didn't prepare. Perhaps it was superstition, not wanting to tempt fate, or more pragmatically just not wanting to waste time – whatever the reason, I didn't do a lot of work researching Paris and what I might do with two weeks to spend there. Less even than if it had been a weekend city break, in which case I would almost certainly have looked out a few guidebooks and done a bit of googling to work out what to see.

When we gathered at Edinburgh airport I had only a vague idea that I would look for sport-related images and not follow any guidebook-driven itinerary of 'must-see' sights. Which is not to say I didn't carry a few non-sports thoughts in my head as I checked my bag in. I'd been to Paris before, after all, and I had a list of places that meant something to me. In no particular order there was the Musée de l'Armée at the Hôtel des Invalides, the Pont-Neuf, the Musée d'Orsay, Père Lachaise and Rue du Petit-Musc. The Musée de l'Armée, or more specifically the attic collection of fortification models, was something I still vividly remembered seeing on a family holiday in the 1970s. The Pont-Neuf was the setting for *Les Amants du Pont-Neuf*, which was and is one of my favourite films. The Musée d'Orsay is an obvious place to visit but I particularly wanted to see Whistler's *Arrangement in Grey and Black No. 1*, which I'd written about for a class assignment. Père Lachaise is also on many people's Paris list but, rather than paying homage to Oscar Wilde or Jim Morrison, I wanted to go and see Chopin's grave, because my wife Lorraine had written a radio play about the composer. And finally there was the very ordinary Rue du Petit-Musc, close to where we would be staying near the Bastille. Lorraine had briefly stayed in an attic apartment there when she was hitching across France, years before I met her, and I'd said I would try to pay it a visit.

Considering the tension in the build-up in the preceding week, the flight was uneventful and we reached Charles de Gaulle Airport on the northeastern edge of Paris in the early afternoon. It had the feel of a major hub airport, much like Heathrow; a whole order of magnitude bigger than Edinburgh's airport that we had left that morning, now tiny by comparison. Carrying our bags we boarded a train that took us through the northern suburbs towards the Gare du Nord.

My 'proper' camera was packed away in my rucksack and for some reason I didn't attempt to get it out to take any pictures on the journey into the city, or even use my smaller compact camera or my phone. Strange now to think I could arrive in a new city and take no immediate pictures. Was I too conscious of the finite capacity of my memory cards and a need to ration myself over the two weeks of our stay? If I was, then all I can say is it's all relative. The 20-exposure film I'd taken with me on that family trip in 1976 was a world away from a handful of CF cards that added up to several megabytes of storage and represented many hundreds of potential pictures. Just how many photographs did I imagine myself taking?

I've since dug out the pictures the 13-year-old me took in Paris. They're slides, which must have been taken with the Kodak Instamatic I got for Christmas in 1972. Although we were in Paris for three and a half days in October, from a Sunday teatime to a Thursday lunchtime, I took only thirteen pictures. On the Monday I took a couple of Notre-Dame and then two of the Eiffel Tower, including my favourite of the thirteen, presumably taken from a tourist boat on the river and showing a Métro train crossing the Pont de Bir-Hakeim. I then took one picture from the first level of the tower – I'm sure we walked up the stairs to get there – and two at the Hôtel des Invalides.

The next day I took three in Montmartre – one of Sacré-Cœur, one of the short funicular railway going up the hill, and one of the artists in the Place du Tertre – and then one from the Place de la Concorde, looking up the Champs-Élysées, and one close-up of the Arc de Triomphe. On Wednesday, despite visiting the Palais Garnier opera house and the Louvre, the only picture I took was of the toy yachts on the pond in front of the Luxembourg Palace. I'd like to think I'd take a better photograph today, and not just because I wouldn't have the technical limitations of the little camera I was using then. I'd take the shot from lower down,

Samedi 24 avril / 2010

looking across the surface of the water, and with one of the toy yachts in the foreground.

And that was it. The first five were at the end of a film I'd started on our summer holiday in Wales that year, so I was able to get those developed when we got home, but the rest stayed in the camera until the following August when I finished the roll on our summer holiday to the Netherlands. That meant I only got to see the rest of my Paris pictures ten months after I'd taken them.

Whatever the reason, I took no pictures on the RER train and none on the station concourse at Gare du Nord, where we got off to catch the Métro – Line 5 in the direction of Place d'Italie, at that point simply another place-name without any context. We only went as far as Bréguet-Sabin, one stop before Bastille. Rather like a school party, when we emerged we traipsed behind our two tutors as they led us up the wide Boulevard Richard-Lenoir and down a side street to the hotel that would be our base for the next fortnight. Two sides of a triangle, if anyone had looked at a map.

We checked in and sorted out our rooms. To make the most of our funding we were mostly sharing, two to a room. I was with my Czech friend Petr and, after dumping our stuff, the two of us headed straight back out again to explore the neighbourhood. It was a glorious afternoon and, largely following our noses, we crossed another of the broad boulevards that radiate out from the Bastille and walked down a side street which opened out into a beautiful old square at Place des Vosges.

I still didn't have my camera with me, which seems so odd now. Not just because there I was in Paris, a photography student in a (maybe *the*) city of photography, but also because since that trip I have become a long-term photoblogger. So, again, I'm not sure why I didn't take my camera out with me. Perhaps it was part of thinking I was not and didn't <u>want</u> to be a regular tourist, clicking away at everything, and that there would be plenty of time for more considered Photography, with a capital P, over the rest of my stay. I wasn't in the habit of taking pictures with my phone back then either, whether out of snobbery or frustration with the relatively poor quality of the pictures it took, so I don't even have any phone snaps of the square in the sunshine.

It was very warm that day and I just assumed it was the typical Parisian climate – a month or more ahead of Scotland. It was only on the Monday morning, when I bought a copy of *Le Parisien*, that I found out the weather that weekend had been exceptional and

Samedi 24 avril / 2010

the first really good weather of the year. So much so that it was worthy of a full-page feature in the paper, discussing how long the unseasonably warm temperatures were going to last and including short interviews with Parisians, asking them just what they had done in the beautiful weather.

As we wandered round the square we knew none of this. Paris on that sunny Saturday afternoon belonged in a different world from the Edinburgh we had left that morning – much more relaxed and communal. When the sun shines most places can't fail to look joyous and vibrant but it's funny the way that first impressions have such a lasting impact on our perceptions. In my late teens when I first went to university in Durham it was a cold, dry autumn, heading into a colder winter. So cold in fact that the River Wear froze solid in places and some people (not me) walked across the ice to get to lectures. The following autumn was mild but, while that year's cohort formed the view that Durham was a mild, damp place, to me it was still the cold and dry place it had been the year before, just briefly experiencing some uncharacteristic weather. This was despite the fact I was studying Geography and should have been more aware than most of the differences between weather and climate.

After some time in the park we looked round the rest of the square, with its covered arcades, its cafés and its shops. Petr bought a hat from a street stall and I got a small book of maps from a newspaper kiosk. It included information on public transport – how to get around – but there was no real indication of what we should see. We moved on, further into the Marais district we would come to know very well over the course of the fortnight. Many of the streets were closed off to cars – pedestrianised for the weekend as far as we could make out from the road signs. (Our French teacher back in college had done a good job.) Not wanting to go too far, we completed a sort of loop that took us back onto the southern side of Place des Vosges. We crossed the square again then walked up the Boulevard Beaumarchais, away from the Bastille roundabout, then found a mini supermarket and got a few things before wending back to the hotel.

In the foyer we met a fellow student who was heading out to join some others at a nearby restaurant, so we tagged along and the three of us squeezed in at the end of a large table with about a dozen people. There with our two lecturers, it still felt like a school trip as we ordered from the multilingual menu, all talking in English. Thinking back, apart from Petr, most of us around that table were Scottish. Our classmates from other countries, already well used to being in places where most people didn't speak their language, were noticeable by their absence. Did they not feel a need for a security blanket of familiar faces around them and were therefore much more comfortable doing their own thing that night? Maybe it was just a coincidence.

We latecomers had just placed our orders when a disagreement kicked off at the far end of the table. Something about the quality of the food. 'So bad it isn't worth paying for,' someone was shouting. It crossed my mind, as this was all going on, to wonder what they might be doing to our food back in the kitchen. I mean, I'd seen *Fight Club*. And the *Seinfeld* episode where George talks about the bouillabaisse at Bouchard's. But it looked okay when it turned up, and tasted good. An agreement was reached and some people left before we finished our food and settled up our share of the bill. The staff seemed satisfied with what had been paid but it hadn't been a pleasant first-night dining experience.

Outside we started looking for a bar where we could get a big enough table to fit us all in. The streets were busy and the temperature enhanced the feeling of being abroad. It wasn't often that the weather in Edinburgh was so warm after dark. We drifted along the Rue de la Roquette as the lights came on. Someone seemed to have turned up the volume, too. While the younger members of our group were looking for a lively Saturday night there were others (me) for whom a quiet drink was more the thing.

In the days immediately after returning from Paris I felt a bit depressed. There's always a letdown after a holiday, when you return to routine, but this was more. A kind of slump in mood I was familiar with in the form of post-show blues after putting on an amdram production. For weeks you meet up regularly with the same people and work together on a shared project. There are cast warm-ups and exercises designed to foster trust and team spirit, then the show comes round and for a few nights you're all focused on putting on the best performances possible. You wait in the wings, ready for your entrances and watch the same bits of scenes night after night, briefly audience rather than performer. Sometimes there are quick costume changes, when a particular cast member is ready in the wings to help you swap a jacket or a hat before you go back out on stage. After-show visits to the pub strengthen the bonds.
 And then it's done.
 The last round of applause has died away, the set has been struck, the cast party has finished in the early hours of the following morning, the hangover has receded. What has, for months, been 'rehearsal night' comes round and you don't need to go to the usual venue to hang out with the rest of the cast. Something feels off. That was what I was feeling in the first few days after I got home from Paris. I missed my phone pinging in the middle of the afternoon with messages asking where we were meeting that night to eat. Breakfast back home wasn't a communal affair, catching up with other members of the group and hearing what they'd seen and done the day before. Edinburgh, and I, felt very flat.
 That was the mood that first prompted me to want to produce some sort of book about the trip. A way of reliving the experience

and lifting my spirits. To start with the idea was just a set of photographs, adding to the small selection I had to choose for my documentary unit. I looked into printing options and daydreamed about self-publishing a book that might end up in a bookshop.

But in any case there wasn't time for distractions. There was coursework, not least the big project for the year, the Graded Unit, due at the end of the week after we got back, editing to be done and images to be printed. After that there was my Paris documentary selection and other assignments in the final term. For my fashion module I was going to photograph a series of outfits on a wedding guest theme, which needed sessions arranged in the studio and on location. Where was I getting the time to work on a book about the Paris trip?

And even when all the work was handed in there was the end-of-year exhibition to organise, which took us on into June. By then I knew I'd been accepted onto the BA course starting in September. This meant the summer felt like a break, a time to watch the World Cup and take pictures just for fun, rather than work on a new project. In the autumn new assignments came thick and fast and my Paris book was put on the shelf of future projects, something to do when I had more time.

In October, for the first time since the trip, I did something with a few of my Paris images. A group came together on the Flickr website and organised an exhibition in an Edinburgh tea shop. The café simply wanted some pictures for its walls and each person was to provide five or six images. It had potential to be eclectic, with no overarching theme.

Liberated from college constraints, I picked five of my Paris pictures to give a selective-colour treatment. Selective colour is probably most famous from its use in *Schindler's List*. The image is converted to black and white, with only an isolated detail left in colour, often a bold tint, like the young girl's red coat in the film.

Samedi 24 avril / 2010

It's the sort of technique people love to hate. It had been done thousands of times before, even then, but it hadn't been done by me. It turned out to be a useful lesson in not letting artistic snobbery get in the way of trying something different even if people say it's jumping on the latest photography bandwagon (see also: HDR or long exposures of moving water). Those people included myself, though, as internalised negativity can be just as damaging as external critique, and while I think I've now escaped it when it comes to my photography, it's been a tougher nut to crack in writing, and in particular in producing, my Paris book.

That busy Saturday night in April 2010 we went to a traditional-looking bar close to the Bastille monument. It wasn't rammed but only had small round tables and was a bit too staid and lacking in atmosphere, even for the quiet types, so after standing around for one drink we moved on to a cocktail bar on the corner of Rue de Lappe that had plush seats, large tables and big windows. It felt to me like we were more at the heart of things, watching the bustle outside, but it was still too quiet (and pricey) for some, so they pushed for us to move on again and look for somewhere livelier. They certainly found it at Tape, a tiny, chaotic bar with loud music and staff who had a haphazard way with drinks measures. The guys behind the bar behaved more like they were throwing a party than running a business. The same order cost randomly different amounts from one round to the next but at least it was all cheap. So we stayed a while. Tomorrow it would be time to take out our cameras and start photographing Paris properly.

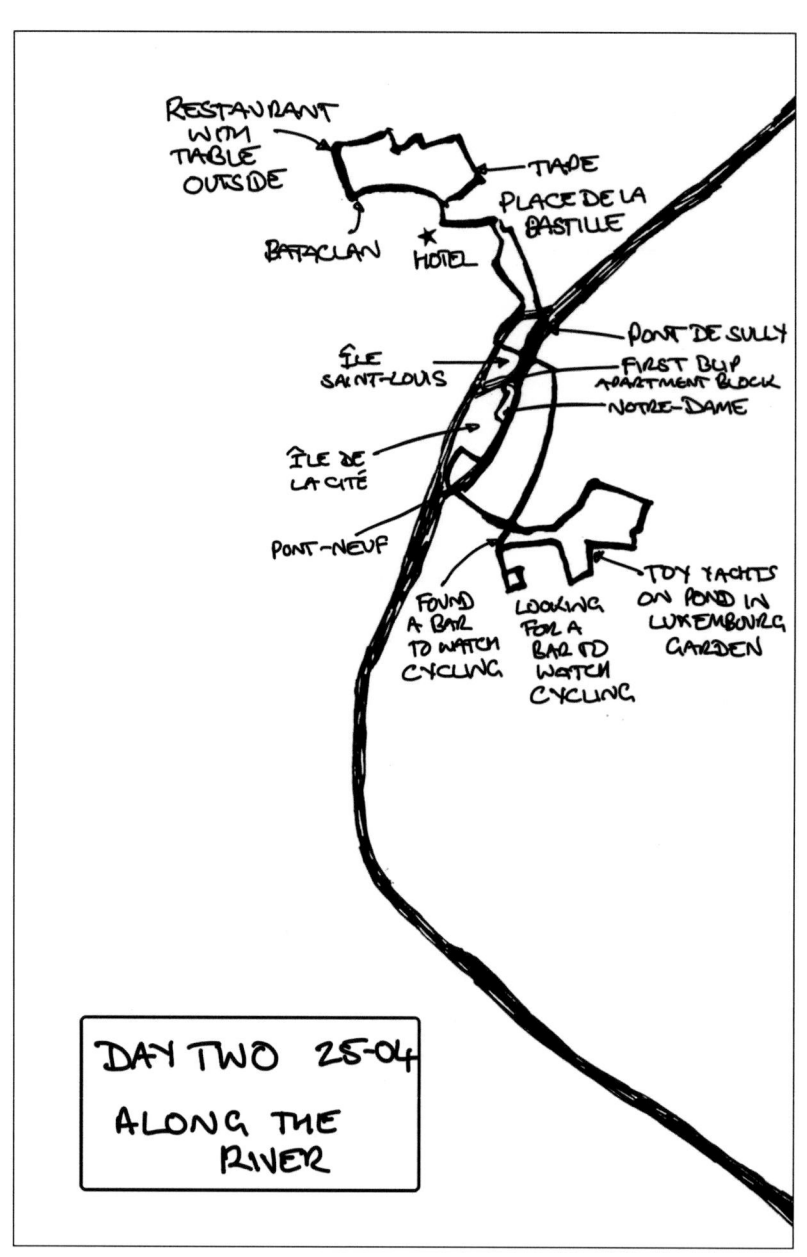

Dimanche 25 avril / 2011

Day two, and our first full day in Paris didn't start off quite as warm as the day before. It was established that breakfast would be a time to touch base with our tutors, discuss progress with our documentary projects, our plans for the day and, I suppose, check that no one had gone missing.

Without any specific ideas of places to go Petr and I decided to head for the river and then see where that might lead us. Maybe we'd try and find a bar or café later in the afternoon that was showing the cycling. One of the classics in the pro cycling calendar was taking place that day – Liège–Bastogne–Liège – and Petr wanted to see how in-form Czech cyclist Roman Kreuziger would get on after his top-five finish in the Amstel Gold Race the previous weekend. It sounded like a good plan. What could be more French than an hour or two in a Parisian café watching cycling on TV?

But that was for later in the day. To start with we walked the short distance to the roundabout at the Place de la Bastille and then headed down the tree-lined Boulevard Henri IV. I thought of Daniel Auteuil, who played Henri in the heavily fictionalised film *La Reine Margot*, based on Alexandre Dumas's 1845 novel. The film was an extravagant costume drama, full of scandal and intrigue, which I first saw on the big screen in Edinburgh's Filmhouse in the mid 1990s. I remembered being swept along by the story as it showed the machinations of Catherine de' Medici, wife of Henri II, during the religious turmoil of sixteenth-century France. To strengthen her position she arranged the marriage of her daughter, Marguerite, the queen of the film's title, to Henri of Navarre. The wedding, on 18 August 1572, brought many Huguenots – Calvinist Protestants and supporters of Henri – to predominantly Catholic Paris. Less than a week later thousands of Huguenots were killed in what became known as the St Bartholomew's Day massacre. All graphically portrayed in the film.

The boulevard led straight to the river and continued over it on the Pont de Sully. The wide bridge crosses the upstream end of the Île Saint-Louis, the smaller of the two river islands at the heart of Paris. Rather than immediately crossing the other section of the bridge over to the Left Bank we branched off along the southern side of the island. Unlike Île de la Cité, with its dramatic public buildings, Île Saint-Louis is modest, filled with neatly ordered streets of apartment blocks. They occupy one of the prime locations in the city and have property prices to match. We walked past the Polish Library in Paris, closed on a Sunday morning but advertising an exhibition about Chopin.

My wife's radio play, *A Rose for Chopin*, is a fictionalised account of Chopin's visit to Scotland as he sought refuge from various problems, not least of which was the disruption in Paris during 1848's 'Year of Revolution'. It's easy to think that France got rid of its monarchy in the tumult of the French Revolution, sparked by the storming of the Bastille in July 1789, but like tipping over Jerry Seinfeld's proverbial Coke machine it actually took several attempts to get rid of the kings and queens for good. Louis XVI was executed on the guillotine in what was briefly known as the Place de la Revolution (now Place de la Concorde) in January 1793 and his queen, Marie Antoinette, met the same fate in October of the same year. However, a little over two decades later the monarchy was restored, briefly while Napoleon was in exile on Elba and then more permanently after his defeat at Waterloo in 1815. In 1830 the more liberal constitutional monarchy of Louis Philippe replaced that of the unpopular Charles X and then the 'February Revolution' of 1848 replaced Louis Philippe with the Second Republic. Much of the aristocracy in Paris fled, including many of Chopin's wealthy students, and concerts came to a halt. Chopin, with his health failing, lost his livelihood. He was invited to London by two Scottish sisters – Jane Stirling and Katherine Erskine – and crossed the channel in April 1848. He would spend three months in London and then four more in Scotland before returning to Paris, where he stayed until his death the following October.

Chopin had done well to leave Paris when he did. In the weeks following his departure the radical reforms introduced by the new Second Republic were increasingly opposed by reactionary forces, leading to civil unrest. The working class who had driven the February Revolution increasingly felt that their ideals were being betrayed and undermined, and things came to a head in June 1848. A scheme had been set up in Paris to provide work for the unemployed – the National Workshops – but it was soon overwhelmed by the numbers looking for work, not helped by landowners not paying the taxes that had been levied on them to help fund the scheme. On 23 June a decree came from the committee chaired by Comte de Falloux that the National Workshops would be closed in three days' time. The working class of Paris took to the streets, barricading thoroughfares and arming themselves by seizing weapons. Three days of fighting led to 4,500 deaths as the insurrection was suppressed. In the aftermath 4,000 people were sent into exile in Algeria. In the December presidential elections Louis Napoleon-Bonaparte, nephew of Napoleon I, won a dramatic victory. Three years later he successfully staged a coup and established the Second Empire, which would last until 1870 when the monarchy was finally toppled.

On our Sunday exploration Petr and I continued on to the end of the Île Saint-Louis. The bridge that connects the island to its larger neighbour was closed to traffic and a band was playing; the sound of brass filled the open space. I looked across the narrow waterway and took my first photographs of the trip: the apartment blocks opposite on the Île de la Cité. Their many windows brought to mind *Life: A User's Manual* by Georges Perec, which I first read back in the late 1980s when it was translated into English. My girlfriend at the time, Margaret, read it in French and we compared notes as we went through the book. Time and again we found that the English version had captured much more than the simple literal meaning of the words, so it is no surprise that David Bellos's translation won awards. In the book the inhabitants of a fictional Parisian apartment block, 11 Rue Simon-Crubellier, 'somewhere' in the 17th arrondissement in the northwest of the city, are described in great detail as the interwoven stories of their lives are told within a series of complex and carefully constructed patterns. The chapters capture the building and the people within it at a specific point in time – just before 8 p.m. on Monday, 23 June 1975.

The picture I took of the Île de la Cité tenements on the Quai aux Fleurs has something of the same feeling about it. What lives are behind all those ornate and fashionable windows? And what has happened in the fourteen-plus years since I took the photograph? Fifteen Bastille Days, fifteen Christmases, fifteen New Year's Eves and who knows how many birthdays. Probably some births and deaths, certainly moving-outs and moving-ins. There's a young woman out on a balcony towards the bottom of the picture while two floors above her an older woman leans on her rail looking down. Is she about to speak to her neighbour or merely watching her? Are they just on nodding terms when they see each other in the building or do they stop to chat on the stairs? The only other signs of life, right up in the seventh floor roof-top flats, are a couple of open windows. Are they both in the same flat or are they garret neighbours with the same thought to let in a breeze on a mild Sunday morning? Presumably up there, under the roof, it gets pretty hot as the grey slates heat up. Elsewhere the closed windows give no clues to the lives of the residents. How much I wished for Perec's ability to slice away the front of the building and see the stories within. Another moment in time, just after 11 a.m. on Sunday, 25 April 2010, captured for ever by the click of my shutter.

This moment has become more significant for me as it was the first picture I posted on the Blipfoto website. I found out about Blip from another student later on in the trip and decided to sign up when I got back home. The principle is to post an image a day, taken on the day you want to post it for. At that point, in 2010, you could only start posting from the day you signed up. So I assumed I'd be starting post-Paris. But when I tried to create an account I discovered I'd already set one up just before Christmas the previous year and done nothing with it. I think I must have created the profile early in the morning one day, before I'd taken any pictures, and then rather than immediately taking a picture to post I'd decided to wait and then forgot about it. All of which meant I was able to post pictures from Paris after all – back-Blipping as it's called – as long as it was still just one picture per day, and the pictures were posted for the specific days when they were taken. With no pictures at all from the day we arrived, the photo of the apartment block on the Île de la Cité, taken early on the second day, became my first Blip.

Whenever I take stock of my time on Blipfoto, usually prompted by the marking of another year's worth of images or by reaching a significant number of Blips, I go back to the picture where it all started. Since Paris, Blipping has become a constant in my life. To start with, after catching up on the two weeks in Paris, I only Blipped images I'd taken for some other reason, and so it wasn't a picture a day, every day. I'd post an image when I'd taken it already for a college assignment or a personal project. It wasn't until later in the year that I thought I'd try and see if I could manage a picture every day for a month. And now it's quite some time later and I haven't stopped. More than five thousand days without a break. Nearly fifteen years of photographs, documenting my life. A little like a Perec book.

Back to 25 April 2010, just after 11 a.m. I put my camera back in my rucksack. Maybe the two women on the balconies were out listening to the band playing on the bridge. Petr and I stood for a while and listened too but I didn't take any more photographs.

Plenty of other people were taking pictures, with all sorts of cameras. Was I still thinking I'm not a tourist and therefore shouldn't be taking holiday snaps? As I've already said, back then I rarely took pictures with my phone but, unlike the day before, I now had two cameras with me and yet both stayed in my bag. So, as well as the nervousness over filling up my memory cards, was there also, despite my limited pre-trip research, too much awareness of all the photographers who had gone before? An internalised pressure from thinking what would Cartier-Bresson have taken, or Brassaï, Atget, Doisneau or Kertész? A feeling that here I was in Paris, aspiring to be a proper photographer, whatever that meant, and couldn't take ordinary pictures.

Something of a similar feeling prevented me writing words for this book. I felt intimidated by other writers' works about Paris. But over time I've come to recognise my imposter complex and tried to call it out.

While I'm happy to learn about facts, deep down I feel something different about art. However many times I read about the importance of artistic practice, I find it hard not to believe that real artists don't work at it. I feel sure that, somehow, really good work just comes to them. I wonder what is at the root of that thought. Something in my middle-class upbringing that separated artistic endeavour from legitimate work. A view that sees creativity not as a continuum but as an exchange between two distinct groups – the creators and the audience. Also a product of capitalism peddling a narrative that art is made by other people and we, the consumers, need to buy it with the money we earn from 'proper' jobs.

Petr and I left the musicians and walked past the back of Notre-Dame and down the side of the cathedral to the open square in front of the twin-towered west facade. No doubt one of Europe's, if not the world's, iconic buildings. Something emphasised in 2019 when the fire in the roof captured global attention and charitable impulses in a way that more pressing and systemic problems like climate change and poverty still don't.

I didn't take any pictures. It was a Sunday and it didn't feel the right day to gawp around a place of Christian worship. Something else for the list of places to come back to perhaps. Or subconscious resistance to tourist itinerary things that everyone sees because everyone else expects them to? The square was full of people and I watched an old lady scattering crumbs on the ground in front of the statue of Charlemagne. Pigeons swooped in to peck at the food. Moments later the birds flew off as a guide clapped his hands to get the attention of a group of young tourists. They listened intently as he scattered his crumbs of history. I took photos of both, pigeons and people, attempting to make a connection but not completely sure about the outcome. It needed more effort to make the juxtaposition work, but at least I was taking pictures.

We left the crowds and walked along the edge of the Île de la Cité to the Pont-Neuf. Like at the Pont de Sully, the bridge here spans the end of the island or rather, in this case, has created it. When the Pont-Neuf was built in the late sixteenth century it crossed the very tip of the island but the passage of time led to the creation of first a sandbar downstream of the bridge and then a land extension of the island. We walked past the statue of Henri IV (he of the boulevard we had walked down earlier), who inaugurated the bridge in 1607, finishing a project first started by Henri III in 1577. The statue was commissioned while Henri IV was still alive but by the time it was finished he, like his predecessor, had been killed, finally, after numerous attempts. He died on 14 May 1610, stabbed by a lone assassin who took advantage of a traffic jam on the narrow Rue de la Ferronnerie that briefly halted the royal carriage. The king was on his way to visit the Duke of Sully (after whom the other bridge we had crossed earlier was named). The statue was finally erected in 1614, destroyed in 1792 during the revolution, then recreated after the

Dimanche 25 avril / 2011

restoration of the monarchy using, among other metals, bronze melted down from the statue of Napoleon on top of the column in Place Vendôme. A more artistic act of restoration revenge than that carried out by Charles II in Britain, who not only brutally executed those who had ordered the death of his father but also exhumed the bodies of those who had died in the meantime and ritualistically executed them in death.

In the early months of 2011 I was still finishing my degree. By the time April came round, Blipping had become a habit. So I took advantage of the ability to quickly look back a year and marked the anniversary of my first Parisian Blip with a picture of our then neighbour's wisteria flowers, a reminder of the blossoms in Montmartre. A few days later I Blipped a picture of the dappled light on Middle Meadow Walk, just across the road from where we used to live, another reminder of the similar pattern of shadows I'd photographed (see p. 108) on the tree-lined paths of the Jardin des Plantes exactly a year before.

The project to do something with my images from Paris had not advanced very far but the idea that the passage of time could actually strengthen my connection to Paris was starting to take shape. Other college students who we were working with on the end-of-year exhibition were on their own trip to Paris at this point, and their images were reminders of places I had visited.

After finishing my degree in June I started noticing more Parisian links and began to make more effort to find them too. This was when I discovered Hemingway's concept of the 'moveable feast'. It captured perfectly the way that my memories of Paris seemed to resonate with new experiences. Paris was always with me so that I found myself noticing streets that I recognised from my visit in a film scene or in the background of an advert. Whether I should have read Hemingway before going to Paris and been better prepared, like some of my classmates, the fact was that

I hadn't. And there was a growing sense that working all this out my own way might be better anyway. Whether that is true or an after-the-fact rationalisation that I've used to make better sense of the narrative of my life, I'm not sure.

Anyway, I knew nothing of Hemingway's moveable feast as Petr and I walked down the old stone steps into the Square du Vert-Galant (from Henri IV's nickname – 'The Green Gallant') that occupies the extension to the original island. This small triangular park, jutting out into the river with its well-established trees, is a recognisable feature in many films set in Paris whose narrative takes them to the Seine. We walked around a bit and then back up the steps onto the bridge. We crossed the road and walked down the other side of the Île de la Cité and around the perimeter of the Palais de Justice. We decided against joining the queue to see the ornate Sainte-Chapelle and instead completed a walk around the block that took us back to the Pont-Neuf.

For me the Pont-Neuf is indelibly linked with Leos Carax's *Les Amants du Pont-Neuf*. No doubt it is one of those films that for specific personal reasons had a strong impact on me when I first saw it at Filmhouse in 1992. We bring all of our past experiences with us whenever we interact with anyone and anything, and those experiences are the lens through which we see the world. Exactly when we first see something, just like the weather when we first live somewhere, is critical to how we connect with it. Or not. Disappointing as it is when our friends and family don't seem interested in a film or book or band we're raving about, what if a different you, of last week or next year, would have shared their sense of 'meh'? Everything we encounter is in cultural context, such as a blockbuster marketing campaign, or the more general mood of the time, the zeitgeist. However, our personal situation can be just as important – the state of our relationships, how things are going at work, whether our team won or lost that

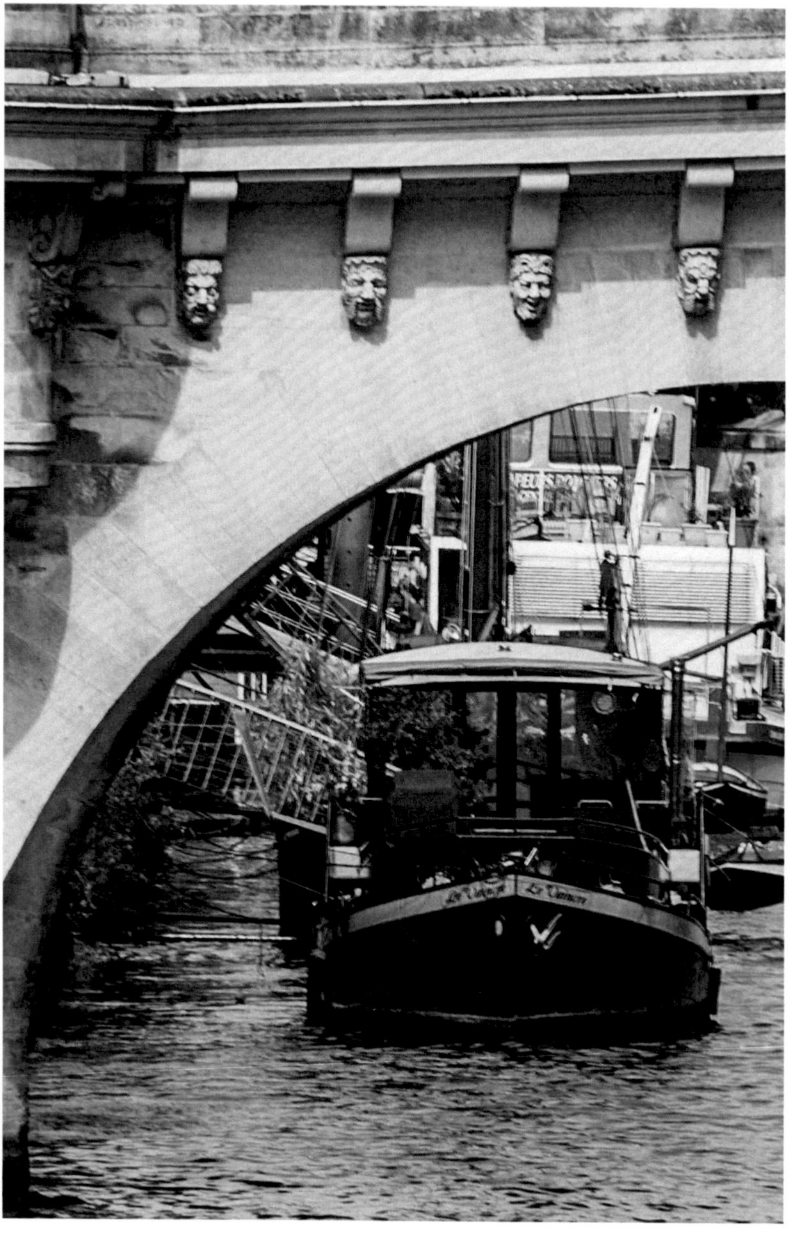

weekend – and sometimes we can choose to forget it all and immerse ourselves in the story, and sometimes we can be distracted by everything that is going on. In one case the film is loved and remembered, in the other it's almost instantly forgotten.

At this point, as if the small circle we had walked had enabled us to build up sufficient velocity to escape the islands, Petr and I spun off across the southern part of the Pont-Neuf onto the Left Bank. The Rive Gauche of student protests, of Hemingway and Fitzgerald.

We walked up the Rue Dauphine, named after the son of Henri IV. This part of the city is dense with reminders of that era of French history. We bought ourselves tuna salad baguettes and headed on towards the Luxembourg Palace at the top of the hill. We still had our plan to watch the cycling later and started paying a bit more attention to cafés and bars as we walked by, to see if we could spot a big screen. A couple of places we looked into didn't even have a TV, so we walked a bit further along streets that seemed less and less promising until we cut across to the long thin extension of the gardens that continues south from the larger park around the palace.

Not just vaguely 'south', though, as it happens, because the Jardin des Grands-Explorateurs continues the straight line that passes through the centre of the Paris Observatory. This line was the meridian for French cartography from the foundation of the observatory in 1667. The Paris meridian was mapped in detail in the late seventeenth and early eighteenth centuries by two generations of the Cassini family, leading to a new, more accurate map of France based upon the line through Paris that continued north to Dunkirk and south to Collioure near Perpignan, close to the Spanish border.

After the French Revolution the meridian became crucial to the attempt to standardise units of measurement used across the country. The new metre was to be defined as exactly one ten-

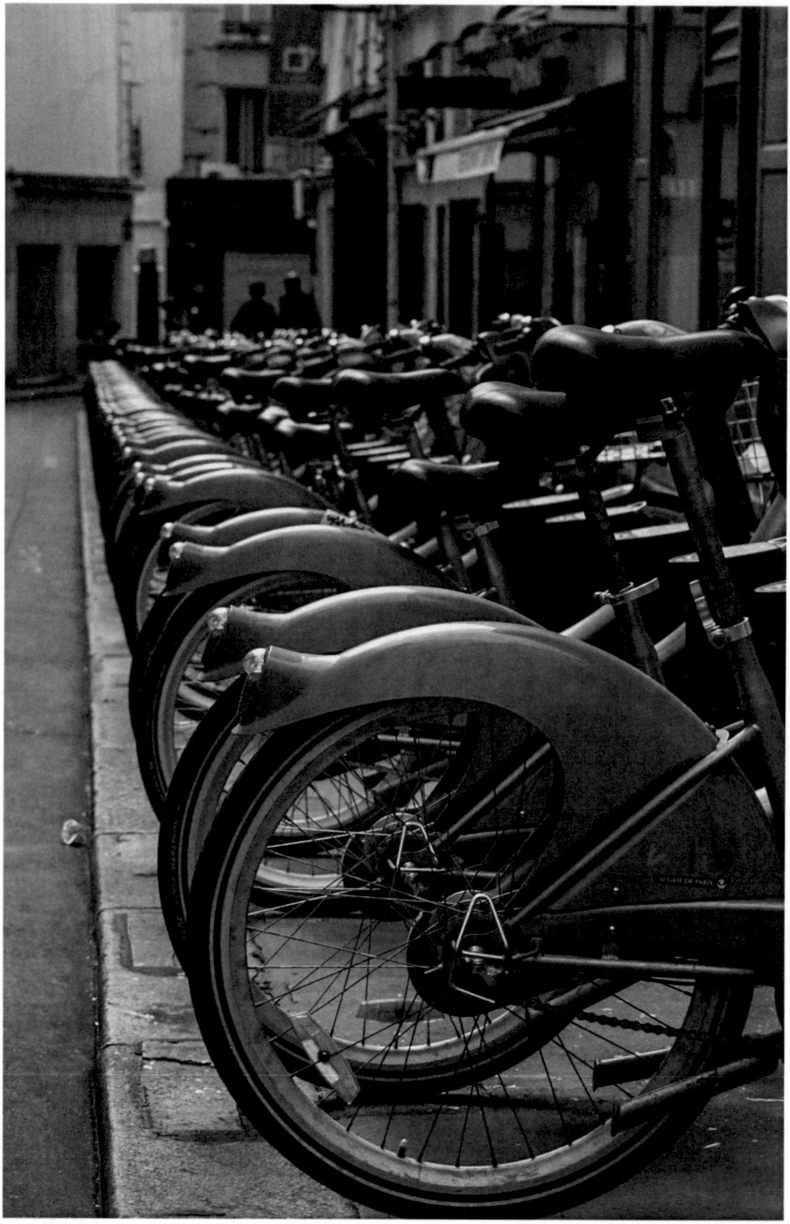

millionth of the distance from the equator to the North Pole, and it was careful measurement of the Paris meridian that was used to calculate Earth's circumference. The Paris meridian and the linked Ferro meridian, defined as exactly 20 degrees west of Paris, were rivals to the Greenwich meridian for the global standard of longitude until the late nineteenth century, when the world officially adopted Greenwich as the prime meridian. France continued to use the Paris meridian for timekeeping until 1911 and for navigation until 1914. Mind you, as part of the deal, the UK was supposed to switch to using the metre and well over a century later I still see our road signs in yards and miles so it isn't just Brexit that has seen the UK go back on agreements with our European neighbours.

Might knowing about the meridian have added something to the walk? Would I have looked for the Arago medallions? They were installed in the mid 1990s to commemorate the scientist and politician François Arago, whose bronze statue had been removed during the Second World War to meet the occupying German forces' demand for copper. The original idea was to commission a new statue on the empty plinth but there was an intriguing alternative proposal from Dutch artist Jan Dibbets. Instead of a single statue, a line of bronze medallions, each with Arago's name, would be placed across the city along the line of the Paris meridian, which Arago had recalculated with greater accuracy in the early nineteenth century. (I presume that recalibration was responsible for the discovery that the neat alignment of roads and park paths northwards from the observatory towards the Luxembourg Palace is a little awry.) From what I have read many of the medallions have now disappeared, as a result of roadworks or redevelopment or theft. The line still exists, albeit invisibly on the ground, and at least one blogger I'm aware of writes about revisiting it every time they return to Paris, increasingly following the line through memory.

This reminds me of the photographic view markers there are in the centre of Edinburgh. They were installed in the 1990s too – obviously a thing in cities at that time – sponsored by a camera manufacturer. Every so often I spot one of them on the pavement in the city centre. There were two trails, red and blue, for the New Town and the Old Town respectively. I've photographed a few of them over the years and have often wondered about trying to find as many of the set as are still in place. Maybe subvert them by taking the most ordinary photos possible from each of the marked locations, looking in the opposite direction from the intended view.

The life story of François Arago seems more than worthy of a cinematic biopic, from his early adventures in Spain while mapping the meridian to his significant contributions to science. It was Arago who negotiated a government pension for Louis Daguerre and Nicéphore Niépce's son, Isidore, in return for the secrets of their photographic techniques (more on them in the chapter 'Mardi 27 avril / 2013'), and introduced the daguerreotype to the wider world in August 1839. I thought I'd discovered a connection from Arago to Edinburgh when I found a reference to a visit to Leith in 1818 or 1819, but further investigation indicates he sent fellow physicist Jean-Baptiste Biot as his representative. Biot also visited Scotland in 1817 rather than a year or two later. After several days at Leith Fort, he travelled on to Shetland to conduct pendulum experiments before returning to London where he was joined by Arago for a meeting with the Astronomer Royal, John Pond, in Greenwich. Perhaps the confusion is caused by the fact that Arago and Biot were joint authors of the published results of the pendulum experiments in 1821. They were very close but parted ways around this time after a disagreement over the nature of light. Written down like that, what a great reason for friends to fall out.

Dimanche 25 avril / 2011

Unaware of the Arago medallions or the Paris meridian, Petr and I walked through the park towards the palace. We stopped at the small boating pond and sat down for a while. A memory came back to me of being there on my one previous visit to Paris and watching children playing with toy yachts. They had set the sails on their boats to catch the wind and released them from one edge of the pond before running round to the other side to gather them in and then carry them back to set them off again. I thought then that those children had brought the toys with them to the park but now I could see there was someone hiring them out. It turns out that the tradition of renting a model boat here dates back to the 1880s. In the 1920s Clément Padeau took over the business and his family ran it for many years, using the same handmade wooden boats. Although a feature of simpler times, the boats are still popular with children visiting the gardens. And again, I took no pictures. On this occasion was I concerned about taking pictures of children? And why did we not hire a boat ourselves?

Instead we sat in chairs and watched the toys crossing the water. Over on the other side we saw two groups of fellow students. We waved and they came over and we hung out for a bit. Some had itineraries already planned out, but Jo and Iza said they'd come along with me and Petr, at least for a while. We were back on our mission to find a bar to watch the cycling. Surely it wouldn't be that difficult to find somewhere showing it on a big screen? After all Liège-Bastogne-Liège is one of the big five European cycling one-day races, known as the Monuments, and therefore almost like a cup final. We headed down to the busier area along the Boulevard Saint-Germain, where we thought we'd have more luck, but it proved not so. Bar staff we spoke to were apologetic and helpful. One barman directed us to a sports bar a few streets away but when we finally found it, an Irish bar tucked away down a narrow street, it wasn't open until the evening.

Dimanche 25 avril / 2011

Eventually we decided we would give up on our quest and just stop for a drink. We picked a likely-looking place on the Boulevard Saint-Germain and went in. The big screen in the back room was showing music videos as we sat down with our drinks and asked in our stumbling French if there was any chance we could watch le cyclisme? 'Bien sur, le cyclisme?' the barman said enthusiastically, and went to fetch the remote control from behind the bar. He flicked through the channels until he came to images of cyclists racing along the roads of Belgium – très bon! We thanked him and settled down to watch the closing stages, as there was still more than an hour of racing to go.

Unfortunately there was no immediate sign of Roman Kreuziger. After a while the pictures showed him back in the pack, with no real prospect of getting to the front. Many of the big names of cycling, familiar to me from watching the Tour de France every year, were in the leading group – the Schleck brothers, Alberto Contador, Alejandro Valverde, Cadel Evans, Philippe Gilbert and Alexander Vinokourov. While we watched Jo finished her drink and said her goodbyes but Iza stayed with us to watch the finish of the race. It felt like the sort of thing Petr and I might have done had we been living in Paris. Later, we did meet up a few times in an Edinburgh pub to watch a stage of the Tour and any time I have watched a cycling road race on TV I've thought back to our afternoon in the bar on Saint-Germain.

Two riders pulled ahead on the last big descent and in the final 500m it was Vinokourov who sprinted away from the Russian Alexandr Kolobnev. A minute further back Valverde just beat local favourite Gilbert across the line. Or so we thought. Cycling was getting its house back in order after years of doping and several leading riders were banned and stripped of their achievements, changing the sporting record. At the end of May Valverde was banned for two years, backdated to 1 January 2010. His results from the start of the year, including the race we watched in Paris, were annulled and Gilbert was retrospectively promoted to third. In July Contador would apparently win the Tour only to be later stripped of that title (and the 2011 Giro), although he continues to deny doping, blaming his positive test result on eating a contaminated steak.

Does such sporting revisionism matter to our memories? In this case neither Petr nor I had much skin in the game, with no personal favourites involved. Maybe it would have mattered more if Roman had been in contention. Sport produces winners and losers, but that isn't all we watch for. It's also about other narratives that play out over the duration of a particular race or match and over the longer term of a season or an individual career. In any event, Valverde's demotion didn't change the winner, only the third place on the podium. And it didn't change the memory, the shared experience of sitting in a Parisian café, watching the cycling on a Sunday afternoon.

We finished up our drinks and waved our thanks to the barman on our way out the door. It was a pleasant afternoon and the route back to the hotel was straightforward – follow the Boulevard Saint-Germain all the way back to the Pont de Sully and the Boulevard Henri VI where we had started in the morning. As it happened, we detoured slightly and crossed the river on a different bridge, where we bumped into another student also heading back to the hotel. We walked up a small side street that headed in the direction we wanted. It turned out that this was the Rue du Petit-Musc – the street that Lorraine had asked me to look out for during my stay. So I took a picture of the street sign as we walked up towards the Bastille. After declining so many more obvious photographic subjects, an obscure but personally significant shot.

On 14 July 2011, Bastille Day, my Blipfoto entry highlighted the direction my thoughts were headed. I'd considered trying to find something French to mark the holiday but hadn't found anything

Dimanche 25 avril / 2011

suitable and resorted to taking some pictures of the ongoing tram works at Haymarket. I like to get a picture early on that could be my Blip, on a 'this is the one to beat' basis, so I was going to use an image of the works until I went past the very grand former Donaldson's School for the Deaf and saw the door standing open. An open door just waiting for you to walk through it. It was one of the pictures that was later selected for an *Edinburgh Evening News* article in August about my first year of Blipping.

That night I went to see *La Rafle* (*The Roundup*) at Filmhouse. Although probably not entirely appropriate for 14 julliet, it was its last showing and I really wanted to see it. It brought back many of the feelings I had during my visit to Paris about the Holocaust in Europe. Obviously I knew about it before I went, and Paris isn't Auschwitz, but maybe that was why my reaction was so powerful. I wasn't particularly expecting it, unlike I imagine you do when you go to the camps. It got me before I was able to close up my defences and I found it hard to hide behind the camera. Instead there were times when the camera seemed both wrong and incapable of saying what I wanted to say.

La Rafle is fictional but based on events that happened on 16 and 17 July 1942 when more than 13,000 Parisian Jews were rounded up by French police. One of the Germans in the film suggests it be done on the fourteenth, but the police say that it should be delayed until after the national holiday. Although many of the reminders of those events that I saw were in the Marais quarter, close by the Bastille, the film focused on people living in Montmartre and the early scenes brought back memories of several visits I made there during the fortnight I was in Paris. And in one of those coincidences that link the fabric of life, one of the foreign Jewish families in the film turned out to be Polish, from the eastern city of Lublin. Which is where my good friend Agni is from. The same Agni I walked round Montmartre with on a sunny May evening the year before, taking photographs of the same streets that were up there on the screen.

The film followed some of the Jewish families, first to the Vélodrome d'Hiver (or Vél' d'Hiv'), close to the Eiffel Tower, and then to an interim camp where they were held before being put onto trains taking them east to the death camps. As it says at the end of the film, only a handful the 13,000 survived to the end of the war. However, the plan had been to arrest 24,000, so many avoided being rounded up, often saved by the support of other Parisians. While some locals were portrayed as being antisemitic, others showed their humanity and bravery in doing something to help. In the film there were moments at the end, after the war, as people looked at pictures of the dead, searching for their families, that were clearly intended to evoke strong emotions. Which they did. The walls of photographs the same as those up in the Shoah museum I visited in Paris. But the sequence that I found most moving was the scene in the velodrome when a group of firemen came to check the hoses in the building and instead turned on the taps and distributed water to the thousands crammed in there. The firemen then gathered messages to take out to friends and relatives, with the support and encouragement of their commander. I ended my Blip entry for the day with an exhortation to myself to get the book written that had been in my head in one form or another since my return from Paris. I was a little disappointed in myself at the lack of progress.

After the film I set myself the task of finding out more about the events portrayed on screen. Where was the velodrome where the Jews were gathered and the firemen turned on the hoses? Had I been anywhere near it? It turned out that it had been badly damaged by fire in 1959 and completely demolished shortly afterwards. There was still a memorial, though, preserved when the building was demolished, and I had unknowingly been very close to it when I got off the Métro at Bir-Hakeim station to go and see the Eiffel Tower.

Although the film was showing in Edinburgh in July 2011, it had premiered in France the previous March and had fuelled a national discussion about the role of the French authorities in the 1942 Roundup. Back in 1994 President Mitterrand had said that the actions of the Vichy French government were nothing to do with the French state, which had been effectively dismantled by Pétain and only reconstituted after the war. But just a year later the new president, Jacques Chirac, reversed that position and formally admitted French responsibility for the persecution of Jews in France during the Second World War.

Another film released in 2010, *Sarah's Key*, explored elements of France's national dilemma in grappling with the wartime past and its consequences. The film is based on a novel by Tatiana de Rosnay (who coincidentally shares my birthday) published in the USA in 2007. *Sarah's Key* uses the events of the Roundup in a fictional account of one Jewish family caught up in it, with a parallel story set in the present in which an American woman becomes obsessed with finding out the details of what happened to them.

Back in 2010 we'd gone back to the hotel and Petr and I joined a group of a dozen or more that headed up Boulevard Richard-Lenoir towards the Oberkampf district looking for a place to eat. There was nothing very promising in the first few blocks so we went for a drink in an interesting-looking bar with some eclectic oriental features, big old posters on the walls and large brown leather tub chairs. It had a friendly atmosphere but we were too big a group and stood around awkwardly below its high ceilings until we'd finished our drinks and then moved on. The name of the bar, the Grand Café Bataclan, meant nothing to us.

In 2011, as the year turned to autumn, I continued to look for Paris connections. In October I went to see Woody Allen's *Midnight in Paris* and although I enjoyed the locations I wasn't convinced about the magic realism element of the film. Having watched it again, though, I've changed my mind and now appreciate the way it keeps going back to an earlier 'golden age' in which people are themselves looking back to when things were 'better than today'. A creative, cinematic way to explore the historical layers in the city, the urban palimpsest. My Blip image for the day made parallels between Edinburgh's Festival Square and Paris, and later I met up with Petr before my wife and a friend of hers joined us. They'd been to a concert by a Doors tribute band. The Doors, whose lead singer Jim Morrison is famously buried in Père Lachaise. When you start looking there are connections everywhere.

Before the end of the year, shortly after completing a full year of Blipping without a break, I met up with Anita, the person who introduced me to Blipfoto in the first place. We talked about each other's experiences since finishing college and how we were managing to make a living as photographers. Or not. We also

Dimanche 25 avril / 2011

looked back to Paris and I was surprised to hear that she had been disappointed by her visit. With much stronger links to France and many previous visits, it had not been the novelty for her that it had been for me. Something about how the brain reacts to new experiences, giving more attention to something fresh and taking the familiar much more for granted. The way in which the outward journey to somewhere brand new seems so much longer than the return trip.

There is a theory, first described in 1890 by William James in his book *The Principles of Psychology*, that explains why time appears to speed up as you get older. The idea is that the brain experiences new sensory input more vividly than it does familiar things. When you're very young, just about everything you see, hear, touch, taste and smell is new so time passes slowly, one day containing many new experiences, each an individual sensory marker. As we get older the number of new things decline and into adulthood the rhythms of days, weeks, months and years can mean a lot of time flashes by. In a nine-to-five job individual days can follow the same pattern, all contained within a larger weekly pattern, from Monday mornings to Friday afternoons. Even the weekends, with their apparent freedom, can follow their own routine, with regular activities such as housework, sport, movies or dinners creating their own pattern, which leads to a feeling that the years are racing by. The proposed solution is that you should do different things, and the more new things you do to stimulate your brain, the more you will manage to slow the apparent passage of time. All of which might have been the reason why, on that November morning, Anita seemed so unimpressed with her time in Paris and I was so enthusiastic. And hearing myself, I felt a renewed enthusiasm for the project of writing a book and resolved, again, to get it done. November 2011. Just saying.

Anita and I also discussed identity and memory and a bunch of other concepts – in my caption for my Blip for that day I hope that we will meet again soon to continue the conversation but sadly it never happened and, like a number of the people I was in Paris with, we lost touch in the decade and more that has passed. After we'd gone our separate ways – and with me being too shy to ask friends if I could take their picture for a Blip – I was on the lookout for a suitable image so took a photo of the Flodden Wall, close to the Pleasance. The wall was built following the disastrous defeat suffered by the Scottish army led by King James IV at the hands of the English in 1513. There was a very real fear of an English invasion and therefore Edinburgh's defences were strengthened. There was also a commercial imperative, to control smuggling, and therefore the walls included both the Grassmarket and Cowgate areas of the burgh. Although work began in 1514, the wall wasn't completed until 1560 when it enclosed 140 acres and protected a population of around 10,000. It remained the limit of the burgh until the eighteenth century. In this it echoes the development of Paris, which grew outwards slowly as a series of walls were built and then superseded, first for defensive purposes but later, like the Flodden Wall, also for commercial reasons to regulate and tax trade.

Still on our quest for a restaurant in 2010 we headed up the hill of Rue Oberkampf, a strangely Germanic name at the heart of a French city. It was named after an eighteenth-century German-born French industrialist best known for creating patterned textiles – the famous Toile de Jouy – in his factory southwest of Paris. As is the way with these things, it wasn't clear if we were headed for a particular place or just looking for anywhere that struck enough of us as suitable. I hope it was the latter because otherwise someone had deliberately led us to sit outside a café on a busy road junction where Rue Oberkampf crossed Avenue de la République. Hardly a peaceful spot, on a dark street between tall buildings and with tons of traffic passing by, but they did have a long table outside that was big enough for the whole group.

It was another difficult-to-manage eating experience in which the practicalities meant we ended up splitting into subgroups up and down the table. Maybe not as uncomfortable as the situation the night before but still less than ideal, not least because it had taken us so long to even get there. But the food was all right and I liked hearing about other people's days. Headed back, the streets were quiet and dark, the shops closed and shuttered. Our route led us onto the Rue de la Roquette and past the restaurant where we'd gone the day before.

And then we ended up at Tape again. Just as wildly chaotic as it had been the night before. Was it all part of an act, along with the graffiti on the walls and the loud music, aimed at attracting a younger clientele, or was it genuinely as disorganised as it seemed? It still appeared to be operating three years later, although the shutters were down when Lorraine and I walked by in the afternoon in 2013. Google Street View lets you scroll back through time, and I can see it had a makeover sometime between then and September 2014 – was it just a refresh or did the chaos catch up with them and new owners took over but retained the name? It was still there in 2015 and 2016 but by the following year it had transformed into a cocktail bar, which looked to still be going strong the other side of the pandemic the last time the Google cameras went by.

Dimanche 25 avril / 2011

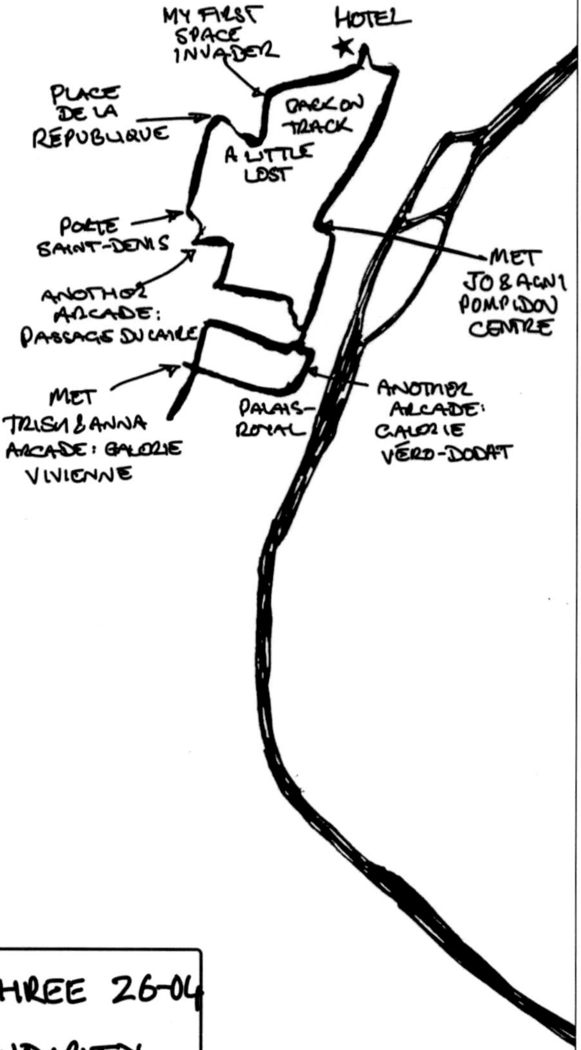
MY FIRST SPACE INVADER
HOTEL
PLACE DE LA REPUBLIQUE
BACK ON TRACK
A LITTLE LOST
PORTE SAINT-DENIS
ANOTHER ARCADE: PASSAGE DU CAIRE
MET JO & AGNI POMPIDOU CENTRE
MET TRISH & ANNA ARCADE: GALERIE VIVIENNE
PALAIS-ROYAL
ANOTHER ARCADE: GALERIE VÉRO-DODAT

DAY THREE 26-04

SERENDIPITY

Lundi 26 avril / 2012

At breakfast we discussed getting ourselves weekly Métro passes. Having personally walked everywhere since the journey from the airport, I realised it would make getting further afield much easier. So shortly afterwards a number of us dutifully joined a queue at the nearest Métro station and one of the French speakers in the party explained what was required. One by one we got our passes. And then, perversely perhaps, I walked back out of the station and carried on on foot. I went down to the Place des Vosges again but this time headed westward towards the centre of the city.

I walked in a direction vaguely parallel to the river without ever seeing it, along the narrow streets of the Marais. After a while a massive modern building loomed up ahead, all external scaffolding and pipework and in vivid contrast to the old-style streets I'd come along. The Pompidou Centre was originally known as the Centre Beaubourg but was renamed after the death in office of Georges Pompidou in 1974, three years before the building was officially opened. Some still refer to it as the Beaubourg out of antipathy to the former president. (The faultlines in French politics run very deep.) The centre is completely uncompromising and was the first major inside-out building in the world, with its utilities in full view rather than concealed within. They are colour-coded: green for water, blue for air conditioning, yellow for electricity and red for access (lifts and escalators). It is closing in 2025 for a five-year renovation programme.

As I walked round the side of the building I noticed two familiar figures just ahead of me – Agni and Jo. We laughed at the coincidence of bumping into each other. In a city of two million residents (and a wider metropolitan area with five times as many), not to mention hundreds of thousands of tourists, I had somehow managed to meet two of the twenty-six people I knew. They were going to the modern art gallery inside the centre and asked if I wanted to join them. Before we went in we looked around a tourist shop on the other side of the square. I'm not quite sure how it happened but someone picked a random, very ordinary postcard and then we thought it would be funny if one after the other we each bought single copies of the same card. I don't think the shop assistant even noticed.

We crossed the open square in front of the centre and joined the queue to get in. There were no bags allowed inside so I checked-in my daypack, including my big camera, which means the only photos from inside, or from the viewpoint up on the roof, had to be taken with my small camera or, a bit of a novelty for me, with my phone. It probably says more about me than the quality of the modern art on display that the most memorable things about the visit are the views from the top floor and the expensive cup of tea we had in the rooftop café. A massive gold flowerpot loomed above the tables as the three of us discussed where we might go next. Agni wanted to stay and look round another suite of galleries but Jo and I had both had our fill of art. She was going to Notre-Dame but I wanted to go somewhere new so I thought I'd go west. At breakfast I had had nothing more than a vague idea about sport on the streets. I wasn't the only one struggling for a theme, though, and I suspect our lecturers knew that many of us might end up with a nebulous set of street photography images rather than anything more structured.

Lundi 26 avril / 2012

Even so, I was optimistic and on the lookout for sporting images as I passed the glass entrance to Les Halles shopping centre and continued on. A few kids were kicking a football around in a small square but it felt too impromptu to be called sport. And, again, it's potentially problematic photographing children in public. What were the laws and etiquette in France? I wandered into a covered arcade – like Les Halles, built to protect shoppers from the elements but a century and a half earlier and with an elegance lacking in the modern underground complex. While clearly nothing to do with sport, the arcade architecture made for some interesting photographic possibilities so I was composing a shot looking down the row of shops when someone I recognised walked into frame. It was Anna, closely followed by Trish – two more from our group. Unlike me, they had a very deliberate plan. They were going round as many of the arcades as possible. Trish had done her research and had identified the arcades as a potential documentary topic. She was always the best prepared and her workbooks were not only a thing of beauty but also perfect exemplars of the value of creative preparation. After I got home, I came across the Paris work of Walter Benjamin and in particular his Arcades Project. The Eiland and McLaughlin English translation is a massive book, running to more than a thousand pages. Although there are a few essays in there, the bulk of it is bringing together Benjamin's research on the Parisian arcades, in the form of hundreds of his notes and reflections and citations from others' work. These were organised according to theme into sub-collections, called 'Convolutes' in the English version (from the German term 'Konvolut' used by Benjamin's friend Theodor Adorno when he organised the material after Benjamin's death). The essays were manageable but the rest of the book was completely overwhelming. I sat and looked at it, thinking was this the sort of thing I would have to do before I could write my own Paris book?

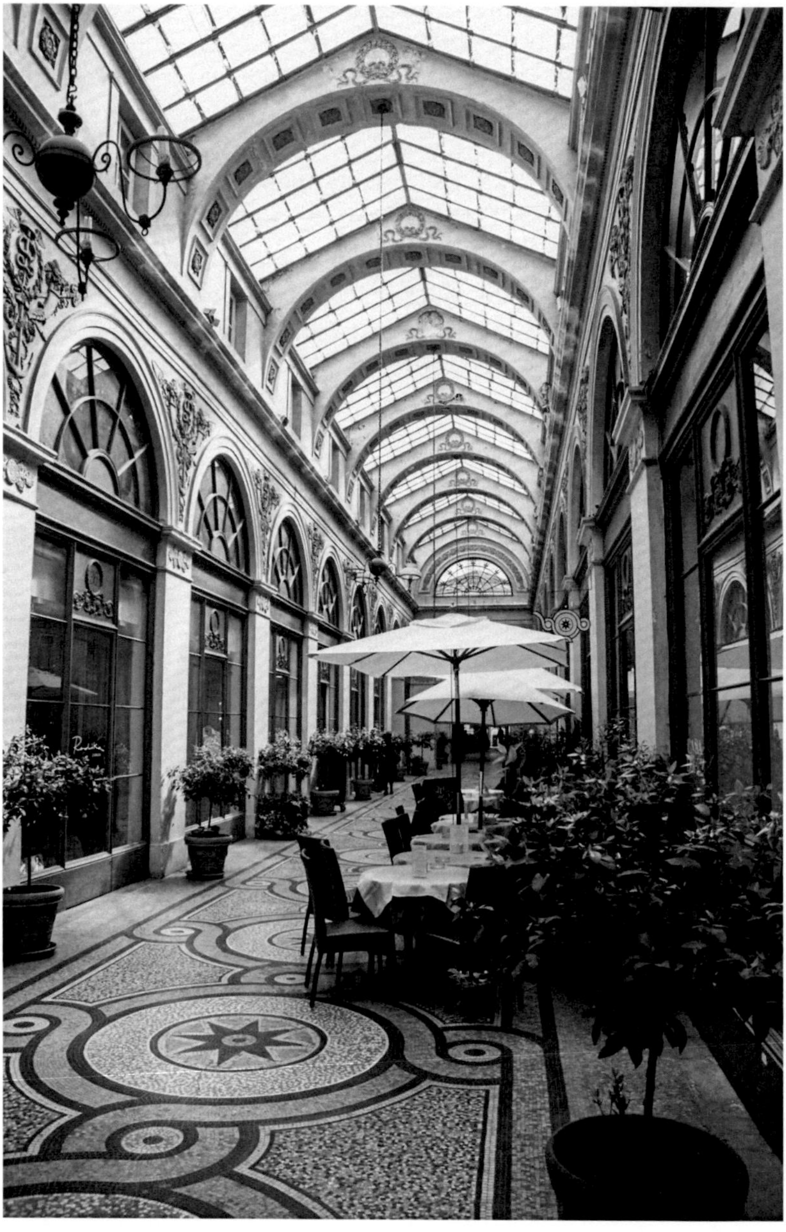

Lundi 26 avril / 2012

In early 2012 I still had the selective-colour prints I'd had done for the tea shop exhibition. None of them had sold during the show, so I'd brought them home and put them up on the wall of my room. (Study? Office? Let's just call it a room.) But a few years later I got a message via my website from someone who remembered seeing the exhibition in the café and wanted to buy one of the prints if I still had it, which I did, and so made a sale.

Looking at them then, I had a plan to take advantage of the extra day, 29 February, as a day for creativity.

Only it didn't happen.

We did buy a secondhand mirror to complete our then living room, tins of paint for the bathroom and some shelf-lining paper (aka suitably coloured gift wrap) to go on some bookshelves. I cut the paper to size and stuck it into place, which gave a sense of achievement but nothing that felt really creative. In the evening I found myself wondering what to Blip and went back to the project that I described then as continuing to nag away at me without ever getting properly started – my Paris book. By then I was clear it was going to be a book of some sort and although I felt drawn to creating something physical I speculated that it was increasingly likely it would be digital.

I recognised my usual problem, then and still the case – the difficulty of making a selection. However, I also acknowledged that, just like writing a story or a novel, I really needed to make a start and then I could always move things around, shift things in and out, replace things that didn't look right. Always easier when there is something there to edit. I also debated whether to include some sort of map, or maps plural, showing my wanderings across the city during the fortnight, mostly in the eight central arrondissements but sometimes into the outer ring of twelve and even briefly beyond, to the edge of the 'banlieues' (the suburbs). Would the maps be an essential part of the whole, or merely incidental, perhaps a backdrop to the images? A bit like the effect I produced in my Blip that day, with a central map showing where I went on different days surrounded by a selection of small printed images.

I wondered how much text I should write. I was already thinking that it would be more than just captions. Would I start with an introductory essay before all the pictures or would I fully integrate text and pictures? So many things to think about but, as I wrote in my Blip, it would be two years in April since I was there and more than enough time for anyone to mull over an idea before getting on and doing it. I also wondered if procrastination ran in the family. My father is a retired History lecturer and has had a project to write up the minutes of a local nineteenth-century agricultural society on his to-do list for years. As of this writing, unless he's been publishing in secret, it remains undone.

Lundi 26 avril / 2012

Sharing where I was in my process on Blip was helpful. I got not just some cheerleading on the book idea (working title at that point: 'Le Plan') but also a pointer to check out Guy Debord's Theory of the Dérive.

Debord was writing in the 1950s, during the early days of what is now known as psychogeography, and defined the dérive (from the French for 'drift') as 'a technique of rapid passage through various ambiences'. For Debord one or more people would drop 'their usual motives for movement and action' and instead 'let themselves be drawn by the attractions of the terrain and the encounters they find there'. He referenced the earlier work of Paul-Henry Chombart de Lauwe, who had described the tightly constrained urban worlds of Parisian residents, plotting their journeys on a map. One of them, a politics student, spent a year largely within the confines of a triangle whose corners were her flat in the 16th arrondissement, the School of Political Sciences and the home of her piano teacher.

Debord and the Situationists in the 1950s had a strong political element to their work and this remains a feature of contemporary psychogeography, such as the anti-Thatcherite work of Iain Sinclair in London, but there is also another, less didactic strand that can trace its roots back to Baudelaire and beyond. As psychogeography has moved out of academia to become more mainstream, this more aesthetic, creative and more personal strand seems more accessible and therefore has become more prominent than the overtly political aspect, at least in popular perception.

Exploring Parisian psychogeography also led me to the leftwing historian and philosopher Éric Hazan. Hazan had been a surgeon before he became an author and established a publishing house. Many of his books were about the geography and history of Paris and the first – *The Invention of Paris* (published in French in 2002 and translated into English in 2010) – caught my attention.

The book starts with a discussion about the nature of internal boundaries within the city and the different ways that districts are separated, sometimes by a clear line on the map and other times by a more gradual transition. Hazan then moves on to the main part of the book, a methodical geographical and historical journey through the city. He describes the way that the centre of Paris grew in tightly constrained concentric circles, as determined by the city's walls.

Hazan then goes on to write about Red Paris, and the barricades, as he goes back in time looking at their role in Parisian insurrections. As part of my coursework I'd done a series of landscape images at battlefield sites across Central Scotland. What interested me most were not the places where the battlefield had been preserved but rather those where the current landscape appeared indifferent to the historical events which had taken place there. Perhaps a different, better-prepared version of me might have chosen the barricades as the subject of his Parisian documentary project and travelled the city to photograph their historic locations.

Looking back before 1848 I would have needed to refer to paintings of the barricades but the brief June Days uprising of 1848 were the first Parisian protests to be photographed. The early photographer Charles-François Thibault took three daguerrotypes looking down a street with a series of barricades. The first two pictures were taken early on the morning of 25 June 1848 and the third was taken the following day, after the barricades had been stormed by government troops and the insurrection suppressed. Two of the images were copied to create wood engravings that were published in the periodical *l'Illustration* shortly after the events took place. (The technology of the day meant that it wasn't possible to directly print from the daguerrotypes.) The original captions describe the two engravings as showing 'La barricade de

Lundi 26 avril / 2012

la rue Saint-Maur-Popincourt', presumably as documented by the photographer himself.

Detailed investigative work by the French academic Olivier Ihl identified the building where Thibault took his photographs as actually being on Rue du Faubourg-du-Temple, looking towards the crossroads with the Rue Saint-Maur where the first barricade has been set up. Rather as bus stops are named for the closest intersecting street instead of the street they are on, so Thibault titled his image. Notably he used the singular definite article for the barricade on the Rue Saint-Maur, which he presumably saw as the main subject of his photograph. If he was looking down the Rue Saint-Maur and seeing several barricades, would he not have titled the picture 'Les barricades de la rue Saint-Maur-Popincourt'? Unfortunately, at the time of writing (although I have told them), the Paris Musées website contains exactly this error: the titles of the two images held at the Musée d'Orsay have been changed from 'Barricade' to 'Barricades'. Whether it arises from people using this source or making the same mistake themselves, this error has rippled through the internet, onto sites such as Alamy and Wikimedia Commons. The third of Thibault's images is held in the Musée Carnavalet, which correctly identifies the barricades as being on the Rue du Faubourg-du-Temple, but this image seems less popular in searches and derivative articles, particularly in English.

The last section of Hazan's book provided me with another prompt-that-never-was in his chapter on the visual image. It gives a whistle-stop tour through depictions of Paris which again might have been the basis for a series of contemporary photographs paying homage to classic images. But rather than giving me a documentary subject, would more knowledge of the great photographers that had gone before have actually hindered me in Paris, my ability to take photographs paralysed by their reputations?

Probably. Even reading Hazan's book had a similar effect on me in 2012. On the one hand it was encouraging to discover a book that seemed to explore similar ideas to the ones I was wrestling with; but on the other, there was his book, already printed and in the bookshop. His credentials, living in Paris for decades, completely trumped mine.

Hazan also discussed Baudelaire's concept of the flâneur and his (for back in the nineteenth century it was exclusively a male preserve) unguided wanderings. The term has been popularised and artists have encouraged people to use various creative means to explore urban landscapes in different and unexpected ways. While the goal is undirected exploration, in order to try and circumvent deliberate or subconscious guiding of the walk (walking is still the primary means of exploration) various structural schemes have been used to attempt to create truly random routes, if that isn't too contradictory. You might follow a rigid series of directional instructions drawn up in advance, determining each choice of path by rolling dice, or superimpose a map from a completely different location. For example, you might take the basic directions from following a map of Paris to walk between two locations – first left, second right, second left and so on – and use those to determine a walk in Edinburgh.

The concept of the flâneur resonated strongly with me as I thought back to my days in Paris. Much of my time had been spent exploring on foot and, without a detailed guidebook to follow, my journeys were frequently impromptu and vague, heading in a rough direction and seeing what I found. A city like Paris, one of the most familiar cities in the world, is never going to be terra fully incognito, however little preparation the visitor has done, and I was no different. I had the memories of my one previous visit, back when I was a teenager, complemented by movies I'd seen and smatterings of historic general knowledge. No different from

Lundi 26 avril / 2012 65

anyone visiting an unfamiliar city, bringing their personal idea of the geography they expect to find.

I had left Trish and Anna in the arcade and walked on a bit further, but not immediately finding anything very interesting I turned back. Probably too soon as I was heading towards the Place Vendôme, the Palais Garnier opera house and the wealthy boulevards of Haussmann's mid nineteenth-century redesign of the city. Now, instead, I was walking back towards Les Halles and saw Trish and Anna again, sitting in a café. I went in to join them for a drink and then decided to explore a bit together.

We were only a short distance from the northern entrance to the Palais-Royal and went through a passageway into the relative tranquillity of the gardens, with their fountains and tree-lined walkways. Later, when I got home and had started Blipping, a picture taken here was my photo for the day, looking down the lines of carefully sculpted trees in the main courtyard. At the far end of the gardens the paved piazza contained a modern art installation with lots of black and white columns of different heights and some interesting water features. Trish and Anna were following the directions in their *Rough Guide* as they looked for the next arcade on their list – the Galérie Véro-Dodat, supposedly one of the oldest and prettiest of the arcades. We went out the other side of the Palais-Royal and then doubled back down a tiny side street where we paused to look at some intricate paper sculptures in a shop window before finding the entrance to the arcade they were looking for. It was pretty enough, with wooden panelling and black-and-white tiled floor, although having not seen many others I couldn't say it was the prettiest. At the far end both Trish and Anna were very taken with the shoe shop that was there. Not just any shoe shop, they explained, this was Christian Louboutin, maker of the iconic red-soled footwear. While they looked at the shoes in the window I photographed an ornate brass door knocker.

We continued on our way. Trish and Anna had one more arcade on their list for the afternoon. We walked through the gardens above Les Halles and then up the lively Rue Montorgueil. The shops were all still open and the pedestrianised street was very busy. We stopped at a patisserie and walked on, eating our purchases. Reaching the Rue Réaumur, we checked their map and zigzagged our way to the Passage du Caire. By the time we got there the shops inside had either already closed or were just closing and there wasn't much time to look around before they started closing up the entrances to the arcade itself.

We walked down the hill and turned left onto the Rue Saint-Denis. We passed several sex workers standing in shop doorways, their cropped tops, short skirts and thigh-length boots incongruous amongst the sedately dressed late afternoon shoppers. We were enjoying walking so we decided not to use our new travel cards. Took a right onto Boulevard Saint-Martin and headed east. The wide pavement was elevated above the busy road, and looked like a pleasant walk back towards the hotel, but when we got to Place de la République we went awry. We'd intended to walk down Boulevard du Temple but somehow turned onto Rue du Temple instead. In our defence it was still early in our stay and we still hadn't got to grips with the Parisian road pattern of circular hubs with roads radiating out in all directions rather than a more linear network of criss-crossing streets. Whatever, we didn't pay enough attention to our Temples and walked for several blocks before we realised our mistake. Still, it was possible to cut across to Boulevard du Temple or its continuation Boulevard Beaumarchais, without having to retrace our steps back to Place de la République. As a result we took a route along back streets. Anna and Trish found a leather shop that made beautiful handbags and while they were in the shop deciding whether to buy one, and if they could photograph the man working on his latest bag, I wandered further down the street.

On the corner I saw, or at least registered, my first Parisian Space Invader, which merited a photograph. When I rejoined the others Trish told me there was a huge number of them all over the city, all created by the same person – an anonymous artist called Invader. There was a website that listed them all. But although I continued to see and photograph them during my stay, I never did go online to find out where they all were. Once again, the accidental discovery was better than searching them out or ticking them off on a list. Eventually we reached Boulevard Beaumarchais and got back on course. Finally, after a long day's walking around the city, we were back at the hotel.

As 2012 continued there were further reminders of Paris, some of which I Blipped, like the new cake shop near Haymarket station that had an icing Eiffel Tower in the window. Shortly afterwards on the same day I met Petr at the bus stop, as the universe did its best to nudge me into action. In April I won a pair of tickets to see a new adaptation of *The Marriage of Figaro* by D. C. Jackson at Edinburgh's Royal Lyceum Theatre. This version was set in the world of finance in Edinburgh and gave a modern twist to Beaumarchais's original. The same Beaumarchais who is remembered in the Boulevard Beaumarchais that I crossed almost every day when I was in Paris in 2010.

Beaumarchais's life reads like a play itself, and one was written by Sacha Guitry but so far never produced on stage. It did, however, become the basis of a film – *Beaumarchais the Scoundrel* – directed by Édouard Molinaro and released in 1996. Beaumarchais was born Pierre-Augustin Caron in 1731, the son of a watchmaker. After his watchmaking skills brought him to the attention of the royal court in Versailles, he married a wealthy widow and took on a new name, Pierre-Augustin Caron de Beaumarchais, to sound more aristocratic. His influence at court grew, along with his wealth, and he moved into an expensive townhouse on the Left Bank in 1763. He spent time in Spain then returned to Paris, where affairs financial and romantic brought him into conflict with some powerful people, but things improved when the new king, Louis XVI, set him to work as a spy across Europe. He also was involved in arms-running for American revolutionaries in their war against the British.

The first of Beaumarchais's three Figaro plays – *The Barber of Seville* – was premiered in 1775. The sequel, *The Marriage of Figaro*, was not seen in public until 1784. Both were critical of the ancien régime and were elements in the rising tide of opposition to the king.

Beaumarchais bought a large patch of land close to the Bastille and was in the process of building a new, larger mansion there when events across the road heralded the start of the revolution in 1789. He was still able to move into his new home in 1791 but then spent time in prison before travelling abroad, seeking to buy arms for the French revolutionary army.

Lundi 26 avril / 2012

In his absence he was again declared an enemy of the state and spent two and a half years in exile before he was able to return to Paris in April 1796. His mansion on the Boulevard Saint-Antoine had fallen derelict by then but he restored it and lived there with his family until his death in 1799. It was bought by the city in 1818 and the house demolished to create a section of the Canal Saint-Martin. There's a statue of Beaumarchais in a square on the nearby Rue Saint-Antoine. Reading about it, I wondered why I hadn't seen it in 2010, but it had been away for restoration and didn't return until the autumn of that year.

Later in April and on into early May there were images shared online from the latest group of college students on their own Paris trip. Their visit coincided with the French presidential election campaign, although sadly not the final result and they missed the exuberant street celebrations following Hollande's victory, which made for some great photos in the news media.

But clearly, interesting as they all were, none of them inspired me to start work on my book and on Bastille Day 2012 I was once again berating myself for my lack of progress. My Blip for the day highlighted that it was TWO YEARS since the trip – typographically shouting at myself because I still hadn't produced even a first draft. Using Blipfoto's 'one year ago' feature, I commented that I'd been talking about it then too. My Blip was a similar physical desktop picture to the February one – backgrounded with a large map of Paris and including a small selection of my photos scattered more or less in the right geographical positions. There were also some works of fiction – Perec's *Life: A User's Manual*, the copy of Patrick Süskind's *Perfume* that I read on the plane to Paris, and *Sarah's Key*. The DVD of *Les Amants du Pont-Neuf* was there, along with museum guides, Parisian newspapers and minor souvenirs. In there too was *The Invention of Paris*, that I had only recently finished reading.

Lundi 26 avril / 2012

I thought about the way Hazan's book had undermined my self-confidence and why this lack of confidence stifled so many of my creative projects. I believe I want to do them and yet I don't seem to get them done. Was it to do with the large chunk of time I felt I needed to set aside to get properly started? I suspected it would get easier to keep going once I was under way but I also wondered if it was something more fundamental about not wanting it to turn out wrong. If I didn't ever produce it, it would remain this perfect thing in my head. Whereas, if I did create it, would it turn out to be a disappointment? At least I was aware enough to recognise that while the answer to that would almost certainly be yes to begin with, that disappointing first draft would get better after revisions. Without that initial, flawed version there would be nothing to work on.

I also wondered why, instead of working on said first draft, I had spent Bastille Day evening watching the highlights of the latest stage of Le Tour and arranging an elaborate still life of Paris-related material for Blipfoto. I even thought about giving up Blipfoto and using the extra mental space to create My Paris Book (sometimes it felt like it had capitals). A bit drastic as I approached my second year of Blipping and I'm glad I didn't do it. I noted that we'd talked about the same sort of thing at Socrates Café, a regular casual philosophy meetup I go to – how lack of self-belief prevents us doing things. It wasn't belief in the success of the endeavour that was critical but faith that even if it all went wrong it still wouldn't be a disaster. Something I think I struggled with then, and can still find difficult. I think the young boy who liked being right became an adult who worried that if he was wrong he might cease to exist. Preserving an idea in its perfect but intangible state keeps it, and me, safe from criticism. Which means it never appears at all.

As before, though, I found support in the Blipfoto community. Some people let me know that they recognised the same issues in their own blocked creativity and others encouraged me to remember that it doesn't have to be perfect. (Something my wife encapsulated much more recently when she said I should think of it as the first draft of my *first* Paris book.) And in the course of the conversation with Blippers I remembered my paternal grandfather who, looking back, seemed to take the attitude that just making something was good enough and didn't let himself be constrained by perfectionism. I remember inheriting the wooden toy fort he made for my father. It had what appeared to be, even to my young eyes, some incongruous details – a flagpole in what was clearly a painted cotton reel and a space inside the castle keep with a pair of sliding wooden doors, more wardrobe than great hall. But it gave me hours of fun as I overlooked all that amidst the escapism of play.

Another Blipper, who had also commented back in February, praised me for writing two very engaging pieces about *not* writing the book and said that she was convinced because of these that when I did write it, it would be marvellous. She identified completely with the tyranny a procrastinated perfect can hold over a lumpen actuality and admired my honesty in admitting it. She also said I should make a start, however rubbish I felt it was bound to be, and then see where that would lead me. She stopped Blipping years ago so I have no way of telling her that finally I took her words to heart, wrote the book and found the process led me to unexpected places, just as she predicted it would. Her advice – as much, she said, for herself as it was for me – was to promise someone I love that I would do a first draft for their birthday, or enter a competition, or, if I could find the willpower, set myself a specific deadline – do one month's research then write 200 words a day or something. I could even use Blip as a testing ground, sharing my writing and the images that inspired it.

And then another Blipfoto friend, someone whose wonderful portraits I had admired but who I had never met at that point, joined the thread to say she found my honesty inspiring but that my overthinking was getting in the way. I recognised the overthinking as something I was too often guilty of and thought that a solution might be to document my creative struggle more publicly. That would make the project more visible and I would feel more accountable because more people knew about it. In psychology this is known as a Ulysses contract – an agreement made with my future self. It comes from the story of Odysseus (Ulysses to the Romans). In Homer's epic poem the *Odyssey*, Odysseus made a pact with his men that, when they approached the Sirens, his crew would all have their ears blocked to resist the creatures' songs. Odysseus, however, would be able to hear them but would be tied to the ship's mast. He insisted that his men should do everything they had to, to prevent him leaving the ship, no matter how much he struggled and pleaded with them. In the context of a personal project that you're having difficulty finding motivation for, a Ulysses contract often involves just telling lots of people about it, knowing that they'll ask you how it's going and that you don't want to experience the shame of having to tell them that it hasn't been done.

The following week, at an event marking the 70th anniversary of the 1942 Roundup, President Hollande recognised it had been a crime committed 'in France, by France', and emphasised that the deportations in which French police had participated were offences committed against French values, principles and ideals. He praised former president Jacques Chirac for telling France back in 1995 that it needed to face up to its history and recognise the years of collaboration with the Nazis, rather than try to pretend it had never happened. Hollande visited two small parks near where the Vél' d'Hiv' had been, to commemorate the Roundup, although I hadn't known they were there to visit in 2010.

I was still watching the Tour that week too, and on the final stage Norwegian Corner was packed with flag-waving Vikings. Paris looked wonderful in the sunshine. I wasn't a fan of Blipping what you're watching on TV, and it's become ever more frowned on, in fact all but outlawed on the site now for copyright reasons, but I made an exception that afternoon. Team Sky orchestrated the perfect lead-out for Mark Cavendish to take his fourth straight Champs-Élysées win, and Bradley Wiggins finished safely, with no last-day mishap, to confirm his yellow jersey. And he really did need to confirm it as, despite all the chickens being counted after the last mountain stage and the time trial, even by the man himself, slip-ups are always possible. Someone could step into the road or he could hit a pothole. Get so badly injured that he couldn't finish the race. Unlikely, yes, and a deeply unjust way to lose the Tour, but it could have happened. Or am I just a natural pessimist? Anyway, nothing went south so it was a great day for British cycling on the Champs-Élysées.

A few months later, in September 2012, I finally got myself a copy of *A Moveable Feast*. It was written years after Hemingway lived in Paris, although based on two trunks' worth of notes and writing he had done at the time and which had remained unclaimed in the Hôtel Ritz for almost two decades. He died before the book was published but it firmly established the titular idea, that Paris was a feast that a visitor there carried with them for the rest of their life, to enjoy whenever they wanted. The version I bought was the Restored Edition, published only a couple of years earlier and a reworking of the material by Hemingway's grandson. It was two years since my visit, hardly the decades that had passed for Hemingway, but it was enough time for me to start to appreciate how Paris resonated in my consciousness.

Back in 2010, on that first Monday night, I joined another large group heading out for dinner. This time, having learned the lesson of the night before, we only walked to the end of the street and the Cuban-themed place on the corner. But we were still sat at another long table that made it hard to talk. I decided that next day a smaller group would be better.

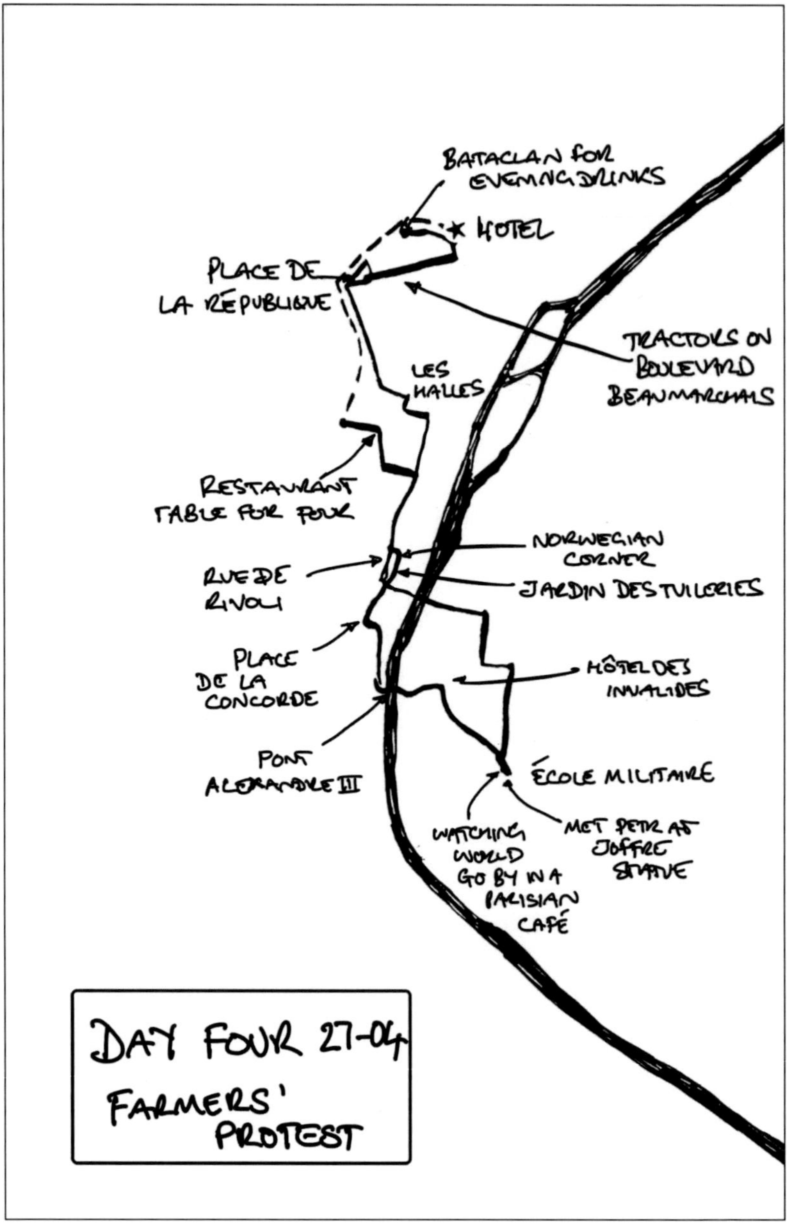
BATACLAN FOR EVENING DRINKS
HOTEL
PLACE DE LA RÉPUBLIQUE
TRACTORS ON BOULEVARD BEAUMARCHAIS
LES HALLES
RESTAURANT TABLE FOR FOUR
NORWEGIAN CORNER
RUE DE RIVOLI
JARDIN DES TUILERIES
PLACE DE LA CONCORDE
HÔTEL DES INVALIDES
PONT ALEXANDRE III
ÉCOLE MILITAIRE
WATCHING WORLD GO BY IN A PARISIAN CAFÉ
MET PETR AT JOFFRE STATUE
DAY FOUR 27-04
FARMERS' PROTEST

Mardi 27 avril / 2013

After breakfast there was some time with our tutors to discuss progress on our projects and look at some of the photographs we'd taken so far. As a result it was almost eleven by the time Petr and I set out from the hotel. We were headed towards Bastille once again when we found a queue of cars at the end of the street. The road was blocked, with a policeman standing guard, but there was no trouble getting past as pedestrians. Out on Boulevard Beaumarchais the only traffic was a seemingly endless parade of tractors. Lots of people were watching them go past, including young students with brightly coloured rucksacks, old ladies with their shopping baskets and office workers in suits. Many of them were applauding as the farmers went by and it seemed that everyone was taking photos, whether with their phones or actual cameras. We stood at the edge of the Place de la Bastille and took some pictures of our own until Petr decided he'd seen enough and headed off towards the river. I thought I'd follow the tractors for a bit and get some more photographs of the protest.

As I approached Place de la République some of the tractors had started parking up along the side of the road and I took some more shots looking down the lines of vehicles, their massive tyres slightly out of scale even on a wide boulevard. Looking for photographic angles was probably why I didn't notice an interesting curved building set back a little from the main street. The building I missed was the Cirque D'Hiver, the oldest circus building in the world. To a photographer, it is also noteworthy as the location for one of Richard Avedon's most popular images.

'Dovima with Elephants' was part of a series of images taken for *Harper's Bazaar*'s September 1955 issue. Avedon was staff photographer there from 1946 to 1965, and the thinly veiled inspiration for Fred Astaire's character, Dick Avery, in the 1957 film musical *Funny Face*. In the film, Avery is on a shoot in a New York bookshop when he discovers a new talent. Watching the film again recently I saw that the model in the shoot was played by the same Dovima whom Avedon photographed. Avery takes his discovery, Jo Stockton, played by Audrey Hepburn, to Paris as the creative circles overlap. Prompted by the film, I looked again at the picture of Dovima and the elephants, and started to investigate its location. But I was unaware of this in 2010 and therefore didn't stop at, or even notice, the Cirque d'Hiver to pay homage to Avedon, Dovima and those elephants.

Neither was I aware that, as I approached the Place de la République, I was walking into the frame of one of the most well-known images in the history of photography. The very first photograph, or at least the earliest surviving one, was taken in 1826 or 1827 by Nicéphore Niépce using a bitumen process that required an exposure time of several days. Louis Daguerre worked with Niépce and then continued his research after Niépce's death, developing the daguerrotype. This was much quicker but still required an exposure of several minutes and therefore the first daguerrotypes are largely empty street scenes, as even a busy street would not show any people if they were not in the same place for the majority of the exposure time. (Ironic, given that current French privacy laws risk effectively removing people from Parisian street images once again.) I'd actually already studied Daguerre's famous Boulevard du Temple image, probably taken in the spring of 1838, which includes a man stopping to have his shoes shined – something which meant he paused long enough to register in the

Mardi 27 avril / 2013

long exposure. This is the photograph that many people credit as the first to capture a human being but once again my lack of preparation for visiting Paris meant I wasn't remembering the connection as I walked up the street.

The road layout in this part of Paris has changed considerably since Daguerre took his famous picture. Using some meticulous detective work, Daguerre expert Jacques Darcy-Roquencourt, along with Françoise Reynaud and Catherine Tambrun from the Musée Carnavalet, has determined that the camera was probably set up in Daguerre's studio on the top floor of the building that housed his diorama, behind what was then the Place de Château d'Eau and today occupied by the National Gendarmerie buildings on the northeastern side of Place de la République. The investigative team used Daguerre's 14-inch (355mm) lens to take pictures looking across the square and down the Boulevard du Temple. They then placed these images against the modern streetscape – reversed, as they have to be, because daguerrotypes are mirror images – and showed how the layout has changed.

Passing between the lines of tractors at the end of the boulevard I could see there was a rally taking place in the square. In the paper the following day it said there had been more than a thousand tractors and 11,000 demonstrators. After the speeches the crowd started to form up across the street, all wearing the same white tee-shirts with a slogan in green – 'fauché comme les blés'. Its literal French translation is 'broke like wheat' but more generally it means someone who is completely without money – just like a deserted wheat field after the harvest. In the context of a protest organised by the farmers' union the metaphor was more visceral.

The media coverage explained the farmers' grievances – volatile grain, sunflower and rapeseed prices meant they were getting back less than it cost to produce their crops. A farmer from northeast France was quoted on the publicly funded TV news channel France 24: 'We can no longer make a living out of what we produce. It costs 150 euros to produce a ton of wheat, which we sell for 100 euros. We're losing money. EU subsidies make up for part of that, but they're getting smaller and smaller. All of the tractors you see here belong to banks. A new tractor costs 50,000 euros, but by the time we've finished paying them off they're too old and rundown to be worth anything.' As they gathered you could see the range of banners and placards with their handwritten slogans and several effigies of French president Nicolas Sarkozy, or Sarko as many described him. Some tractors had the sorts of road signs you see at the end of a French village, where the name of the village is crossed out when you're leaving it – making the point that the system was killing their communities. The crowd moved down the boulevard, setting fireworks off into the air, followed by the tractors. I saw men carrying strange metal poles, like some sort of hook attachment for a trailer. I couldn't see what they were for until the march set off and one of them swung his pole over his shoulder and smashed it down onto the road as if using a pickaxe, setting off a loud firecracker.

Mardi 27 avril / 2013

In 2024 there were similar protests in London, apparently provoked by proposed changes in the taxation system, rather than the systemic problems of modern agriculture. At the time of writing Labour's idea is to remove the exemption from inheritance tax for agricultural land that was introduced by Margaret Thatcher's government in 1984, which incentivised some people to buy up farmland, pushing up prices and notional value, without changing the income it can generate. Worse still for farmers, as opposed to wealthy landowners, is the same problem that those French farmers were protesting about in Paris back in 2010 – farming doesn't pay. Costs have increased but food prices have not risen to match. Farmers are angry with their situation and have been provided with a cause to rally behind, a cause that really serves the interests of the rich. Much like the people who were poorer as a result of globalisation and stagnant wages but voted for Brexit to express their anger.

I finally decided I'd had my fill of tractors, crossed Place de la République and headed down Rue de Turbigo towards the city centre. At the top of the street, just round the corner from the square, I passed a small phalanx of riot police waiting beside a newspaper kiosk, helmets, shields and tear gas making them seem like modern-day legionaries. They were clearly waiting out of sight but ready in reserve in case of trouble. Unsure of the rules around photographing the police in France, but absolutely certain I couldn't talk my way out of any difficulty in French, I didn't use my camera.

Early in 2013 I went to the opening of a photography exhibition in Edinburgh. *La Culture Parisienne* was put on by that year's BA Photography class at my old college. The pictures were mostly the ones the group had shown in Paris the previous spring during their exchange visit (this was introduced post my year's trip). Despite a successful London exhibit in 2012, the college had withdrawn the funding and so the students were trying to raise the money themselves. You could argue that that was fair enough, as they stood to gain most, but the college also benefited from a raised profile in London. Just another symptom of the pressure the FE sector was under as the SNP government robbed College Peter to keep its funding promises to University Paul. And the students were stuck in the middle.

Seeing pictures of Paris of course made me think again of my Paris book.

In April 2013 I posted my 1000th Blip. It had become a well-established part of my routine, as well as a daily reminder of Paris, where it all started, and the project that never seemed to get off the ground. (Another Paris habit which had stuck was not adding milk to my tea. In Parisian cafés they often brought tea without milk and after a few times asking them in my stumbling French to bring some milk I tried it without and, finding it tasted fine, thought I would just drink it black. By the time I got back I was used to it. At first no doubt an affectation but now just part of who I am.) On the anniversary of the trip I posted several Blips that referenced the same day exactly three years previously, like the spring sunshine in Edinburgh on 24 April that reminded me of the sunshine on our first day in Paris.

Later in May I wrote a bit more on the nature of Blip anniversaries. I'd photographed the neighbour's wisteria flowers but then, as I was about to post the Blip, I thought I remembered Blipping them before. If so, and me being me, I would probably have to find something else. I had a quick check and, yes, I had Blipped them before but it had actually been more than two years previously, on the anniversary of my very first Blip, in Paris. Interestingly it was more than a month earlier in the year. So, despite the apparent repetition, I thought it would be worth Blipping it again after all, with some thoughts on the changing seasons.

Mardi 27 avril / 2013

I had believed the seasons were getting progressively earlier but here was clear evidence that the wisteria was flowering a whole month later than two years previously. And although the Parisian wisteria I reminisced about had also been in flower above the slopes of Montmartre in the first week of May, Paris is almost 500 miles south of Edinburgh. In my 2013 Blip I wrote that there was a rough approximation that spring moves north at about sixteen or seventeen miles a day. An idea that deftly combines the temporal with the geographical in a way that feels instinctively illogical and yet also describes what we can see all around us. I see now, though, that the sixteen-miles-a-day figure is based on US observations. In the UK the data collected by the Woodland Trust, using submissions to its Nature's Calendar website tracker, estimates spring's northward march closer to 2mph and therefore nearly fifty miles a day. Which would put Edinburgh less than a fortnight behind Paris, rather than the whole month I believed to be the case in 2013.

The differences I'd observed did bear out the variations in the arrival of spring, though. While 2010 was a little late, compared to a 2001 baseline, 2011 was at least a month early and 2013 was back around the baseline. Two pictures in two years is some way behind the picture a day, every day, that Harvey Keitel's character Auggie Wren takes in the film *Smoke*, but they're both examples of the way that photographs of the same thing can tell a story. Auggie takes the same picture on the corner of 3rd Street and Seventh Avenue in Brooklyn at the same time every day, when he opens up his cigar shop. At one point he tells a customer he has more than four thousand pictures in albums. When I first saw the film that seemed an unimaginable sequence of pictures to take but Blipfoto has made me much more aware of the relationship in sheer numbers between days and years as my entries have racked up – 365, 730, 1095, 1460, and on, and on. More than 5,000 without a break at this time of writing, and even though most of mine have been taken in different places, in 2015, shortly after we moved to the seaside at Portobello, I took one hundred photos of the same view – the sea and sky at the bottom of our street. They were taken at different times of day, but the pictures were the same and different in an Auggie Wren sort of way.

After a morning with the protesting farmers in April 2010 I was walking, flâneur-like, in the vague direction of the city centre. Despite the pass in my pocket that would've got me on the Métro for 'free', it didn't occur to me to use it. After all it was a beautiful sunny day and I was beginning to get to grips with the starburst pattern of the boulevards, how they radiated out from key squares and roundabouts. It had led us astray the day before, so I knew a small mistake could slowly take you further and further out of your way without you realising it, but I still felt okay with my sense of direction as I walked down Rue de Turbigo, a wide tree-lined street whose diagonal direction cut across the grid of adjoining streets to create a series of off-kilter junctions. Feeling hungry I stopped at a baker's and bought a pain au raisin, a simple transaction for which I was pleased to be able to use some of the French phrases I had learnt for the trip.

In early June 2013 I was composing a picture on Bruntsfield Links in Edinburgh. I felt there was something a bit New York – Central Park rather than Auggie's Brooklyn – about the view across the Meadows. I framed it looking towards the Quartermile redevelopment of the old Royal Infirmary site to show how the evening sun picked out the glass tops of the new buildings. It was a lovely evening and I'd taken the camera out with me to look for a Blip. As I was considering my shot, just like in the arcade in Paris I saw a familiar figure walking towards me. It was Matthew, one of the two tutors who came with us in 2010. He had news. The merger that had formed Edinburgh College out of the three Edinburgh FE colleges – Stevenson, Telford and Jewel & Esk – had led to the loss of many senior lecturer positions. He could have applied for a management role but that would have meant no teaching and so he was leaving. On our course some of my fellow students questioned the value of Matthew's classes. They often included things that were not strictly on the syllabus, therefore unnecessary in a box-ticking, transactional view of education. However, for me and several of my friends on the course, his was exactly the sort of teaching that encouraged you to find out stuff just because you wanted to know about it, not because there would

be a question on it later in an exam. To the accountants who run so much of edu-biz these days and see students only as customers, that appears to be something of a luxury but I think it is the way to encourage the sort of enquiring minds that can create the unexpected and make real discoveries. I told Matthew about one of my teachers at Durham whose lectures always rattled along, full of anecdotes and ideas. He explicitly told people beforehand not to take notes, just listen and think, but every time you could see people desperately scribbling as they tried not to miss anything. He was right, though. It was better to try and follow his train of thought running through the hour and then talk about it later over a coffee with other students. We'd done exactly that after many of Matthew's classes, in the college canteen.

When I bumped into him Matthew was walking home from Leith as part of his training for walking the West Highland Way. It was linked to the Ragged University and we talked about walking as an activity to give space for thought and for coming up with ideas. Something I recognised from when I used to walk to work every day, and one of the things I missed most when I left my nine-to-five. Heading our separate ways, I went back to taking my Blip and then, walking home, I thought once more about the Paris book, trying to make more sense of the rough ideas in my head.

Back in 2010 I took the pastry out of the bag to eat as I walked. Soon I passed the entrance to the underground shopping centre at Les Halles, then, reaching the Rue de Rivoli, turned right and walked along the covered arcade-like pavement on the north side of the street for several blocks. Across the road was the back of the Louvre but I stayed on my side of the street, briefly out into the sunshine to cross the square in front of the Palais-Royal where I had been the day before and then back into the shade. Three more blocks before the long stretch of buildings across the street came to an end at a busy road junction that will always be Norwegian Corner to me. Since Norwegian cyclists started to have some success in the early 2000s, Norwegians have travelled to watch them in the Tour de France, congregating in a prime spot on the final circuit where the riders come back out of the Louvre tunnel and slow to take the corner onto Rue de Rivoli.

In June 2013 among the films I saw at the Edinburgh International Film Festival was *Paris Countdown* (*Le jour attendra* – literally 'the day will wait'), largely chosen on the basis of its setting. It was very hip, with some splashy violence, and a few glimpses of the streets of Paris during a car chase sequence. I was sitting right behind the director, who was there for a brief Q&A after the film finished. He kept referring to his two leading actors as comedians, but I'm guessing he was caught out by a 'faux ami'.

   A month or so later, on Bastille Day, I read my Blip post from the year before and couldn't fail to notice the similarities. I still hadn't completed the first draft of my Paris book. Now, in 2013, I was again disappointed at my lack of progress but found a lot to say about Chris Froome winning that day's stage of the Tour de France on top of Mount Ventoux. And a week later I Blipped the TV and my laptop again. Was this going to become a tradition? We'd talked about that at Socrates Café and I supposed they had to start somewhere: once is an isolated incident, the second time is the beginning of a sequence. The Tour is another example. In 2013 it was the centenary and the race delayed its entrance into Paris until the early evening to provide a night-time conclusion. The circuit also included going right round the Arc de Triomphe rather than turning just short of the top of the Champs-Élysées, a change they subsequently kept. I left my Blipping to concentrate on the conclusion of the race – and noted that it was also the 114th anniversary of Ernest Hemingway's birth.

Walking along the Rue de Rivoli in 2010, imagining the peleton racing by, I passed Angelina's, the fancy café a friend back in Edinburgh had recommended for an afternoon tea. It was under scaffolding but still open and looked enticing, selling amazing cakes and pastries. I decided it wasn't a place to waste on your own – I should try and persuade some of the others to come back later to share the experience. So I crossed the road and into the Jardin des Tuileries. I walked through the gardens and then down a flight of steps that took me under the road that leads from the Place de la Concorde to the Louvre tunnel. (Another part of the familiar laps at the end of Le Tour.) The steps led down to the Quai des

Mardi 27 avril / 2013

Tuileries beside the river and another flight of steps led up from the lower level of the Passerelle Léopold-Sédar-Senghor, an elegantly designed footbridge.

On the Left Bank the Musée d'Orsay was only a short distance away but instead I headed in the opposite direction. I zigzagged along some ordinary-looking Parisian streets, stopping to photograph another Space Invader. I reached the Hôtel des Invalides complex and went in by a side entrance. It seemed too good a day to be in a museum so I stayed outside in the gardens and photographed the ornamental bushes around the gold-dome-topped building that houses Napoleon's tomb (famously the subject of Margot's going-away gift for Barbara in the 1970s sitcom *The Good Life*).

I sat on a bench in the gardens and wondered which direction I should go in next. It's not far from the military mausoleum at Les Invalides to the École Militaire – from Napoleon's final resting place back to the institution where, as an awkward teenager, he first studied to be an artillery officer – and that was the way I headed. Across the road from the grand eighteenth-century facade I sat in the shade of the statue of the First World War general Joseph Joffre and looked across the park towards the Eiffel Tower. A cluster of laughing tourists on Segways posed for a group photo in front of the Mur de la Paix (Wall for Peace). Behind them, half a mile away at the other end of the Champs de Mars, the Eiffel Tower loomed large. There was a real feeling of a grand plan, a city with a design to it, on a monumental scale.

In the late summer of 2013 I put the book project on hold for the best of reasons. Lorraine and I decided to go to Paris for a few days to mark my 50th birthday, combined with a visit to London so she could go and see Fleetwood Mac at the O2. The concert was the night we arrived in London and while she went to the gig I headed to Soho, where I was meeting some people for dinner. I had time to kill and so went to Soho Square. I know London quite well because I did a postgrad at the LSE in the 1980s, but the last time I'd been was in 2010 with people from college. Three of us had been shortlisted in a national photography competition and had come down together, with one of our tutors. None of us won but it was a good trip.

So I was wandering round the square – looking for Kirsty MacColl's bench, a memorial to the singer in a place she referenced in one of her songs – when I bumped into Anna, one of the students on the Paris trip. She'd moved to London after college and like me was killing time before meet someone. Of course we had a catch-up and I was now in danger of being late.

I was a little nervous as I was meeting someone I had got to know through Blipfoto but never met in person. I needn't have worried, though, as I had a great evening with Juliana, her husband and a couple of their friends – women I'd also never met but was familiar with because they'd both been the subject of some of Juliana's wonderful portrait Blips. I talked a bit about my ideas for the still-not-written Paris book and the way the upcoming weekend would help to cement things in my head. They'd arranged a small birthday cake as an early start to my celebrations. Later I went to meet Lorraine at the tube station. She'd had a great night too (albeit no cake.) The next day was spent mostly on the South Bank. A bit like being in Paris, sitting in a café with a drink watching the world go by.

The next day we took the Eurostar and arrived right into the heart of the city at the Gare du Nord. It seems strange that the tunnel is so ordinary now. When I was growing up it was just a mad idea of Napoleon's that had never happened. Something that belonged in a world of steampunk science fiction.

Our hotel was walkable from the station and after unpacking our bags we headed straight back out. First, we went down to the Place de la République, which looked a bit different when it wasn't full of angry farmers. We walked on to the Bastille, along streets that were still very familiar to me. After a sit down on the steps of the Opéra building we went to Rue du Petit-Musc. Lorraine's memory was vague about exactly which building housed the apartment she'd sofa-surfed in thirty years earlier but we took a few pictures and then bought pastries from a nearby patisserie. Lorraine had a much clearer memory of looking in the window last time, a hitcher with very little money and certainly none for fancy cakes. So we bought what we liked the look of and took the cakes down to the Quai de la Tournelle and sat there eating them in silence with sticky fingers as we looked across to the islands in the middle of the river.

We were more or less opposite the block of flats that had reminded me of *Life: A User's Manual* and been the subject of my first image on Blipfoto. I took another picture, to mark my return. At that point it was still not quite three years of uninterrupted Blipping – a picture a day, every day – and just as in a Perec novel, there are many other stories. I've seen the same apartments photographed by other Blippers and commented on the connection. It is a very recognisable view, more often included on the edge of a picture of Notre-Dame from the Left Bank.

We crossed the river and into the Marais, where we bought falafels on the Rue des Rosiers and ate them as we wandered along. In a park we stopped and watched kids playing table tennis on outdoor tables and had a drink in a café opposite the statue of Marianne in the centre of Place de la République on the way back to the hotel.

The next day was my birthday and so started in the hotel with cards and presents, including a tee-shirt with the surnames of the members of The Jam on it. We went round the corner for breakfast and then down to République again, but this time we headed in a different direction – up the Avenue de la République towards Père Lachaise. Past the corner café on the junction with Rue Oberkampf where I'd had dinner on the first weekend in Paris back in 2010. At the top of the hill, close to the cemetery entrance, we looked for a florist and Lorraine bought a single white rose – a rose for Chopin, after the title of her radio play – to lay on his grave. We also stopped by Jim Morrison, Édith Piaf and Oscar Wilde, and then visited the infamous Mur des Fédérés ('Communards' Wall').

The whole of that corner of Père Lachaise is filled with memorials to the turmoil of twentieth-century European history and the struggles between Left and Right and between the two great European powers of France and Germany. There are several dramatic sculptures to the victims of the Nazi death camps, some I hadn't seen the previous time and some of which I had photographed in 2010. When I took those pictures I had been unaware that a short distance over my shoulder was the memorial to the Communards. Against this wall was where 147 prisoners were shot at the end of the suppression of the Paris Commune in

1871. It has been a place of great symbolic significance to the Left in France ever since.

The Commune was a very short-lived revolutionary government that came about after France's defeat at the hands of the Prussians in the process of creating modern Germany. It was a national humiliation and arguably prompted the severe French terms laid out in the 1918 Armistice that then gave Hitler the sense of German grievance that he exploited in the lead-up to the Second World War. But the Commune was also about the fight between Left and Right within France – a battle the Left lost, either due to lack of equipment and men, poor leadership or perhaps because of the redesign of the city that had followed the 1848 uprisings. Some claim that Haussmann's wide boulevards, like the ones we had walked along from the hotel, were consciously designed for military purposes. Intentional or not, there's little doubt that they did allow for the rapid deployment of government troops brought in from outside the city by train, and restricted the opportunities for the barricading of narrow streets that had been a feature of earlier insurrections. Although Haussmann occasionally argued for the strategic advantages of his design in his dealings with the French government, he later claimed that that had merely been the best tactic to secure funds and was not his real motivation. His true goal, he said, was to implement the desire of his emperor, Napoleon III, to create a better connected and more beautiful city for its residents and visitors to enjoy. Whether you take him at his word or suspect a more reactionary objective probably depends on your broader political views.

There had been changes in the cemetery since I was last there, most notably the transparent screen protecting Oscar Wilde's grave from graffiti and lipstick, but it was just as fascinating a place to wander round, peaceful and yet busy with tourists congregating around certain memorials, taking pictures and then moving on.

We too moved on, down Rue de la Roquette towards the Bastille, stopping for lunch about halfway down the street. Further on I was back into more familiar territory, passing bars and cafés I

Mardi 27 avril / 2013

had visited in 2010, including the graffiti-covered Tape. In the Place de la Bastille there was a protest against landmines: a pyramid of single shoes signifying lost limbs. Lorraine and I signed the petition and got a sticker. Then we made our way onto the islands, walking along the north side of Île Saint-Louis this time and then onto Île de la Cité. There were long queues to get in to Notre-Dame but Lorraine had visited it before and I was happy to just sit outside on the terracing for a while looking at the spectacular front of the building and watching the people jostling around, still reminding me of pigeons.

We went over the Pont-Neuf and briefly along the Rive Gauche before heading back across the river. There had been a lot more padlocks added to the Pont des Arts bridge since I'd last seen it. We went into the Louvre courtyards, out into the Jardin des Tuileries and then on to the Place de la Concorde for a view up towards the Arc de Triomphe. On the way back towards the hotel we stopped for a quick drink in a Scottish pub that was showing an English football game. Later we had a birthday dinner for me in a restaurant on the corner of République – steak frites, if I remember rightly.

In 2010 I was just having a drink of water, sitting in the shade of the Marshal Joffre statue on the edge of the Champs de Mars, when Petr walked by. It turned out he had arranged to meet a few of the others at the same statue. We sat and waited and compared what we'd been doing since we separated back at the Bastille. Petr had been photographing cyclists, looking to capture a sense of movement and with the Eiffel Tower in the background to clearly place the pictures in Paris. Soon we were joined by Sophy, Sam, Graeme and Scott and, after a quick group picture, we left the dazzling expanse of gravel in front of the École Militaire and headed to a corner café. Very Parisian, we sat out on the street, our chairs all with their backs to the café, tables in front of us and an uninterrupted view. The city is the show, the café customers the audience, our drinks the price of admission.

Which is where we sat for a while. It was late on a Monday afternoon and I was effectively being paid to watch the world go by instead of sitting at my desk in the Royal Bank of Scotland designing IT systems and writing computer code, clock-watching until it was time to go home. I savoured the moment and the way a different path taken had led me somewhere I'd never imagined a few years before. Then, I had been firmly in the corporate groove with no thoughts of leaving.

We finished our drinks and Scott and Sam decided to head back to base. There was a Métro station just across the road and they could take Line 8 all the way to Chemin Vert, close to the hotel. The rest of us headed off down the wide avenue towards the river.

At the front entrance to the Hôtel des Invalides we admired the upper windows that looked like soldiers' heads then took a path

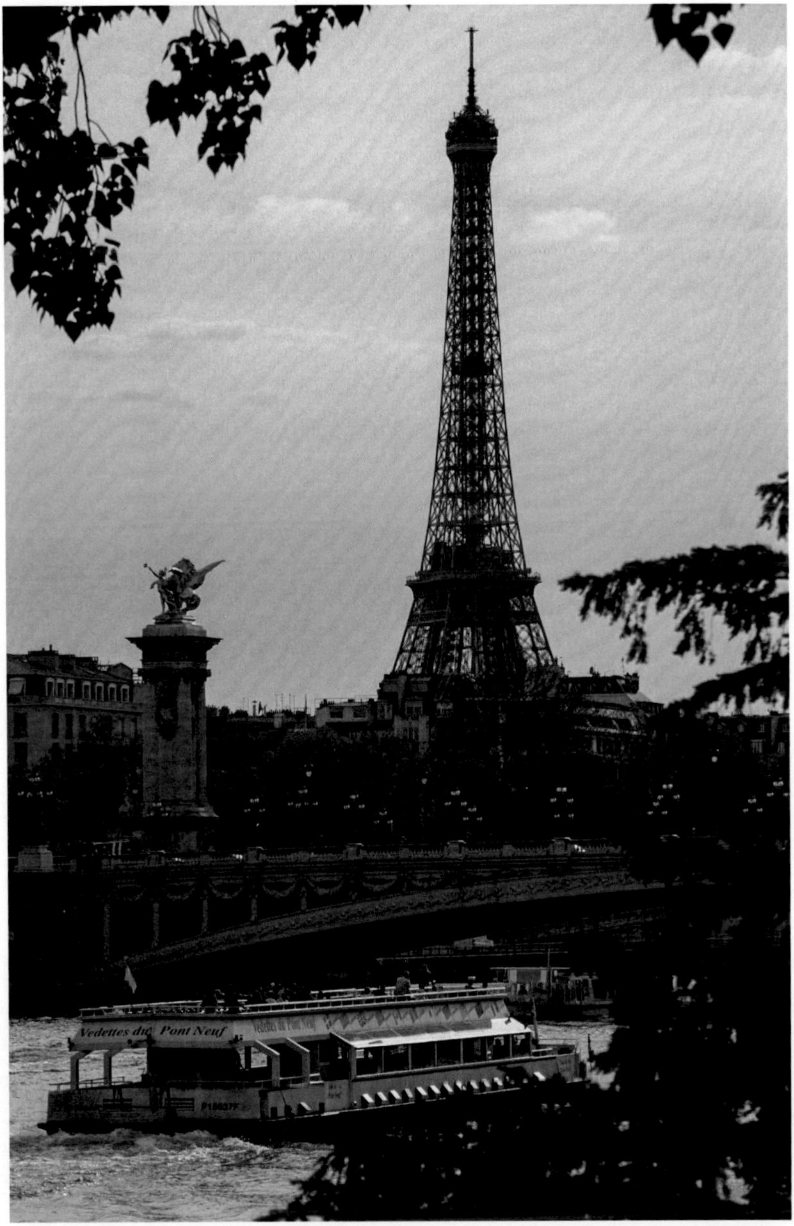
Vedettes du Pont Neuf

along the edge of the park in front of the formal gardens, reminiscent of those London parks with their pavement-less roads, full of cars driving through the middle of open green space. Under the trees men were playing pétanque, the clicking of the metal balls rising above the low buzz of the traffic. Some of the men were casually dressed but others wore suits – presumably they'd stopped by on their way home from the office. Further on youngsters on inline skates practised their moves, legs criss-crossing between plastic cups laid out in a pattern on the tarmac.

We reached the river and the extravagant grandeur of the Pont Alexandre III, with its golden statues on tall columns at the four corners of the bridge. A popular spot for photoshoots, not to mention blockbuster films and music videos. There were views towards the Eiffel Tower in one direction and upstream towards the Louvre. The four of us headed in that direction, stopping briefly at Concorde. It was impossible not to think of a long line of cyclists crossing the cobbles on the final stage of the Tour. We looked up the Champs-Élysées towards the Arc, but rather than walking up the hill – something for another day – we got away from the evening traffic via the ornate gates of the Jardin des Tuileries.

Just inside the entrance I saw an interesting sculpture over by the north wall. It looked familiar for some reason and I went to check it out. The sculpture was *La Foule* by Raymond Mason and I realised that the reason I recognised it was that I'd seen an exhibition of Mason's work in the City Art Centre in Edinburgh. It had been a really good collection of his bas relief works depicting the Parisian fruit and vegetable market. Those had been in colour but this bronze sculpture of a crowd of people had much of the same feel to it. I subsequently discovered that that exhibition had been in the autumn of 1989, more than twenty years before my visit to Paris, and yet the memory of the work was still in my head. As was a scrap of school French. I asked Sophy about the meaning

Mardi 27 avril / 2013

of the French title. She confirmed my guess at the English translation – *The Crowd*.

We walked on through the gardens towards the Louvre, pausing to look back towards the Champs-Élysées and the Arc de Triomphe at the top of the hill. Behind that, in the distance, was La Grande Arche at La Défense, the third arch in the line of the Axe historique, a stunning feat of urban design that spans three centuries. Also on that line is the modern glass pyramid at the Louvre that is the setting for Various Important Scenes in Dan Brown's *Da Vinci Code*. With Paris, the tapestry is just so wide, the cultural connections everywhere – almost every direction you look in points towards a book you've read, a film you've seen, a painting, a sculpture, a photograph, a news story, a sporting triumph (or debacle – I'm Scottish and a Leeds United fan), not to mention memories from previous visits.

At the glass pyramid I took a quick photo. As it turned out, it was one of the few photographs of people from our group that I took during the fortnight. Again: did it feel too much like being on holiday, taking those sorts of pictures? I was supposed to be a photographer, whatever that meant, rather than a tourist.

Leaving the courtyards of the Louvre, we stepped out onto the Rue de Rivoli and I found myself back in a very similar area to where I'd been just twenty-four hours earlier. We were now looking for a place to eat and I knew exactly where to go. I led us across the gardens above Les Halles shopping centre – built on the site of the old market that was the inspiration for Raymond Mason's colourful bas relief sculptures that had proved so memorable. We passed the sculpture of a giant face and hand (Henri de Miller's *Écoute*) and onto a street I'd walked up the day before – the pedestrianised Rue Montorgueil – which was indeed full of places to eat.

We looked at a few very touristy menus and picked a slightly more French-looking place. A table for four was no problem and when they brought us a copy of the menu in English, emboldened by Sophy's presence, and her fluent French, we said the French menu would be fine. Perhaps Sophy would have had an easier time if we'd got the English one, not having to answer numerous questions from the rest of us. It felt good to do our ordering in French, three of us admittedly with a bit of pointing. Things were going well. We ordered a bottle of red. The server commended Sophy on her French.

The food was good but not spectacular – I had swordfish with potatoes and vegetables – but four sitting round the same table, sharing a bottle, all involved in the same conversation was a markedly more pleasant dining experience than the last three large group meals had been. It was a chance to get to know each other, especially Sophy, who'd been a last-minute addition to the group. Someone had dropped out and rather than waste the place it had been offered to students in years below ours, as long as they spoke French (presumably so the college could justify their late inclusion). Several days in, we had begun to settle into our environment and no longer needed the security of the large group.

In 2013, on our last full day in Paris, Lorraine and I headed out in the opposite direction from the hotel, towards the Palais-Royal and then on to the Tuileries. We sat in an outdoor café there, eating clafoutis in honour of the role the dessert had played in the play Lorraine had performed in at that year's Fringe – Yasmina Reza's *God of Carnage*. The play includes the consumption of some leftover clafoutis that Lorraine's character, Veronique, has supposedly made the day before and she talks about her recipe for the dish. Lorraine had a go at making the edible prop, not method acting so much as a practical way to have the right thing to act with on stage. Each member of the cast and crew made their own version of the dish for one of the dress rehearsals or the six actual performances. Having looked into it more, it turned out that

Mardi 27 avril / 2013

technically what she made wasn't a clafoutis at all, as that should only be made with black cherries. Hers, using apples and pears, is actually called a flaugnarde but both are fundamentally a sweet pancake with fruit mixed into the batter that is then baked. Simples. But when we walked through the park and saw the sign advertising clafoutis, we had to have the real thing.

Across the river, there was an event on the riverside promoting urban fitness. We watched people doing aerobics for about as long as anyone can then headed up to the Rodin Museum, which was on our list of places to visit. The sculptures in the house and garden are wonderful to see close up, and not just the most familiar ones, like *The Thinker*, which have entered into the common lexicon. Although busy the gardens still felt relatively peaceful. Afterwards we walked a short way to the edge of the Champs du Mar for a view of the Eiffel Tower, just as I had been doing when I bumped into Petr three years before, and then headed back in the direction of the hotel, more or less retracing the route I had taken with Petr, Sophy and Graeme. Lorraine and I didn't go to exactly the same restaurant on the Rue Montorgueil but ate at one close by.

The next day we walked up to Gare du Nord and got the train back to London, then walked to King's Cross for the connection to Edinburgh. On our way back we gave our solicitor the go ahead to put our house near Haymarket up for sale, moving things on in our lives. Two weeks later I was Blipping about the trip again, sharing an image of a map of where we went in Paris. We had gone everywhere on foot, from the moment we got off the Eurostar on the Friday afternoon until we got back on it again on Monday lunchtime. I was irritated that the new Google Maps route-drawing software didn't seem to show the distance travelled but I calculated that it was somewhere around 22-23 miles, criss-crossing the central arrondissements of the city. In fact, I'm sure

Mardi 27 avril / 2013

we made at least a brief visit to eleven of the inner twelve, just missing out on the 9th, but also adding in the 20th.

Walking everywhere worked well at keeping the relative locations of different places clear in our heads. Our time in London beforehand was also spent mostly travelling on foot. Only Lorraine's trip to the O2 and back was done by tube, everything else was Shanks's pony. Also in my Blip was a pile of books about Paris that I hoped to use in writing my 'long-planned book', as I described it then, in the middle of October 2013. On the screen with the map I added a quote I'd found at the end of an article criticising the Champs-Élysées. 'Today if I'm asked by first-time visitors where they should go in Paris, my advice is clear. Love the Louvre. Marvel at the Marais. Elate at the Ile de la Cite. Get an eyeful of the Eiffel. But as Lewis Carroll said of the *frumious bandersnatch*: shun the Champs Elysees.'

For a moment I felt almost recognised, vindicated. We didn't go inside the Louvre, and although we went to the others all we saw of the most famous street in Paris was the view from the Place de la Concorde. We had just done Paris 'right', without even trying. However, the more I thought about it, the more I disagreed with the article. The writer had taken exception to all the new and very expensive shops on the street and how un-French it had become. It was now a place for tourists, looking for a Paris that didn't exist.

Except, it does exist, as it is, with its over-priced real estate and international brands. It might be dripping with artificiality and marketing but who's to say that those layers of meaning, like a Russian doll, aren't as real as the other Parisian locations on his list?

Ruling somewhere out of a visiting itinerary, especially a place you can visit for free, was actually counter to my preferred approach. Go see it for yourself. See what you think. It might be full of the same shops you can see in New York and London but it still leads up to the Arc de Triomphe. It is still the street the Tour de France cyclists race up and down. It is still Paris.

Unfortunately, despite the renewed impetus the book project received from the trip to Paris, life then got in the way. Lots of people came to look round our house, but I don't think most of them really grasped what it had going for it. The rooms were small, especially the bedrooms, but it was a self-contained house, on a quiet cul-de-sac, with its own garden out the back complete with a little summerhouse, all ten minutes' walk from Haymarket and not much further again to Princes Street. I suspect it would be more desirable now, since the pandemic, as people have placed more value on private outdoor space. Nevertheless, as people say, you just need one buyer, which we had and so we sold up and moved out in November 2013. We'd lived there fourteen years, the longest time either of us had lived in one place, and we'll need to stay where we are as I write this for another four years to beat it, which will take me to my mid sixties. My father, on the other hand, has lived in the same house for more than fifty years. I'd need to live to be a hundred, and stay put until then, despite the second-floor tenement stairs, to match that. Some predictions I've seen have the sea coming halfway up our street by 2050, so there's that too.

In 2010, after our meal, we went to get the Métro – my first opportunity to use my travel card. It was just a few stops to République and then a quick change onto another line took us to Bréguet-Sabin, close to the hotel. Later on Petr, Sophy and I went out for a drink, back to the Grand Café Bataclan where we'd been with the large group on Sunday night. This time we sat around a small table on the worn leather chairs and enjoyed it properly.

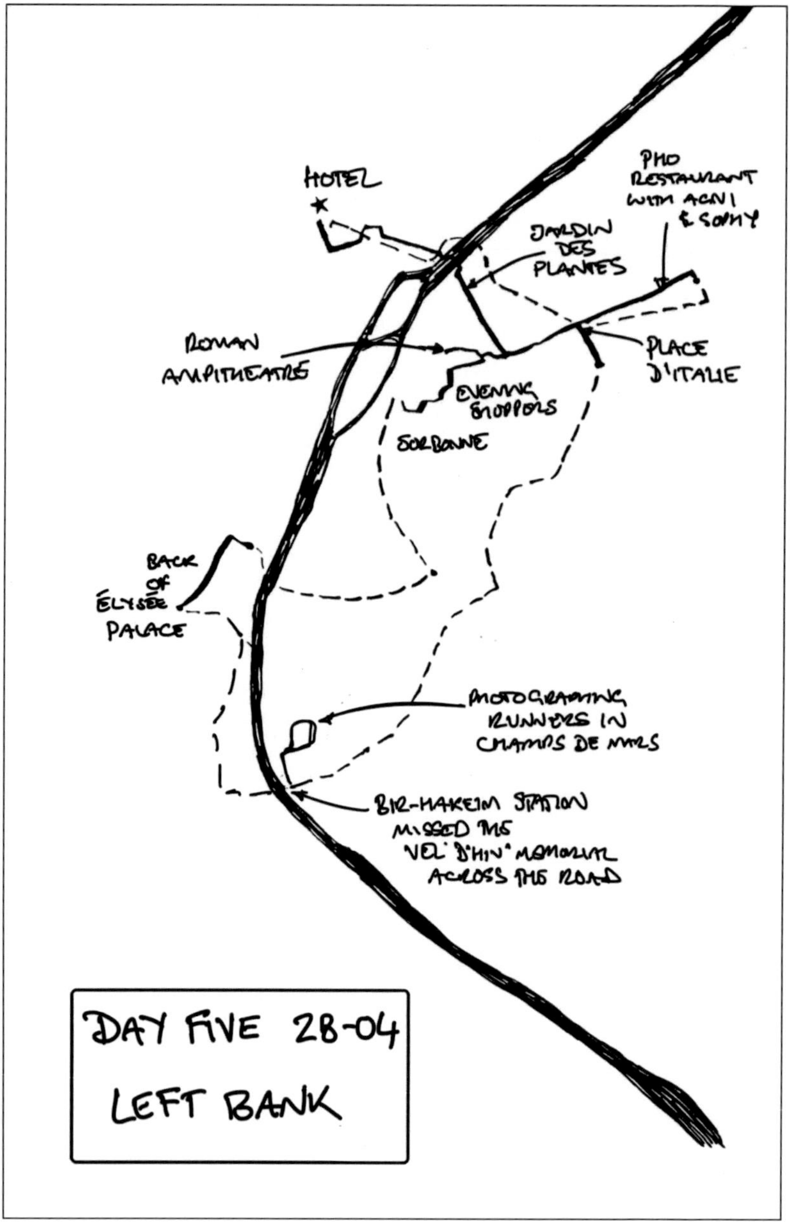
HOTEL
PHO RESTAURANT WITH AGNI & SONNY
JARDIN DES PLANTES
ROMAN AMPITHEATRE
PLACE D'ITALIE
EVENING SHOPPERS
SORBONNE
BACK OF ÉLYSÉE PALACE
PHOTOGRAPHING RUNNERS IN CHAMPS DE MARS
BIR-HAKEIM STATION MISSED THE 'VEL' D'HIV' MEMORIAL ACROSS THE ROAD
DAY FIVE 28-04
LEFT BANK

Mercredi 28 avril / 2014

The day began with a formal 9 a.m. briefing from our tutors, outlining exactly what we needed to produce and how we might go about getting it. Maybe the vagueness of the responses we'd given the day before had prompted them to give some stronger guidance. With the football club behind-the-scenes idea dead in the water, I still thought I would look at maybe capturing sport on the streets, but I really just lacked a clear idea and was going to see what happened. Meeting over, people split up into small groups and headed out in different directions. After two days of serendipity, I turned down an offer from Sophy and Agni to explore the Left Bank with them and went out on my own, trusting to fate that I would bump into someone I knew at some point in the day.

It started well enough, as it was another fine day, and I walked from the hotel to Place de la Bastille and then alongside the last stretch of the Canal Saint-Martin down to the Seine. I crossed the Pont d'Austerlitz, named after Napoleon's great, arguably greatest, victory. Immediately on the other side of the bridge was the entrance to the Jardin des Plantes, the botanic gardens. The tree-lined paths were busy with walkers and runners, and after photographing the dappled sunlit corridors I sat on a bench for a while to watch the world go by, sometimes more than once, as joggers returned for another lap. A low-key example of sport in the city but better than nothing to make a start.

I left the park and wandered south, before turning west at the Place d'Italie, the old exit from the city for the road towards Italy but now a large roundabout where the older tenements of the inner city met the taller and more modern buildings further out. Walking along the street I saw a Métro line appear from below ground and I decided to jump on a train. Several stops along, many of them above the streets rather than below, I got off at the stop before the river – Bir-Hakeim.

In February 2014, with the fourth anniversary of the trip looming, I was still on my own case about the lack of progress. The idea I'd taken from Hemingway – the Moveable Feast – was established in my mind as a way to make a virtue of the years that had passed, as I had more examples of how my enjoyment had continued in the time since the trip. But while the concept was there, the writing wasn't. I wrote that it should surely be possible to fit in just a couple of hours over the course of a weekend. At that stage I was still trying to write about what I actually did when I was in Paris, with the hope that I could then introduce the stuff that had happened since, things I didn't know about when I was there but had resonated with me as I discovered them for myself afterwards.

I started to wonder if I was describing a more personal form of tourism. When you let yourself be drawn to the things that attract your attention instead of following the guidebooks written by those who have been there before. All the things you *must* see. Do we tick off these lists so we can better connect with others when we get back? When someone asks what you saw, is it more satisfying for both of you if you saw the same things? Does it apply more widely to life, the things we see and do? Are they what we really want or are they the things we're told by others that we mustn't miss. And what about bucket lists? Copying someone else's just seems wrong, as does resorting to the most popular places on other must-see lists, but almost by definition these are places you haven't been to yourself yet, so you have to find out about them from *someone*. Someone who has at the very least read an account of someone who has actually been.

There's of course an element of pilgrimage, of quest, especially when the places are scattered all over the globe. But are some people missing the point? Is it really about seeing that specific Mayan temple or the Grand Canyon or the Great Barrier Reef? Or is the real experience your journey to get there, the things that happen along the way? Those moments when you miss a bus connection and spend an afternoon in a café with someone you'd otherwise never have talked to. Modern travel can fool us into thinking it's the destination that matters, and while that's obviously true when the journey is for a specific purpose, like work or a family gathering, when the journey is optional, taken for leisure, if the A to B is too quick, too easy, then hasn't the travelling been lost?

There are companies that recognise, and market, the journey as well as the destination. They offer tours that take you from place to place with varying degrees of assistance and comfort along the way. But what does this sort of packaged quest actually do? Are they smoothing over too many bumps in the road, the things that don't quite work, and failing to create a genuine narrative? I found myself wondering what was the point of travelling to see something else in another part of the world. Why travel at all? It sounded like one of our Socrates Café questions. We're only here on earth for a limited time, so shouldn't we explore the place?

Except there is so much to see everywhere, things I've never seen in a city I've lived in for almost forty years. Is the Colinton Tunnel any less worth visiting than the Jungfrau Tunnel? If we're going to travel, what do we think we'll get from seeing things in person, from standing in front of a specific waterfall or building that we can't get from watching it on film? A film that might swoop over the edge of the waterfall or up the side of the building in ways that would be physically impossible in person. Time and again in Paris I felt the history around me without being able to pinpoint where the feeling came from. Why was it interesting or resonant or meaningful or weird to stand in the space where gladiators had fought or in front of Chopin's grave? What are people capturing when they stand in front of Notre-Dame and look up at the ornate carving? Maybe just marvelling at something made by other beings, the way we might look at an ant heap in the forest. And everywhere, now, taking photographs, proof that we were there.

Or maybe not. Many of the contenders in that year's World Press Photo competition were rejected because of 'manipulation'. It was strange, though, where the line was drawn. Should they have rejected every image on a 35mm camera or its full-frame digital equivalent that didn't use the 50mm lens that is accepted as closest to the field of view of human vision with that size of negative or digital sensor? Any pictures that use flash? Why are post-production manipulations such an issue when the manipulations *in* production are just accepted? I can guess the answer. It's about trying to reclaim the veracity of the photograph, something that is crucial in the world of photojournalism, if not in art.

And so, with this sort of brain music leading my thoughts off in strange directions, a week went by and I was still wondering why I could easily write about wanting to write but still not do the writing itself. I came up with a new scheme – I'd do an hour a night that would slowly build up until the first draft was completed. Although, if I hadn't found two hours in a weekend, how would an hour every evening be any easier? And all this was to be the jumping off point for what I was increasingly seeing as the more interesting stuff. The way that the trip was like Hemingway's moveable feast and was leading me to think about the nature of tourism.

I carried out an inventory of my reference material, including my lengthening shelf of Paris-related books. When we moved we'd put the bulk of our stuff into storage, but I'd kept back a couple of boxes of Paris stuff which I had with me in our rented flat off Ferry Road. I think it's obvious now that the accumulation of books was a proxy for doing the writing. As my reading broadened it only cemented the belief that there was always another book I needed to read before I could really get started. And in fact, writing this chapter now, I seem to be struggling in a very similar way. In 2014 I repeatedly re-wrote a summary of the two weeks in Paris without making any real progress on the broader structure, and I've just been doing it again.

I started speculating as to whether there was something deeper going on. Had something changed my brain, altered my ability to concentrate and made it harder to focus? Back then, I was clear where I thought the blame lay: mobile devices that provided an unending array of short-term distractions. But these issues, this feeling of not knuckling down and pushing through, felt like it had always been there. I was a child who grew up in the 1960s. Had I been praised too much for results rather than effort? What was important was getting the right answer, not the effort you made. I wonder if that is what it is, with me, rather than any particular technological factor. I think I've spent too much of my life only doing things I'm good at and still looking for praise for getting things right.

It explains my attraction to little computer games, with their small rewards every time you solve a puzzle, which of course doesn't last and I have to move on to the next one. I know they're designed to work this way, but I also loved them when the puzzles and games were on paper. I remember hours spent playing paper-and-pencil games of cricket, just like Tom in *The Good Life* (except he at least had been working physically very hard in order to justify his bunking off). I suspect games have always been an escape for me, a way to manage anxiety. External requirements, whether in education or in a job, were strong enough to overcome my fears, at least to an extent, but for self-motivated tasks, such as writing a book about a fortnight in Paris, it was always easier to hide in games than test myself in the world.

Round and round I went. In the spring of 2014 another anniversary of the trip got nearer. This was during one of the periods when I was doing 'morning pages' – three pages of handwritten, uncensored, uncritical writing every morning, as described in Julia Cameron's book *The Artist's Way*. The idea is that the stream-of-consciousness exercise gets all sorts of things out onto the page, freeing your mind to be more creative. It's all about keeping on writing until you've done your pages for the day, even if you have to resort to writing 'I don't know what to write' repeatedly until something comes to mind. For a writing project such as mine, it didn't often feel all that useful.

Mercredi 28 avril / 2014 113

Looking back now, however, something that came to the fore was my attempt to work out a structure for the book. I switched between a chronological and a thematic structure and then back again. But in the end I think the repeated writing-about-writing diluted the drive to get the book done. The words *about* it became a surrogate. By the time the fourth anniversary of the trip came round I was really no further forward.

Back in 2010 I was still thinking of my sporting Paris idea and I looked for more joggers, this time on the gravel paths of the Champs de Mars, hoping to get one with the tower in the background, as Petr had done earlier with his cyclist. The idea was better than the pictures, but perhaps I didn't stick at it enough. Should I have stayed longer and tried harder? I could've played with my own brief and explored different angles, both literally and creatively. But I didn't, and instead caught the Métro again, this time towards the Champs-Élysées area.

Crossing a road junction I was approached by two policemen who asked to look inside my rucksack. They gave it a cursory inspection before letting me continue. For a moment I wondered why but then realised I was in the street that led along the rear entrance to the Élysée Palace, the French president's official residence and close to the British and US embassies. I walked around the block and into one of the gardens on the corner of the Champs-Élysées and the Place de la Concorde, where I sat to eat some lunch and think about where to go next.

I decided to cross back to the Left Bank and hopped on the Métro again. This time I got out at Cluny-La Sorbonne and went up the hill to the Place de la Sorbonne. It was a small tree-lined space, off the Boulevard Saint-Michel. I sat on a bench in the sun. There was an octagonal pond with a single fountain and leading towards the elaborate west entrance of the Sorbonne Chapel were two thin rectangular ponds, one on each side of the square. Down the centre of each was a line of small fountains, the white water like plumes on Napoleonic shakos. Some young boys were playing with a football, throwing it into the fountains in order to soak each other as it landed in the water. People sitting in the café on the edge of the square twitched but said nothing as the splashing got closer. I looked at my map and considered where to go. Then the sun moved behind a building, putting me in the shade, so I moved on again. The Panthéon was nearby, so I headed there. The sign on the gate said it closed at five, in just ten minutes' time, so it would have to be something to come back to another day, and instead I wandered on to the Latin Quarter.

I saw another of the Space Invaders on the corner of Rue de l'Estrapade and then walked down the pedestrianised Rue Mouffetard. It felt like a market in a small town rather than a street in a big city, with shops pushing in on both sides, full of life and colour.

Coming to the bottom I turned uphill, back towards the river, and walked up the Rue Monge, the main thoroughfare through the arrondissement. The street was busy and many of the shops were open, especially the ones selling food. People were smartly dressed, presumably coming home from work and buying something to cook for their tea. It reminded me most of being in Prague, many years before – the same after-work-buying-evening-meal buzz about the place. It was striking how many small specialist shops there were and how different the pattern of shopping seemed to be compared with home. So many people buying fresh food in small amounts as they walked from shop to shop instead of driving the car to the supermarket and stocking up for the week with ready meals.

Later I learned that the impression I'd formed was true and designed to both reflect and shape French food culture. Paris, and the rest of France, had strict planning regulations limiting the proliferation of supermarkets. At least it did. Soon after I was in Paris the regulations started to relax and I wonder now whether the residents of the Latin Quarter are still shopping in small shops or are now going to the supermarket much like most people in the UK. At least was that was the pattern before Covid. Did the constraints of lockdown reintroduce people to local shops and create a habit that has continued since? It's always difficult to know how typical your own circumstances are. The small specialist shops seem to be doing well on my local high street, but are they bucking a general trend?

Back then, on that Tuesday early evening, in the bustle in the street, I saw a sign pointing to the Arènes de Lutèce, a reminder of the Roman settlement of Lutetia, a familiar name from childhood Asterix books. Through an archway between a hotel and a small café a passageway led to a circular gravelled arena, with some sections of terracing on a couple of sides. In the shade of the buildings it didn't look particularly exciting as I walked around. I

Mercredi 28 avril / 2014

was surprised there were no men out playing pétanque in what looked like an ideal place. It felt a bit too well-ordered and ordinary to be the remnants of something almost two thousand years old. Although the terraces are nineteenth-century reconstructions, and many of the original features have been lost, it was almost eerie to have stepped away from the post-work shoppers into a space where the residents of Roman Paris had gathered.

In June 2014 I went to see *Finding Vivian Maier* at Filmhouse as part of the film festival. It was the UK premiere of this fascinating film about the discovery of the street photographer's work only after she'd died, and one of the directors was there. I Blipped about it, with a photo taken on our way out of Filmhouse. I thought I'd just grab a quick shot of the poster and then crop it, but there was a couple standing beside it, with their faces obscured and their shadows slightly reminiscent of the photo of Vivian on the poster, so I left them in.

The film inspired me to return to the Paris book. As I wrote at the time, writing and talking about it wasn't getting it out there and I didn't want the pictures and snippets of text to be found on a hard drive after I'm gone, never having been published in the way I wanted. Although I didn't realise it at the time, this was something of a pattern in the works I'd come across – Hemingway, Benjamin and Perec, all with books about Paris published posthumously. I resolved to get it done, even if the book got created and no one else ever read it.

And in July I met up with Petr in the pub to watch the penultimate stage of the Tour – a reminder of the afternoon we spent in Paris watching the Liège–Bastogne–Liège classic. A reminder, but not enough to get a first draft written in time for my 51st birthday, which had been the deadline I'd talked about when

Mercredi 28 avril / 2014

I wrote in my Morning Pages about the structure for the book back in March. Come September, I was little further forward.

And then we moved to Portobello in December. We'd spent almost exactly a year looking for a place. The very first flat that came up, in January 2014, increasingly looked like the one that got away as nothing better turned up in the following weeks and months. It had just felt wrong to go for the first one we saw. We widened our search area and started looking over the water in Fife, where we could get a lot more for our money in somewhere like Burntisland. We very nearly bought the lower half of a very grand house close to the railway station but doubts about leaving Edinburgh finally persuaded us against. I've wondered more than once how that might have turned out, though. Just like we can see Burntisland across the Firth of Forth from our flat, we could have been living somewhere with the reverse view across the water to here.

In 2010, despite the Left Bank life and colour all around me, it felt a bit flat on my own so it was great to get a text from Sophy. She and Agni were still taking pictures but maybe we could meet near Place d'Italie? That meant turning back on myself but as I didn't have any specific plans I headed southwards. This time I noticed a poster stuck to a tree. Using my basic French I could see that someone had lost their dog – whose name translated as Raspberry – the previous Friday lunchtime, from a street on the other side of the Place d'Italie. Had a lack of success over the weekend prompted them to extend the search down the Avenue des Gobelins and add the handwritten offer of a reward to the bottom? I wonder if Raspberry was ever found. Did she go on to enjoy a long life in the 13th? It's just about possible that she's still alive today, although she would have had to have been just a pup back in 2010.

> Nous avons perdu Framboise le 23 avril 2010 rue Bobillot à Paris à 13h30.
>
> Si vous pouvez nous aider à la retrouver, si vous l'avez aperçue, contactez nous au :
> 00 00 00 00 00
> Ou au 00 00 00 00 00
> RECOMPENSE

Another message from Sophy said that she and Agni were now down Avenue de Choisy, heading into Chinatown looking for a place to eat. I caught up with them as they were waiting for a table. Working on the principle that a busy restaurant is more likely to be a good one, they'd picked a place with a queue outside. It was Vietnamese, rather than Chinese, or more specifically 'pho'. Everyone around us was eating very similar bowls of broth with noodles, meat and vegetables. We ordered from the same short menu. I chose a chicken broth that came with a great plate of leaves, bean sprouts, chopped chillies and other sauces. Mix to your own taste. Never having eaten it before, I couldn't tell whether it was a good example or not but it tasted great to me – a bit different without being too weird. Is that the ideal sort of cuisine – something a bit beyond your personal palette but not so bizarre that it risks being inedible? Maybe we can say that about everything we 'consume' – books, films, theatre, art – best if it's different but not too different. We had a very enjoyable meal, although we couldn't linger too long as the queue now stretched down the street and others needed our table.

With no particular reason to hurry back to the hotel, we walked further into Chinatown. It was an interesting change after the tourist sights of the city centre – very modern, with high-rises and lots of concrete – and yet the residents were out on the streets, sitting around, talking. The weather was warm – the first days of spring – so maybe people were taking advantage of it to sit outside, having been cooped up over the winter months. A group of old men were sitting on a bench in an open space beneath some tower blocks. It seemed too intrusive to stop and take a picture, but one of them saw Agni's Kiev 88 film camera (a Russian Hasselblad clone) and called her over. He insisted she take his picture. He also got some of his friends to agree to be photographed. I wondered what had caused this reaction: old-style camera, young woman, or a bit of both? Either way, I with a modern DSLR was definitely neither.

With the evening starting to close in, and our walk having taken us close to the southern edge of the city, we looked for a Métro station. Back at the hotel there was still time for a drink in the Place des Vosges with Sophy and Graeme in one of the arcade cafés on the square. A chance to compare progress, or lack of it, in our assignments.

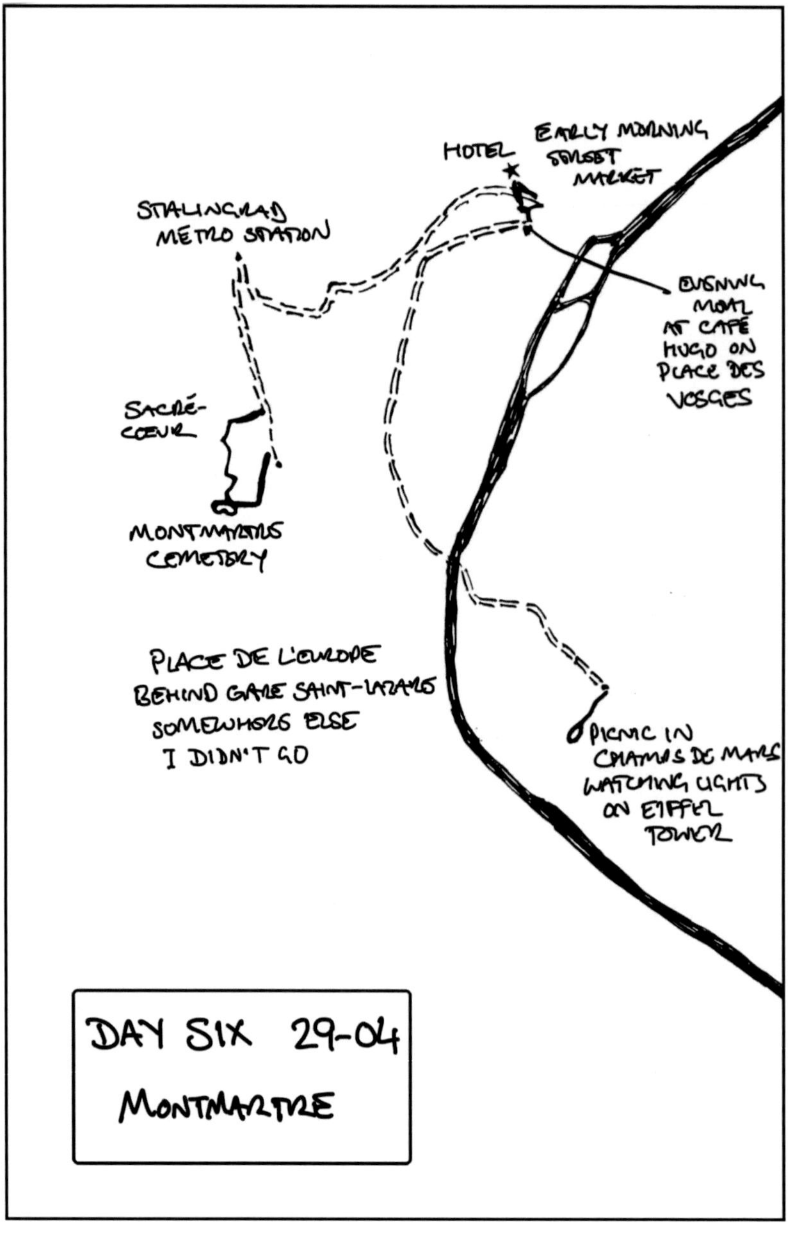
HOTEL
EARLY MORNING STREET MARKET
STALINGRAD METRO STATION
EVENING MEAL AT CAFÉ HUGO ON PLACE DES VOSGES
SACRÉ-COEUR
MONTMARTRE CEMETERY
PLACE DE L'EUROPE BEHIND GARE SAINT-LAZARE SOMEWHERE ELSE I DIDN'T GO
PICNIC IN CHAMPS DE MARS WATCHING LIGHTS ON EIFFEL TOWER
DAY SIX 29-04
MONTMARTRE

Jeudi 29 avril / 2015

Inspired by the shops on the Rue Mouffetard the day before, I decided to get up early and go out before breakfast to photograph our local market in the space in the middle of the Boulevard Richard-Lenoir. When I got there the traders were already unloading things from their vans and setting up their stalls.

There was loads of fresh produce, as well as some clothes, shoes and other household objects. I wandered round with my camera but, unlike Agni in Chinatown the night before, a lot of people waved me away before I could take a picture. Were they just fed up of tourists taking their pictures? After all this was their daily work, not an event staged for visitors. There was an exception – the man on the stall selling sea salt was enthusiastic about getting his picture taken and we had a brief conversation, introduced ourselves and said where we were from. Me a student photographer from Edinburgh – 'ah, oui, Écosse' – and him from Brittany, near Nantes. He explained a bit about the salt, that it was collected from the sea, using the sun to evaporate the water. I remembered visiting some salt pans in Malta on a geography field trip so I was able to understand the process he described, even if I didn't know all the French words.

Considering how far we were from the sea I was surprised at how many fish stalls there were, and at the range of fish. The vans unloading had addresses in Normandy and Brittany on their sides. I wondered how their business worked. Did they drive the refrigerated van straight from the coast really early that morning, having landed the fish in the middle of the night, or was there an intermediate temperature-controlled warehouse in Paris so they didn't have to get up quite so early? Not really something to ask a market trader, with the possibility it would be perceived as a slight on the freshness of their fish, let alone in a foreign language you could barely speak.

As the produce was arranged, boxes emptied, prices chalked on boards above the stalls, the first shoppers started to appear. They were mostly older people, many with wheeled trolleys. Perhaps keeping their small kitchens, with a lack of storage space, stocked with fresh food. Catching up with the news and the gossip from the traders. It felt like a much more connected world than the supermarket shopping we did back home, but one that, as I've mentioned, was being replaced in France too. And it isn't quite as simple as that, anyway. Some supermarket cashiers still have time to chat, something that was especially noticeable during

Jeudi 29 avril / 2015

lockdown, when going to the shops was many people's only regular in-person social interaction.

After the 'mistake' of doing my own thing the day before, I joined in the planning discussions around the hotel breakfast table. Six of us – me and Petr, Agni and Jo, and Sophy and Sam – decided we would go up to Montmartre, a short Métro ride away. Well, rides plural actually, as a change of line was needed at the interestingly named Stalingrad station, a picture of which taken by a student on the previous year's trip had stuck in my mind.

It's a classic case of place-names changing over time. The first station, opened in January 1903, was on an above-ground section of Métro Line 2 (then called Line 2 Nord) and called Rue d'Aubervilliers. A few years later a separate station on the underground Line 7 opened close by, named Boulevard de la Villette. In the 1940s the two stations, along with a new station on Line 5, combined to form the Aubervilliers-Boulevard de la Villette station. Shortly after the end of the Second World War the station was renamed again, this time commemorating the pivotal Battle of Stalingrad. This is the name that has stuck, despite the Russian city changing its name from Stalingrad to Volgograd in 1961. Although in 2013 the Volgograd city council introduced a formal return to the wartime name on a handful of days each year, to commemorate anniversaries of key events in the war.

Changing trains at Stalingrad from underground to overground, we travelled on three more stops to Anvers station (another battle – the successful French siege of Antwerp (in French, Anvers) in 1832 after the Belgian Revolution of 1830). We headed up the hill towards Sacré-Cœur in a throng of tourists all walking in the same direction. The street was lined with people, almost exclusively men, standing selling just about every imaginable rendition of the Eiffel Tower in plastic or cheap metal. The shops were full of tee-shirts and tea towels. The sorts of things you buy your friends and family to prove that you really had been to Paris. I wondered whether these things now sold in smaller numbers in the era of the selfie. The stream of visitors was well equipped with cameras, round necks, over shoulders and in camera bags, with no doubt many more inside less obvious bags. Not to mention all the cameras that people had in their pockets, on their phones.

All of which came out when we reached the foot of the steps leading up to Sacré-Cœur. How many photos must be taken of this white church every day? A near-constant clicking of shutters floated in the air. (Phones don't actually make that shutter-like noise when you take a digital image; it's added-in.) I've seen artworks that bring together hundreds of tourist images of famous landmarks into ethereal composite images. I wondered what the point was of taking more pictures to add to the virtual mountain of Sacré-Cœurs that must exist on devices around the world.

And then I clicked my shutter.

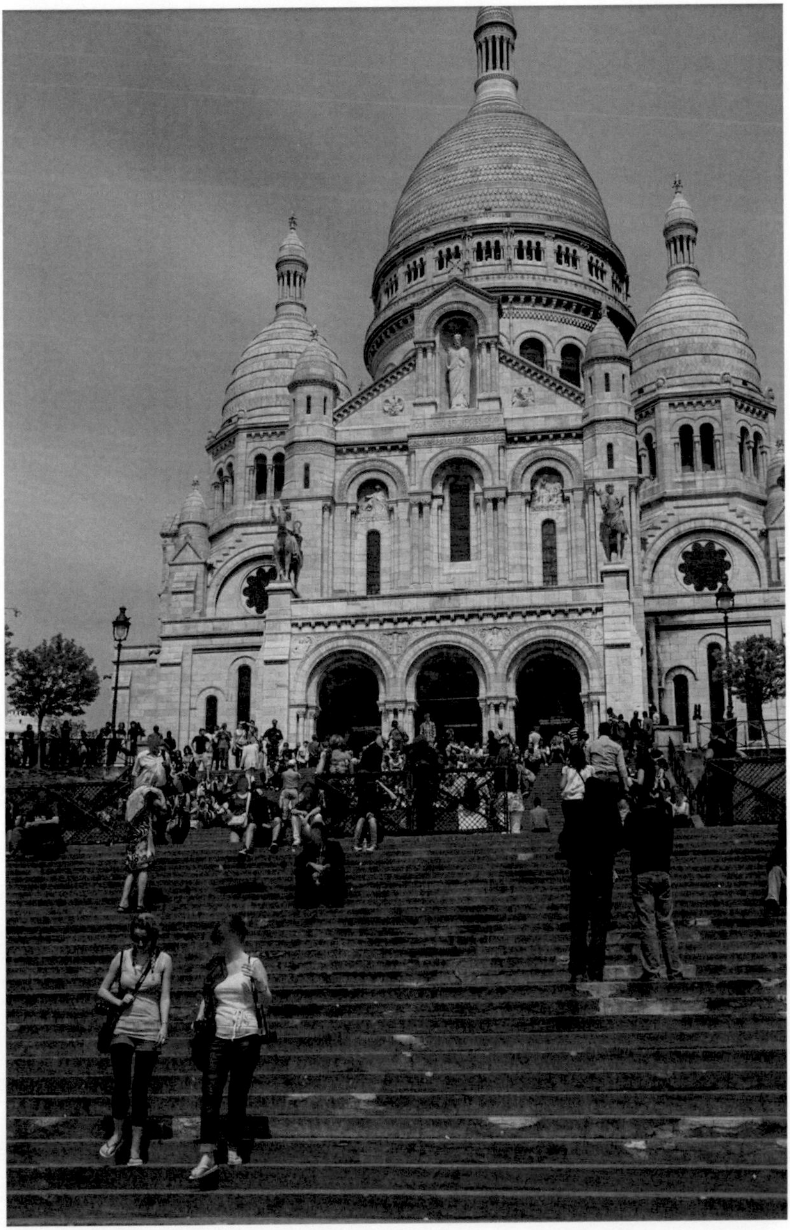

At the top of the steps we looked out across the city. That view must be photographed more than the building itself; irresistible to the eye with so many landmarks merged into a hazy cityscape stretching into the distance. The Sacré-Cœur basilica, photogenic as it is, can be seen as fiercely political in its construction, following the defeat of the Paris Commune in 1871. A symbol visible across the city that the old forces of the political and religious establishment had conquered the radical forces for change. A pretty building is rarely only a pretty building.

On the fifth anniversary of the first day in Paris, towards the end of April 2015, I was deep into my fifty-fifty Blipfoto project, already fascinated by a view that was right on the doorstep of our new home in Portobello. Although the picture for the day was another sea-and-sky photograph, the text was taken up with vivid memories of that first afternoon in the Place des Vosges and the comment that 'Hemingway was right'. Memories of Paris were always there, ready to be unpacked time and time again.

One of those memories was Montmartre, teeming with tourists, many sitting on the steps in front of the church while a nearby guitarist bludgeoned his way through 'Back In The USSR'. We'd soon moved on. I'd watched a couple of English-speaking teachers trying to count their class outside the Église Saint-Pierre de Montmartre. They must have restarted counting at least half a dozen times as the boys wouldn't keep still. Eventually they confirmed that they hadn't lost anyone and set off. Whether they were just visiting or from an English-speaking school in Paris, nothing changes.

The scene reminded me of old photographs taken on the streets of Montmartre, and then later came back to mind when I came across the film *The Red Balloon* while surfing the internet on a Saturday morning. It's a short film filmed and set in Paris little more than a decade after the war. Much of the action takes place in Belleville and Ménilmontant, on streets that are no longer there following urban redevelopment in the 1960s, but there are scenes elsewhere in Paris, including Montmartre. At one point Pascal rides the 96 bus down the hill and past where we had our group meal at the long outside table, that first Sunday evening.

At the same time I first came across *The Red Balloon* I also found a film called *Robin's Saturday* on the National Library of Scotland Film Archive site. This short film, made by Dr Iain Dunnachie, won the Andrew Buchanan Cup for the best family film at the Scottish Amateur Film Festival in 1958. It follows Robin as he travels around his neighbourhood on a tricycle. The neighbourhood is Broughty Ferry, Dundee, where I grew up. Many of the locations are familiar to me and I had a very similar tricycle myself at the same age. Made a couple of years after *The Red Ballon* was released, and filmed in a similar style with a similar musical soundtrack, I feel sure that Dr Dunnachie was paying tribute to the Oscar-winning French film. There's even a moment during a scene on the packed sands of the beach when a man in a collared shirt and long trousers throws a red ball into the air – for a second it looks like a red balloon.

The film has poignancy now that could have never have been foreseen, as one of the places Robin goes is the lifeboat station at the foot of Fort Street. He looks at the lifeboat on the slipway and briefly goes on board before it is hauled back into the shed. That lifeboat was the *Mona*, which capsized with the loss of all eight of its crew in December 1959. The boat had been launched into a strong gale to go to the aid of the *North Carr* lightship, which had broken its moorings off Fife Ness. The lightship's crew were able to drop their spare anchor, however, and were rescued by helicopter the next day. The *Mona* never reached them. The lifeboat washed up on the beach near Carnoustie with five bodies aboard and two more on the sands. The eighth was never recovered. The lifeboat was then taken to a boatyard in Port Seton, East Lothian, where the removable fittings were taken off before it was burnt amid great secrecy in the middle of the night. This was done apparently with the approval of the RNLI, who recognised the difficulty of asking a new crew to volunteer aboard a vessel that had suffered such a tragedy.

In Montmartre I went inside the church. It was cool and quiet in contrast with the rammed street, visitors talking only in hushed tones. Although restored at the start of the twentieth century, the Église Saint-Pierre de Montmartre dates back to the twelfth century and is the second-oldest church in Paris. Back outside I found the others and discovered that six was now only five. Perhaps we should have been more like the teachers and kept better track of our group? The remaining five of us chose a café where we could sit outside, on the Rue Norvins, just beyond the Place du Tertre. Before long we saw Jo walking down the street and she came to join us.

After lunch we headed west. We found a small shop chock-full of curios, like glass eyes and plastic dolls' heads. It was called Tombées du Camion – literally 'fallen from a lorry', a phrase with similar shady connotations to the English phrase 'fallen off the back of a lorry'. I later found out that the shop owner gathered his stock from factories across France that were closing down. He curated it as carefully as a museum, but looked for multiple examples of the mundane rather than single instances of the exceptional. Following the passage of time on Google Maps, I could see that the shop was still operating in 2014. It appears it then had something of a makeover between June 2016 and September 2017, replacing the outsized wooden type shop name with something more stylised, and by April 2019 it looks to have closed. It has been available to rent every time the Google street car has passed by since. They also had another shop back in 2010, out beyond the Boulevard Périphérique, among the northern flea markets, and from what I can see online it is still operating.

In May 2015 my mother died. She had been diagnosed with pancreatic cancer the year before, and although she and my father kept many of the details of the prognosis to themselves it was clear that it was not good. Still, she had treatment through the rest of 2014 and in the spring of 2015 things had been looking up. She'd been getting out for daytrips with my dad and there was talk of a visit to Edinburgh to see our new flat. It wasn't to be, though, and we got a phone call one day to say that things had taken a turn.

Lorraine and I went up to Dundee and were able to see her in hospital. My sister, nephew and brother-in-law also came up from the north of England. My father had been staying at Mum's bedside overnight, so we left him there and went back to the house. The next day Mum was sleeping when we arrived and we sat in the room with her while Dad went out to get a paper. While he was gone, she died. Not an uncommon thing to happen apparently, when someone has been sitting in vigil. When they leave for a few minutes is when the person slips away. My father squeezed my mother's hand as he left the room, presumably the last thing she was aware of.

In the days that followed I used Blipfoto as a way to come to terms with things, much as my father turned to poetry, writing a series of sonnets. And I found myself thinking about my Mum's love of France. She learned French at school but didn't actually go until we all went on a family holiday to Normandy in 1971. We stayed in Caen and I remember going to see the Bayeux Tapestry and the D-Day beaches. Mum enjoyed speaking French, although sometimes found it nerve-racking because she had a good accent but not the vocabulary to match. French speakers often assumed she was more fluent than she was and rattled away in reply to her carefully prepared questions. She was always asking them to go 'lentement' – slowly.

She and my Dad went to Paris for a couple of nights in Easter 1976 while my sister and I stayed with our grandparents in Sussex. We all went back as a family that autumn, on the trip I've already mentioned. In 1981 my sister went to stay with her French pen-pal and I went with Mum and Dad to La Rochelle on the Atlantic coast. From then on my parents visited France at least once a year for the next quarter of a century. Sometimes they went to Dordogne or Provence, taking two or three days to make their way there, staying in small towns and villages, enjoying traditional

Jeudi 29 avril / 2015

French food. On other trips they stayed in the north, returning year after year to Saint-Valery at the mouth of the Somme.

When he turned seventy my father decided he was too old for the long drive to the south of France but they still visited by train and coach, including to Paris in 2009. They stayed in the south of the city, near the Porte d'Orléans, and visited Versailles, Montmartre and the Musée d'Orsay. Mum always liked Impressionist paintings. We had a print of Renoir's *Les Parapluies* on the wall of the dining room in the first house I remember living in as a child.

I made sure I took a photo every day but I didn't actually share any until after Mum's funeral the following week. I found the Blips helped, the connections with friends and strangers. Everyone's lost someone, haven't they? There was no time, probably actually no appetite, for working on the Paris book and I allowed myself some slack come July: no reproachful Bastille Day check-in about my lack of progress.

Back in Montmartre in 2010, Petr bought a pair of novelty glasses in the shape of a bicycle from Tombées du Camion before we continued round the corner to the cemetery. At first we found ourselves a level above, walking over a blue metal bridge on the Rue Caulaincourt and looking down on the graves through the ironwork. At the end of the bridge there were steps that led down to the entrance to the cemetery. It was a peaceful place after the tourist bustle of Montmartre and the trees provided shade. A noticeboard near the entrance highlighted some of the famous people buried there, such as Edgar Degas, Émile Zola, François Truffaut, and we headed in the direction of those we'd heard of, along tree-lined 'streets' of gravestones and mausoleums where cats lazed in the sun and a few other visitors wandered about.

The Montmartre Cemetery had been a quarry for gypsum – the critical element of plaster of Paris – but was later used for a mass grave during the French Revolution. In the early nineteenth century it became one of the new municipal cemeteries that opened up outside the city walls. The cemeteries within the city were all closed and their bodies moved to the catacombs at Montparnasse. The story of the moving of the bodies from the most famous city cemetery – the Cimetière des Innocents – is told in the novel *Pure* by Andrew Miller that came out in 2011 and was another of the books I'd bought the previous year while I was finding excuses not to write.

At Truffaut's grave a small urn was filled with discarded Métro tickets. I wondered what it meant, whether it might just be a way for people to show that they'd made the Métro ride to visit the famous film director's grave or was it perhaps a reference to his 1980 film *The Last Metro*. But his was not the only grave in Paris to attract Métro tickets. Jean-Paul Sartre and Serge Gainsbourg's graves in the Montparnasse Cemetery and Gertrude Stein's in Père Lachaise were other examples. In the case of Gainsbourg it was

Jeudi 29 avril / 2015

supposedly a reference to his song 'Le Poinçonneur Des Lilas' ('The Ticket-Puncher Of Lilas'). There were various theories about what started it for Sartre. One plausible idea was that it was linked to Sartre's support for Maoist activists who stole Métro tickets to give away to people at the time of a hike in fares, but others think it was a reference to a line in *Les Mots* in which Sartre described himself as a traveller on a train without a ticket. Yet others have speculated that it was a variation on the Jewish tradition of leaving some form of marker when you visit a grave, although more usually people tend to place a small stone. Or visitors saw the tickets when they visited in person and thought it was a thing to

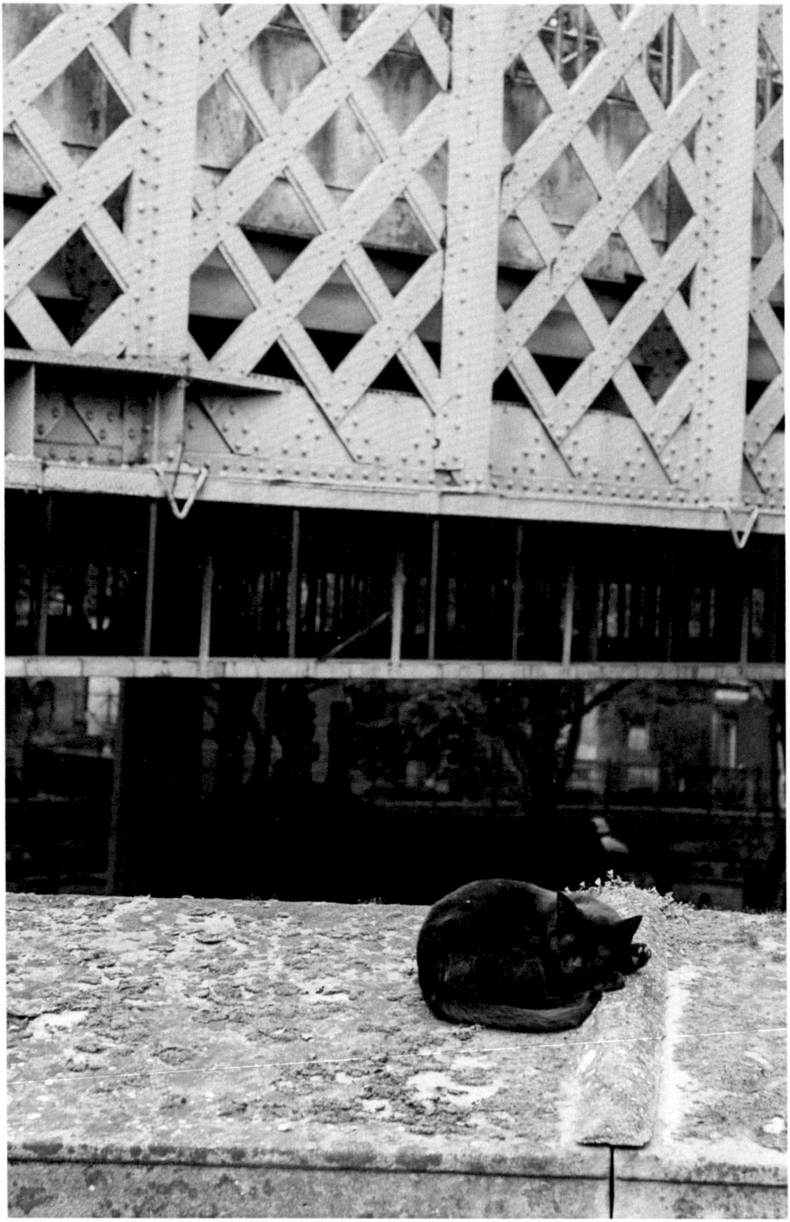

do. Easy if they also had a used Métro ticket in their pocket. The practice has now been curtailed by the Paris Métro switching from cardboard tickets to electronic cards.

Or perhaps it was for none of these reasons and it's just that the sharing of pictures with tickets left beside graves encouraged more people do it. In Edinburgh a recent tradition has developed that students and court defendants should rub the extended foot of the David Hume statue on the Royal Mile, for luck, and tourists can be seen every day rubbing Greyfriars Bobby's nose at the other end of George IV Bridge. While the former may have started organically, the latter seems more likely to be the work of tour guides looking for another story to tell their customers. A less damaging micro-craze took hold during the Covid lockdown in 2020, when a section of Musselburgh beach was planted with sticks. Elsewhere individual artists had left their marks in the sand, or piled up stones into unlikely towers, but this seemed like the work of many people. Did the first person finish their sanctioned daily exercise and then push the stick their dog had been playing with into the sand as they left the beach? Maybe. And maybe others then did the same, not knowing why but liking an activity they could share in space if not in time.

We spent an hour or so in the cemetery. It was interesting to look at the graves of unfamous people. One, for a couple born in the 1910s who both died in 2004, included mention of several family members who were taken in 1942 and were 'never forgotten by us, our children and grandchildren'. It was a warm afternoon and we slowly regrouped on one of the little lanes in the cemetery. I sat on the kerb, watching a line of ants making their way across the 'street'. Eventually we were all back together and ready to move on. Outside the cemetery we split up: Petr and Sam heading for the nearest Métro, at Place de Clichy, and the rest of us walking the other way, towards Pigalle.

Had I gone with Petr and Sam and then carried on beyond the Métro stop, a few blocks later I would have got to the six-way junction at the Place de l'Europe, above the railway tracks heading into the Gare Saint-Lazare. This spot is famous with photographers the world over as the location of Henri Cartier-Bresson's 'decisive moment' image, 'Behind the Gare Saint-Lazare'. The photograph shows a man in silhouette jumping over a puddle, his foot just above the surface, his reflection captured in the water. In the background, a poster of a leaping dancer echoes his pose. (See my recreation of the image during lockdown on p. 207.) Cartier-Bresson took his photograph in 1932, soon after he had got a new Leica 35mm camera. This model was a gamechanger in camera development as it enabled photographers to unobtrusively capture life on the street. He described the scene: 'There was a plank fence around some repairs behind the Gare Saint-Lazare train station. I happened to be peeking through a gap in the fence with my camera at the moment the man jumped. The space between the planks was not entirely wide enough for my lens, which is the reason why the picture is cut off on the left.'

Various people have attempted to work out exactly where Cartier-Bresson was standing when the photograph was taken and several have shared their theories. Greg Neville, writing in his Photography Blog in January 2012 (and since removed from the internet), believed the wooden fence was on the Rue de Liège and surrounding the space between Rue de Liège and Rue de Londres. That placed the leaping man in the triangular garden between the streets. However, looking at the details in the photograph and comparing them with the modern-day view, that doesn't seem quite right. For a start the railings in the photograph appear to match those that are still on the south side of the Rue de Londres, directly above the rail tracks heading into the station.

The angles fit better and the flooded construction site makes more sense if it is work to repair the road surface where Rue de

Londres meets Place de l'Europe and the leaping man is making his way across the junction rather than taking an unlikely shortcut across a private garden. This location was identified by both Michael Zhang, writing later in 2012, and by Thorsten Overgaard in 2017. Overgaard actually visited the Rue de Londres, unlike Zhang who only described it from Google Street View. The location, next to the pedestrian crossing, is now marked on the Google map of the street.

Overgaard used his knowledge of Leica cameras and lenses to also try and work out what lens, aperture and shutter speed Cartier-Bresson used. He shared shots taken from the pavement that he thought were close but not quite right and speculated that Cartier-Bresson must have taken his photograph from a more elevated position, perhaps in the adjacent gardens. Could it have been that the gap in the fence was just above head height and Cartier-Bresson stood on top of something, maybe a pile of earth, to take his picture? If there was road maintenance on the Rue de Londres bridge, is it not more likely that the wooden fence that Cartier-Bresson describes was on the Place de l'Europe itself, temporarily blocking access to the area being worked on, rather than unnecessarily barring access where there was already a metal fence? Was the jumping man, foot tantalisingly poised above the water at the instant that Cartier-Bresson pressed the shutter, taking a well-worn path through the roadworks?

While this image has become synonymous with the 'decisive moment' (despite Cartier-Bresson's own dislike of the term), it is impossible to know whether it was indeed an instant of good fortune or a more carefully composed scene. Many of Cartier-Bresson's early negatives were destroyed and only a single negative of 'Behind the Gare Saint-Lazare' remained from the film he shot that day. If the route across the puddle was a regular short cut, had he already seen one person jump across it and then waited, camera poised, for someone else to do the same?

I think he might have. I learned that the Place de l'Europe was a location where someone specifically looking for street photography opportunities in 1932 would go. In 1876 a painting titled *Le Pont de l'Europe* by French Impressionist Gustave Caillebotte depicted people on the bridge in a style that has much of the look of street photography, even though camera technology was nowhere near making it yet possible. Exposure times had come down from the minutes required for the early daguerrotypes that made people on the street disappear, but it was still the case that people needed to remain motionless while the photographer used a large camera on a tripod, as illustrated by the 'barricade photographs' of the Paris Commune. But by the 1930s Cartier-Bresson was equipped with a discreet hand-held Leica that could capture movement in fractions of a second.

There is evidence from other famous Cartier-Bresson images that proves he did take more than one shot of particular scenes and then choose the best one afterwards. For example, the set of images from Seville in 1933 featuring children playing in a damaged street, taken through a hole in a wall. Two images in particular from the set have become famous, even mistakenly believed to depict the Spanish Civil War, which didn't start until three years later. Other negatives from the set survive and were not selected by Cartier-Bresson, so maybe there was a similar set from the Place de l'Europe and either by accident or design the rest were lost. I'm not sure which narrative best demonstrates Cartier-Bresson's skill as a photographer, though. Capturing a perfect moment with a single click of the shutter might initially appear more impressive, but would that not make luck more significant than the photographer's care and foresight in composing the shot and then waiting for someone to appear in the viewfinder? Maybe the former, based on a single decisive moment, plays into the myth of instinctive creative genius and is more alluring than just working at it.

But on that Thursday afternoon, instead of walking to the Gare Saint-Lazare, I went the other way. Did I miss something? Would I have taken a picture of my own at the same location, and if so, why? Looking for a sense of connection with a famous photographer or a story to tell when I got back probably. In any case, like good tourists, Agni, Jo, Sophy and I stopped to photograph the Moulin Rouge and bought some food to eat on our way.

Our plan was to walk on further, but when it started to rain we got on the Métro. I was going to say underground but at that point it soon became overground again and by the time we approached Stalingrad station we could see that the shower had passed. So had the moment, however, and we just changed trains and went back to the hotel.

Towards the end of 2015 Paris was in the news when a night of terrorist attacks on 13 November made headlines around the world. The connections I had with the places involved made it all seem more vivid, more shocking. I'm sure I'm not alone in that. I had friends who were living in the 10th and 11th arrondissements at the time, where most of the attacks took place. They were all safe, but many people were killed in the course of a terrible night, the largest number of them concert-goers at the Bataclan Theatre on Boulevard Voltaire, the place with the front-of-house café with the comfortable leather armchairs.

Closer to the hotel, and without registering it, we'd also crossed the narrow passage leading to the Rue Nicolas-Appert several times as we walked up and down the Boulevard Richard-Lenoir. Rue Nicolas-Appert is where the satirical magazine *Charlie Hebdo* would later have its offices. Two locations only a short walk apart and both scenes of terrorist attacks in 2015. Following widespread support for the Parisian victims, questions were asked as to why there is always more support expressed visibly on social media when the attacks are closer to home, compared to attacks on the streets of Baghdad or Beirut, for example. I suppose it's just, 'I walked past the top of that street, I sat in that café and had a drink.' And here in the UK I suspect there are more of us with some sort of connection to western cities like Paris than there are to places further away, such as Beirut or Baghdad. I wonder how many UK residents have been to Paris or know people who live there, compared to those who have been to Baghdad or know someone there?

There had been talk of meeting up near the Eiffel Tower, but no details, so Petr and I decided we would get something to eat first. We went to Café Hugo on the corner of the Place des Vosges and had a good meal – their Salade Dalou: smoked salmon, prawns and avocado. Petr had a glass of Chenin blanc and I had a Sancerre. It was still early and there was a feeling that the evening was just beginning as we went down to the Métro to meet Sophy, then back with her to École Militaire and then through the Champs de Mars, looking for the rest of our group. They were sitting on the grass about halfway down the park. It turned out the invitation had actually been for a picnic and most of the others had been there for some time, all bread and cheese and wine. But our late arrival meant we didn't have to wait long for it to start to get dark and the lights to be turned on. The light show is copyrighted and technically not to be photographed, or at least any pictures should not be published commercially. On its website the company that runs the Eiffel Tower reassures visitors that this doesn't apply to personal images on social media – so we all got our phones and cameras out as the lights sparkled.

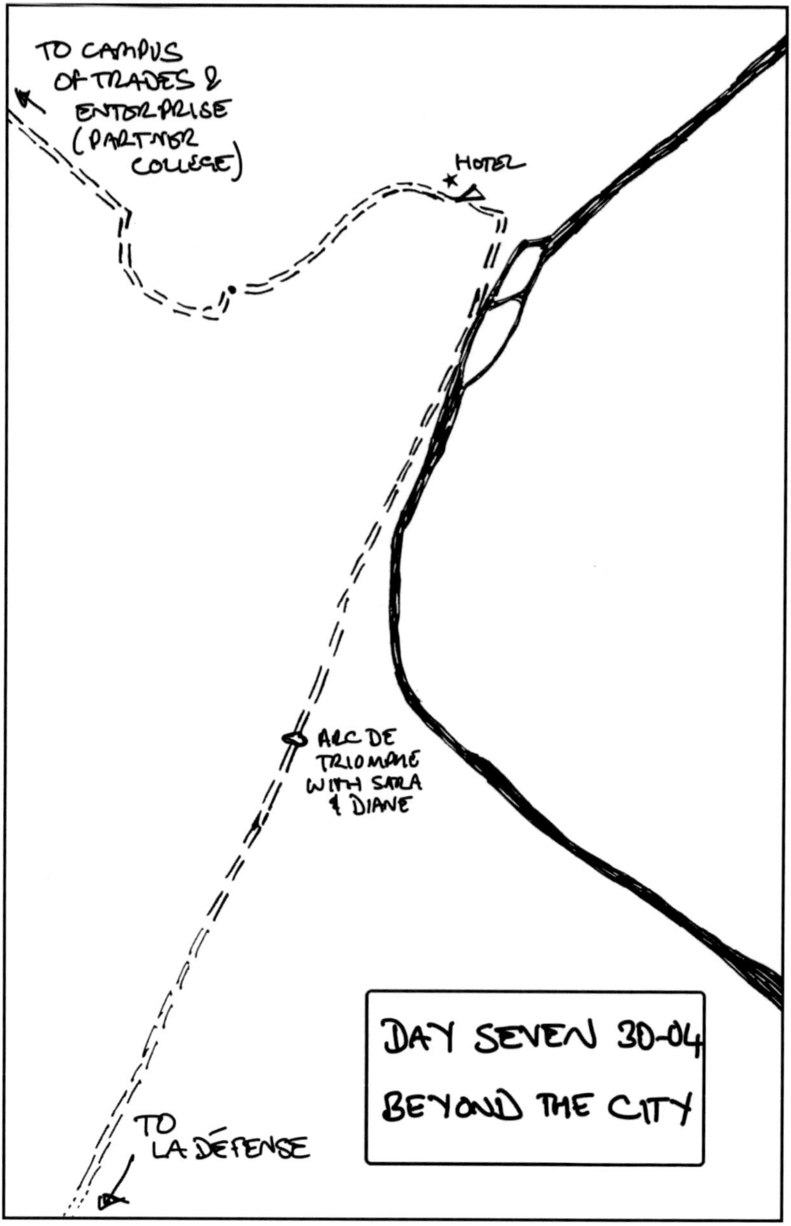
TO CAMPUS OF TRADES & ENTERPRISE (PARTNER COLLEGE)
HOTEL
ARC DE TRIOMPHE WITH SARA & DIANE
TO LA DÉFENSE
DAY SEVEN 30-04
BEYOND THE CITY

Vendredi 30 avril / 2016

As I said in my Blip entry, this was something of a strange day. It started with a trip out to the banlieues, to visit the partner college for our exchange visit. It was like herding cats, trying to get us all onto a bus outside the Métro station at Fort d'Aubervilliers out beyond the Boulevard Périphérique. We did all eventually manage it, only to discover that despite a circuitous route it was only a few stops to the college. We'd have been just as quick walking. I can only imagine the annoyance for the locals, being delayed by this big group of foreigners. It made me resolve to be more tolerant of the groups of Italian teenagers who appear on Edinburgh's buses every summer. Anyway, after all that, when we got there it turned out that the second-year students we'd met on their exchange visit to Edinburgh several weeks earlier were all on a placement week as part of the apprenticeship element of their course. Which was disappointing.

I'm not sure if it was as some sort of compensation for that, or to justify the visit, but we then got a tour of the whole building. As we went round we were told that the French prime minister, François Fillon, had been there the day before to officially open the building, which made sense as it was impressively shiny and new-looking. Several of us thought that would have been quite good for our documentary assignment, but as it was we were shown around the car mechanics' garage and a number of different classrooms. The highlight was the kitchens, where we got to taste some pastries just out of the oven. The photography department was empty, of course, but we were all envious of the room full of sleek new Macs, making our computer room back home look under-equipped.

We went downstairs to the canteen, and after a drink and a snack it seemed our visit was over. It had all felt a bit unplanned. It didn't seem to matter to anyone that none of the students we'd met before were there, though, to be fair, their Edinburgh visit was equally haphazard. We'd just met up in a pub.

So we'd run out of things to see and were free to go. I had a slight snafu on my way back into the Métro, as my travel card kept being rejected, so I missed catching the train with the people I was originally with. I think I was looking a bit lost, so one of my fellow students said I should just sneak through with her on her card. The rule-follower in me was horrified but there were no staff to be seen, and no other obvious option, so I went through the turnstile with her. No alarms went off, no SWAT team descended, and we got on the train.

In 2016 the new year started with a new 'class'. I use inverted commas as it was more of a workshop, all following the course that's in the book *The Artist's Way* by Julia Cameron. It was facilitated by Eugenia, who was doing the exercises along with the rest of us. It was a varied group of people, with different ideas of creativity and different goals. We met every Saturday morning upstairs in Tribe Porty, a new co-working space with a mixture of permanent tenants, casual hot-deskers and classes and groups like ours. For me Tribe had been an important place for meeting people as we settled into Portobello the year before, and I had joined the team that was putting together a TEDx event.

Lorraine and I had made attempts at *The Artist's Way* before. I'd managed to keep the morning pages going for several months in 2014, while we were living in the flat off Ferry Road, between leaving Hampton Place and moving to Portobello, but it hadn't really helped me to progress – which was why, when asked to choose something to work on, I decided to go with a different photography project, rather than returning to my Paris book. I had an idea for a photobook about Edinburgh featuring places that had personal significance for me in my time living there, at that point just over three decades. Only, my mind had other ideas, and when stuck for words doing my morning pages I found myself dragged back to Paris, and my lack of progress, and what I was going to do about structure.

I went back to the work of Walter Benjamin and the concept of the flâneur. Could that provide the framework I was searching for? Benjamin's massive book about the Parisian arcades remained on my bookshelf largely unread. Did I need to read it all before starting to write? Find other books that touched on Paris and how people have connected with it over the years? I'd hit at some point on the book taking the form of a travel manifesto – *Paris Without a Guidebook* – and I still liked the idea. It would encourage people to trust to serendipity when visiting somewhere and the fact that they could take more individual, more specific memories away with them to enjoy in the months and years afterwards, rather than just ticking-off the rest of the world's list of what you're supposed to see.

And I wondered: was it just me who enjoyed seeing what looked like a photograph of the Place des Vosges on the wall of Lilith's hotel room in that episode in the final season of *Frasier*? The sort of thing that made the whole world into a puzzle, spotting pieces and enjoying the satisfaction of fitting them into their proper place? These thoughts led me to back to Perec and *Life: A User's Manual*. The watercolour paintings of harbours around the world that became jigsaws, which were completed, returned to their original locations and erased there, returned back into a blank sheet of paper. The construction and destruction. The ultimately pointlessness of human endeavour, leavened only by the pleasure of the journey between birth and death. A symbol or a metaphor for life. I then disappeared off into an idea for *Porty: A User's Manual* that looked at the inhabitants of one of the beachside tenements. I wondered about using our block, or the one across the street, but later realised that the obvious solution was to use the third block of the original three, Marlborough Mansions – demolished in the early 1970s – in a counter-factual in which the building was saved.

In Paris in 2010 I went back to base before heading out again with Sara and Diane. We got the Métro to the Arc de Triomphe (technically the Arc de Triomphe de l'Étoile, but known the world over as just the Arc de Triomphe). We considered walking up to the top of the monument but in the end hung around at street level for a bit, in the middle of what must be one of the world's most picturesque roundabouts. I got a message from Jo that she and Agni were at La Défense – the modern buildings I could see in the distance down the Avenue de la Grande Armée – so while the others went back to the hotel eastbound on Métro Line 1, I went in the opposite direction and got out at the western terminus. Coming up the escalators from the station I was struck by the sheer scale of the buildings. It was like stepping onto the set of a futuristic blockbuster. I half expected to see flying cars shooting between the skyscrapers or massive advertising screens drifting into view as in *Blade Runner*. The space was out of any human scale.

Daunted by the size of it all, I sat on the steps leading up to the massive modern arch that is the area's most recognisable feature. I looked back towards the Arc de Triomphe in the distance, where I had just been, at the tiny people walking across the vast plazas, and at the pigeons hopping their way down the steps in front of me. I was also, maybe optimistically, scanning the scene for a sighting of Jo or Agni, and after a while I was surprised to spot Agni with her Kiev. When she got nearer I went down the steps to meet her and we spent some time together taking pictures. Some kids were playing football, which I thought might, again, just about squeeze into my 'sport on the streets' thing, but the image I used for Blip was a wide shot that, in a curious way, shrank the shapes by showing their edges and made them resemble children's building blocks nestled side by side.

As the sixth anniversary of the trip approached I noted again the non-existence of a book, by me, about Paris. I looked back at my previous attempts to get something written. Those were mostly describing what I actually did on the trip, which I was coming to realise was really only the beginning of the story I wanted to tell. I was just as much interested in what had happened since and the way the images I carried in my head connected with things in the present day.

For example, there were the recurring connections to the Holocaust – the Shoah, as it is far more often referred to in France – such as the memorial in the Garden of Europe park in Listowel, a small town we visited on a short trip to see relatives in Eire, or the plaque up on the Vigil Cairn on Calton Hill in Edinburgh. The cairn was erected in 1998 to commemorate the vigil for a Scottish parliament that was held at the bottom of the hill, across the road from the Scottish Office building. I remember passing the hut several times, a little awed by the dedication of the team of campaigners that kept someone in it in all weathers. Their campaign lasted more than five years, from 10 April 1992 (the night of a fourth consecutive Tory UK General Election victory) to 12 September 1997, the day after Scotland had voted Yes to the establishment of a Scottish parliament. I was at the official count in the EICC as the numbers came in from across the country.

The cairn includes a stone from the top of Ben Nevis, one from Robert the Bruce's castle at Lochmaben, another from Robert Burns's house in Mauchline that he shared with Jean Armour, and a paving slab from Paris 'used for defending democracy donated to the people of Scotland by supporters in Paris to commemorate the auld alliance'. There is also a stone from Auschwitz with a plaque commemorating Jane Haining, a Scottish missionary who died there in 1944. One of ten Scots who are thought to have died in the Nazi extermination camps, Jane was matron of the girls' home at the Scottish Mission School in Budapest, where she looked after fifty of the school's four hundred, mostly Jewish, pupils. She was ordered to return home but didn't and was arrested in April 1944 and detained by the Gestapo.

I Blipped several times on these kinds of connections and the way that the little details I came across in Paris seemed to bring the history home to me in a way I'd never really connected to before. Are those feelings stronger if the things we saw and did just happened naturally, rather than following a guidebook? Walking its streets is surely the best way to really see a city. Any other means of getting around is constrained: the stops on the underground or the route of the tour bus make it hard to be spontaneous and head off in your own direction.

And as the years pass I realise that, having seen the city the way that I did, I have inside me now a bell that rings almost every day. Paris is everywhere. Recognition comes with other places too, but they're less likely to pop up, especially if they're quite small. Like Český Krumlov. This small Czech town appeared in a Guinness advert in 2013. Seeing it, I remembered the afternoon I spent with Margaret, walking round the old streets there and visiting a medieval house right by the river. Having tea, listening to the Beatles on a record player, eating spaghetti with white cheese crumbled on top of it.

A vivid memory sparked from an unexpected direction. What's its value? Lorraine has a question she asks sometimes: 'How do I know what I've forgotten?' This is almost the opposite of that: 'Why can't I control what I remember?' Because I remember the cheese and the spaghetti and the Beatles, but not exactly how we'd ended up in Český Krumlov. We were staying in Prague with our friend Rachel, and one of her friends (what was her name, was it Olga?) invited us to come with her to her parents' for the weekend. They lived in České Budějovice (home of Budweiser Budvar) and I think they must have suggested Český Krumlov as a place to visit on a Sunday afternoon. I've no idea when I'd last thought of that day before I saw that Guinness ad, but if Paris is a moveable feast, then Český Krumlov is an old sweet, still in its wrapper, that I found in the pocket of my winter jacket on the first cold day of autumn.

In the summer of 2016 France hosted the men's European Football Championships. The ITV Sport studio had a view of central Paris in the background and every evening, watching the pundits, I found myself looking past and around them to catch a glimpse of 'my' block of flats on the Île de la Cité, or trying to work out exactly which rooftop terrace they were sitting on. Reliving the streets and places from both six and three years earlier, though still only a fraction of it all; so many bits I didn't get to.

I wondered what our whole group's travel map looked like. Where we went, in our collective entirety. Like those composite tourist photographs, what would our superimposed tracks across the city look like? Did others explore more of the outer arrondissements, within the orbital and so still 'proper' Paris but beyond the largely central bits I saw? Around Montparnasse, for example, or the Canal Saint-Martin area and the hills in the northeast corner – the setting for much of *The Red Balloon*. Maybe they looked across the city from other vantage points, or visited the flea markets in the south, further round from Chinatown. Strolled the parks and garden spaces in the southern and southwestern sectors that the characters talk about in *God of Carnage* (the clafoutis play)?

As the Euros reached their conclusion, with a win for Portugal over the hosts in the final at the Stade de France, the Tour took over as the main event on my sporting radar. By the time it reached the streets of Paris, Chris Froome and Sky had secured another yellow jersey. On Blip, Bastille Day passed without comment and my end-of-Tour entry made no reference to my Paris book.

But there actually had been some progress. The *Artist's Way* weekly group sessions had finished in April, but some of us carried on with monthly check-ins to try and keep our momentum going. In early July, when we met at Philippa's house, I had agreed to write four 1,000-word pieces, each inspired by a Paris photograph, in time for the next meeting.

At this point I still wasn't clear how the book was going to work. Would it be a continuous narrative piece that developed ideas as it went along or a collection of essays that didn't have quite as much in common? I wondered which days to write about and which four photographs to use. The series of images I'd selected for my documentary coursework had been an amorphous collection of street photographs. Only later did I realise that what they had in common was me. The pictures represented my wandering through the city – being a flâneur before I knew the term.

Day one had no pictures at all, so I wrote about a blank image – a day without photographs on a trip built around photography. For day two I used my first Blip, what I thought of as my *Life: A User's Manual* image. The flats by the river. Flats I now recognise immediately whenever I see them online. The flats Lorraine and I sat looking at as we ate our pastries on our visit to Paris for my 50th birthday. The flats I strained to see over the shoulder of Slaven Bilić when the pundits discussed that day's games at the Euros. I then jumped to day four and a picture of the protesting farmers with their tractors and finished with the mysterious group in the Palais-Royal from day eight.

As I wrote about those four photographs I felt again how my lack of in-depth preparation meant that I was not really immersed in other people's takes on Paris. I'd been quite sure up till now that that had been a good thing, but now I wondered. I thought I'd mainly photographed my own vision and yet it was suffused with secondhand fictions like those of Perec and Carax and the slices of Paris I'd seen over the years when watching the final stages of Le Tour. (Typing that sentence I saw the lone breakaway riders sticking to the smooth line of the gutter up the side of the Champs-Élysées, the peleton behind them rattling over the cobbles.)

Actual Paris, the Paris of history books, was vague in my head. I knew some almost random snippets of knowledge of some of the more significant events in French history – the St Bartholomew's Day massacre, the Paris Commune of 1871, two world wars in Europe. The German advance in the First World War that so nearly reached Paris only to be repulsed at the last minute – something to do with taxis taking soldiers to the front line. The triumphant German conquest of the city in the Second World War – photographs of Hitler in front of the Eiffel Tower. The Allied liberation of the city in 1944 after the success of the D-Day landings. Also a bit about the turmoil of 1848, the Paris of Chopin. From school, the Paris of the Revolution in 1789 and famous names like Robespierre, Marat and Napoleon. A few memories of visiting the Louvre and the Eiffel Tower and travelling on the Métro in the 1970s. The sort of things that anyone of my age, race, nationality and educational background brings with them.

At La Défense in 2010 there were numerous items of modern art scattered around but, again, by not following a guide I later realised I'd only seen a fraction of them. We missed seeing a fragment of the Berlin Wall, tucked away behind some buildings. It was impossible, however, to overlook Joan Miró's *Deux personnages fantastiques* (*Two Fantastic Characters*) and Alexander Calder's *Araignée rouge* (*Red Spider*). The former were

Vendredi 30 avril / 2016

two massive, lumpen figures in glaring primary colours, like childish drawings created in three dimensions. Calder's spider was a thinner steel construction but also loomed high above the passers-by. At the centre of the Esplanade de la Défense was Yaacov Agam's *Fontaine monumentale*, with its brightly coloured tiles and jets of water.

Incongruous amidst the modernity was an old-style merry-go-round inspired by the works of Jules Verne. As it turns out, it was one of a number of carousels across the city and described as a feature of Parisian life for centuries. They can be traced back to the seventeenth century, when the dangerous, sometimes fatal, sport of jousting was replaced by equestrian parades, or 'carrousels'. There was a competitive element whereby riders had to use a lance to spear and collect hanging rings. Riders practised their technique on wooden horses, which developed into circular roundabouts turned manually and used for entertainment by the wealthy. Through the nineteenth century these morphed into first steam-powered and then electric carousels as they became a popular entertainment for all social classes.

    After taking a few more pictures we caught the Métro back to the hotel, where another group meal had been arranged – a bring-your-own picnic in the hotel dining room. We spilled out into the courtyard later as we celebrated the end of our first week in Paris.

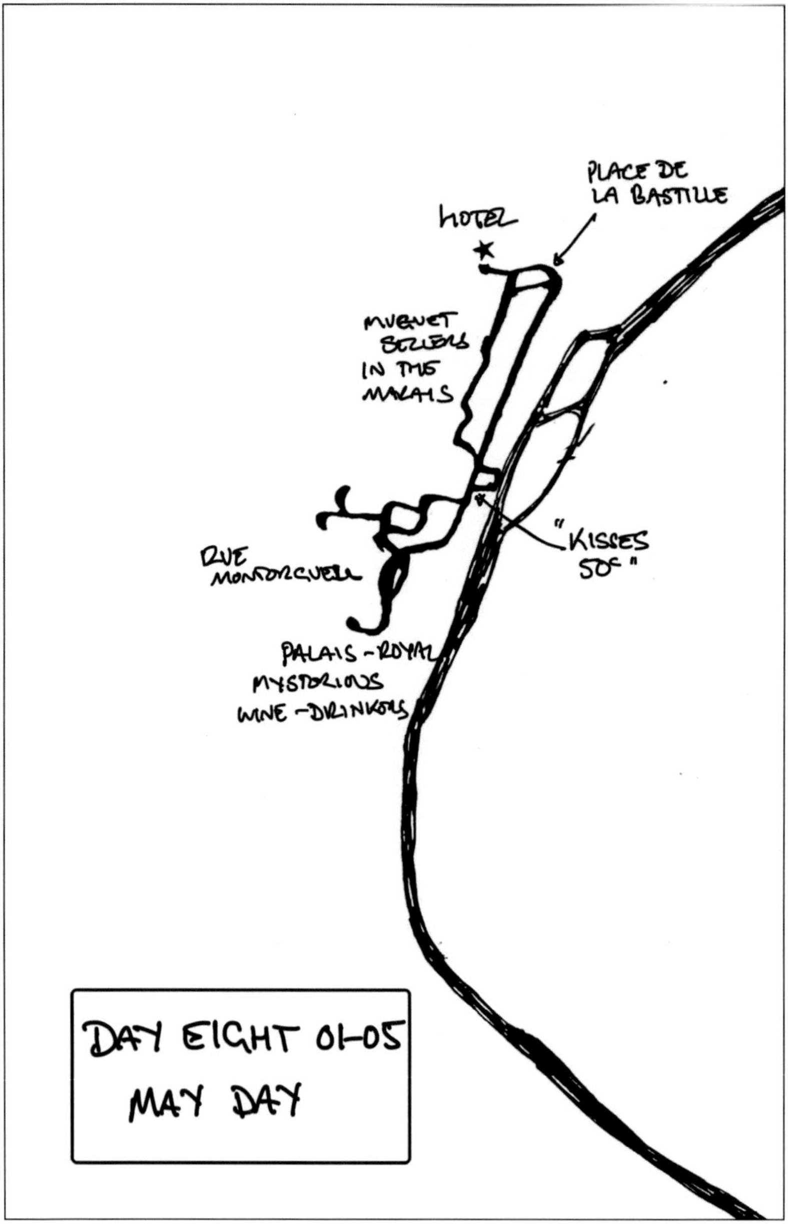
PLACE DE LA BASTILLE
HOTEL
MUGUET SELLERS IN THE MARAIS
"KISSES 50c"
RUE MONTORGUEIL
PALAIS-ROYAL MYSTERIOUS WINE-DRINKERS
DAY EIGHT 01-05
MAY DAY

Samedi 1 mai / 2017

The first of May is a public holiday in France and we were warned that many places may not be open. It might even be difficult to travel around. It was tempting to go looking for political events – May Day particularly associated with the Left – but I resisted and spent much of the day in flâneur mode. Someone had said to look out for flower-sellers on the streets. Although May Day is the Fête du Travail (Workers' Day), it also has a longer tradition in France of being the Fête du Muguet (Lily of the Valley Festival) when you give sprigs of the delicate flowers to your friends and loved ones. It's thought to date back to the reign of Charles IX (the previously mentioned brother of Marguerite de Valois). To encourage the tradition the usual rules prohibiting the selling of things on the Paris streets without a licence don't apply. In theory you aren't supposed to sell too close to a regular florist, and only sell flowers you have grown yourself, but as I wandered around there were several clear instances of the former and, based on the discarded florist boxes left by rubbish bins, quite a few of the latter.

Strictly speaking, I wasn't really a flâneur – a lone explorer of the city – as I set out from the hotel with Agni. She had her Kiev and I had my Nikon. While I was looking for muguet street stalls, she wanted to take portraits and had a short bit of French ready. I wondered again if it was easier to get people to pose for you when you had a more interesting-looking camera. Or are female. Over the course of the day I was pleased to see she had some success, whereas my experience at the market two days earlier had kind of put me off trying again.

We walked the short distance to the Bastille roundabout, where I photographed a market stall laden with flowers. Close by we saw a waiter standing out on the street having a smoke. In his black clothes and white apron, he brought to mind the portraits done by the German August Sander, who wanted to use photography to show a wide cross-section of society. Agni gestured with her camera and he smiled and nodded, but then hid his cigarette behind his back and looked straight at her. She wanted a more natural pose but what were the words? 'Non, avec cigarette. Oui, fumer, et . . .' I searched for the phrase. '. . . regarde ici.' I pointed over to the right as Agni composed the shot. Her shutter clicked. 'Merci beaucoup, monsieur.' He nodded and we moved on, leaving him to finish his break.

In the Marais the narrow streets were full of people enjoying the holiday, many of them carrying bunches of flowers. After a week in Paris the streets were becoming familiar and our route to the Hôtel de Ville didn't need a map. I photographed flower-sellers, a musician with a trumpet and a cool young Parisian having a smoke in front of a street mural of a tiger. In the park around the Tour Saint-Jacques we met a group of women on a hen weekend. Agni took a picture of the bride-to-be, the handwritten sign around her neck offering 'baisers 50 cents', kisses for sale.

Continuing the theme, when we walked into the Église Saint-Eustache de Paris, close by Les Halles, the organist was practising the wedding march. There was one of Raymond Mason's sculptural friezes on the wall. On the floor was a paper-wrapped bottle with a bunch of the ubiquitous muguets. Beside it was a note for Raymond, thanking him for creating his memorial to Les Halles that meant the old fruit and vegetable market that once stood on this site would live for ever. I later found out that Raymond had only recently died. Born in Birmingham, he made his home in Paris and became part of the cultural life of his adopted city. And here he was being commemorated in a very understated and traditional manner, a small bunch of the 'friendship flowers' and a handwritten note. His funeral had been held in the same church a couple of months before our visit. Perhaps the flowers had been left by someone who had been at the service.

Coming out of the church into the sunshine, we headed up the Rue Montorgueil. We were hungry and took a couple of seats outside a café. From our table we could see two very different muguet-sellers. In the florist's across the street an elegant young woman was selling them wrapped in cellophane at €5 each while, sitting on an upturned crate on the pavement a short distance away, a young girl was selling them in paper-wrapped little bunches for €1. I photographed her blowing up a green balloon (an image I would manipulate later in Photoshop, playing with the selective-colour technique). Two very different women, doing the same thing. I wondered what their worlds were like. And, now, what has happened to them in the years since? Perhaps the woman in the shop runs her own business, delivering floral displays to weddings. Maybe the girl on the street got into college where she studied finance and now has a highly paid career. Perec-like stories to be told. There were so many Parisians walking past carrying flowers that day – it was clearly *the* thing to do. It was a street of restaurants and cafés but also flower shops and cake shops, bakeries and butchers, greengrocers and delis. Part of the fabric of a city that didn't allow big supermarkets, back then.

Samedi 1 mai / 2017

We moved on and went inside the Palais-Royal, where I took what became my favourite photograph of the whole fortnight. A group of men, clustered around a bench, all smartly dressed, with collared shirts, suits or at least tailored jackets, even if they have removed their ties. All but one are not facing the camera; instead they're looking across the group at each other, or at the one man who faces forward. He can't see the camera because he's wearing a blindfold. Its composition might make you think everyone had been carefully directed when actually all I did was capture the moment as it played out in front of me. Only later did I see the pattern. Is that the story behind many street photographs? The moment is captured as it is and then, after the fact, significance is layered on top by interpreting compositional arrangements or intriguing juxtapositions of people and objects.

We are back to Cartier-Bresson's decisive moment.

Modern photography encourages us to take multiple pictures at the same time, but the contact sheets of famous photographers of the past show that this is not just a feature of the digital age. The selection of the final image has always been a part of the process. All of photography is about selection after all. The choices made about the precise boundaries of the frame, what is inside and what is left outside. The point of view that can change the perspective dramatically, as can the equipment used to capture the image. During Covid newspapers were full of photographs purporting to show people flouting lockdown rules. Aside from debates over whether the photos being shared were even taken when they claimed to be taken, there was a world of difference between a picture taken with a long telephoto lens looking along a queue, compressing distance to make it look like people are right on top of each other, and another image taken with a wide-angle lens and side-on that shows everyone six feet (and more) apart. People feel they can spot an image that has been tampered with, and maybe they can, but more mundane issues of selection – when and where to press the shutter and then which specific image to use – are just as important in the manipulation of the story told by an image, and near impossible to spot.

I knew my favourite Paris photo wasn't manipulated, but that didn't mean it wasn't mysterious. Were the Palais-Royal men involved in some rite of passage? Was the blindfolded man a groom-to-be, out on a stag weekend, attempting to correctly identify some wine in order to avoid a forfeit? Perhaps he'd always claimed to be the wine expert of the group and his friends had decided to put him to the test. If he guessed correctly then the rest of the day would take one course, but if he was wrong things would take a more embarrassing or darker turn. He might even have been the fiancé of the woman Agni had photographed earlier. They seemed very well turned out for a stag do, even without their ties, so maybe they all worked together in a setting where suits were the norm and therefore saw nothing incongruous about it, even at the weekend. Were they a group of stockbrokers – the old Paris Bourse was just up the road after all – and this was a welcoming ritual for the newest member of the team? If he guessed correctly the group would buy his drinks, but if he was wrong he would pay for theirs. Could they be members of a wine-drinking society and this blind tasting an entrance exam? A little strange to do it out in the open but maybe distractions made it more difficult, the smells of the outside interfering with the bouquet of the wine. Or maybe there was a more exotic, more exciting, even illicit explanation for their behaviour. Hiding in plain sight, could they have been a brotherhood of dapper philanthropists who secretly gave away millions to worthy causes across France? Or criminals. Arms dealers in Armani or drug traffickers in Dior.

That's what I like most about the photograph. We just don't know and the picture can tell almost any story we want. Having taken it, I did consider going over to ask them what they were doing but I'm not sure if I would even have understood the answer. As Agni and I stood watching them, we were joined by a couple of Italian tourists who asked us what was going on. We shrugged, and the four of us speculated a little in a mixture of English and French. The consensus was that it was a stag do.

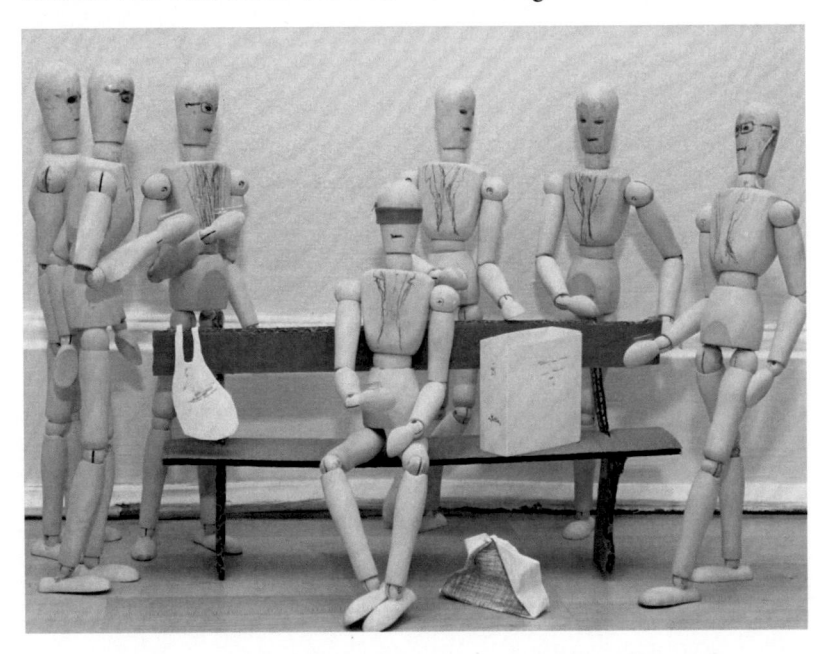

'Le Bandeau' ('The Blindfold') was the picture that I submitted to represent my visit when we got back and was included in the end-of-year exhibition catalogue, one of just four images selected from the trip. In 2020, during the pandemic, it was also the inspiration for the final shot in a series of Blips I took featuring a job lot of bright yellow artist's mannequins I was given (their origin story is on pp. 205-206). The Parisian image came in my mind to symbolise this entire book and for a long time was my choice for the cover, even before a word was written. When I was pursuing the idea of an alternative tourism manifesto, the concept of not being able to see where you're going inspired my working title: *Paris Without a Guidebook*. It's just a shame that this thing with French privacy laws has made me doubtful that it's legal to include it here. But I can share the recreation of the image I made during lockdown.

We left the wine-tasters and the Italian couple and crossed over to the inner courtyard at the other end of the Palais-Royal – the Cour d'Honneur – where a series of outdoor artworks offered some fresh opportunities. There were the reflective metal surfaces of the fountains and the less polished but more intriguing series of different-sized columns arranged across the space. Children and adults alike clambered over and on top of these, taking photos of themselves and of each other. Formally called *Les Deux Plateaux* but more commonly known as the *Colonnes de Buren,* they were created by the French artist Daniel Buren in 1985–86 on the site of a former car park. Controversial at the time, but clearly very popular now.

Among the people posing on top of the columns was a couple with football scarves. Red-and-white for Monaco, so they were almost certainly in Paris for that evening's French cup final. I'd thought about heading out to the Stade de France to take some photographs around the ground but there'd been violence among PSG supporters (Monaco's opponents) in the weeks before our trip so I decided it wasn't worth it. I wondered how far the couple had travelled? Maybe from Monaco itself. Had they checked into a city centre hotel and were doing some sightseeing before the game? If they were fans who lived in or close to Paris, surely they wouldn't come into the centre and wander round a tourist spot like the Palais-Royal rather than head straight to the ground? All this crossed my mind as I clicked the shutter, with them in the background of the picture. Although they might have made a good subject for my 'sport in the city' theme, the shy photographer

I was back in 2010 never considered going over and asking to take their portrait.

In fact, shyness had an impact on the photographs I took for many years. When I was younger I told myself I preferred the candid style of portraiture, shooting from a distance with a longer lens, but I think it was just a way to avoid asking people if I could take their picture, worried about them saying no. At college, taking pictures for assignments gave me the impetus I needed, although shoots were usually pre-arranged and my subjects had agreed in advance. I still found it difficult asking random strangers. For several years I even found it difficult asking friends if I could take their photo for a Blip. I think I've overcome that fear now, after enough times of plucking up the courage to ask. Most people said yes but I think more important have been the no's. The world didn't end, no one confiscated my equipment, friendships remained intact. All that happened was they said they'd rather I didn't take their picture that day. Working at events when I've been briefed to capture the day has also increased my confidence with my camera in hand, and I can now ask people I don't know if I can take their portrait. Most of the time.

In 2017 the book rumbled on in the back of my mind, only coming to the fore when I came across, or sought out, a reminder of Paris. In July we went on a road trip following Lorraine's favourite band, Indigo Girls, as they toured in the UK for the first time since 2009. They weren't coming to Scotland, so Lorraine started looking at where she might travel to see them. The concert in Nottingham seemed a good option. Sheffield the next night was only a short distance away. And having decided to see them twice, adding a few more days onto the trip would mean she could see them twice more, in Birmingham and Bristol. I went with her to the first gig, in Nottingham, and to the last in Bristol, at the legendary (and now defunct) Bierkeller. While I was exploring, taking some pictures at the Clifton Suspension Bridge, I saw a man setting up a shot with an interesting wooden camera on a tripod at one end of the bridge. We got into conversation and it turned out it was a pinhole camera he had bought online. He was taking advantage of the road being closed for maintenance to get a shot without traffic. We talked about photography for a while and I told him about Blipfoto. He now has two accounts on the site, one for digital images and the other for analogue, and has been posting for more than seven years. That makes me feel good, like I passed on a baton that had been passed to me in Paris.

On our way back we stopped at Hay-on-Wye, England's book town, and I found a copy of *Hemingway's France* by Winston Conrad. The book concentrates on Hemingway's time in Paris, although there is some stuff about the south of France too. Conrad uses a mixture of his own pictures and archive photographs.

For a while, as it had before with Hazan, finding another Paris-based book gave me pause and started me doubting myself and the whole idea. However, in his preface Conrad said, 'W. H. Auden once observed that "no two people ever read the same book". Likewise, one might declare that no two people ever live in the same Paris'. Reminiscent of the quote attributed to the Greek philosopher Heraclitus, from the sixth century BCE: 'No man ever steps in the same river twice, for it is not the same river and he is not the same man.' The briefest of research cast some doubt, though, on Conrad's attribution to Auden, so I went to try and find the original quote and see who first applied it to the experience of living in cities.

Julia Kastner, a blogger, delights in quoting Melody Warnick, from her book *This Is Where You Belong*: '"Edmund Wilson once wrote that no two people ever read the same book, and I've come to believe that no two people ever live in the same city", notes the writer Emily St. John Mandel. Our experience of the place we live depends entirely on who we are, how we interact with it, and how we interpret what's happening around us.' Once I got past the layers of attribution, as Kastner quoted Warnick quoting Mandel quoting Wilson, it seemed clear. It was Wilson, not Auden, who first came up with the book-reading angle.

Except, although much of the internet seems to agree, the original quote from Wilson seems slippery at best. Not to mention the fact that Goodreads, high on a Google search for the quote, while crediting Wilson with it more than once also attributes the very same quote to a US author named Diana Tixier Herald, who has laid claim to it as her 'personal mantra', without any reference to Wilson.

But then Diana should *probably* be crediting Sophie Swetchine, a Russian exile who was born in Moscow but lived in Paris between 1816 and 1857. 'No two persons ever read the same book or saw the same picture' is attributed to her in a collection of her work published after her death by Alfred de Falloux in 1862 and translated into English in 1869. Which no doubt led to its, again unattributed, use in the *Overland Monthly*, a Californian literary magazine, in 1875. Falloux, the same man whose committee's decree that the National Workshops would be closed contributed to the 1848 June Days insurrection, was one of many who attended Madame Swetchine's literary salons and his collection of her writing includes many other aphorisms that are quoted online. But not, for some reason, 'No two persons ever read the same book.' There, her precedence is usually overlooked in favour of Edmund Wilson's use of a similar phrase in the preface to a collection of essays published in 1938.

While this all seemed/seems trivial, it got me thinking about the nature of knowledge and the ways that truth can get blurred and lost over time, even more so in the internet era when search engine biases can be impossible to detect beneath their apparent authority. And once I started tugging on this thread I also discovered that the seemingly firm ground of Heraclitus was itself unstable. His thoughts were contained in a single book which has not survived and is only known to us through fragments quoted by later writers. Among those fragments are three related to rivers, but scholars disagree over which of the three are genuinely the words of Heraclitus and which are later interpretations. The 'impossible to step twice into the same river' fragment is known as B91 in the Diels-Kranz (DK) numbering system, the standard system for referencing the works of early Greek philosophers before Socrates. B91 comes to us via Aristotle, Plutarch and Cratylus by way of Plato, and while some believe it is closest to the words of Heraclitus others see fragments B12 or B49a as the original source.

From people stepping into rivers to reading books and then living in cities, I would take it further still and say that no two people will ever visit the same city. Every time I found a new (to me) book about Paris that seemed to overlap with my ideas in some way, I found it difficult to resist the conclusion that it had all been done before. Only recently have I made peace with the thought that my Paris, now viewed in 2025, is a different place from anyone else's Paris, not to mention, harking back to Heraclitus, different from my own versions of the city in 1976, 2010 and 2013, and all the years since.

In July 2017 at a ceremony at the Vél' d'Hiv' memorial President Macron denounced his country's role in the Holocaust and the historical revisionism that denied France's responsibility for the 1942 Roundup and subsequent deportation of 13,000 Jews from Paris. 'It is France that organised this roundup,' he said. 'Not a single German took part.' Like Hollande five years earlier, Macron elaborated on the words of President Chirac, saying, 'It is easy to view the Vichy regime as a monstrosity that grew out of nothingness and returned to nothingness . . . It is easy, so easy . . . but it is wrong. And no pride can be built on a lie.'

On an altogether different note, in September we had a wedding anniversary dinner at our local, the Espy, and then back to the flat for some Champagne and a movie – *Midnight in Paris*. I had a great time (Lorraine says) recognising locations as Gil did his late-night wandering through the Left Bank.

On that late afternoon in 2010, Agni and I left the Monaco fans waiting for the main event of their day while ours was coming to an end, back towards the hotel through the streets of the Marais. That night a group of us went out to eat at Café Hugo, then for a drink in a bar at the Bastille. The football was on TV, having gone to extra time. PSG won, so ultimately it was a disappointing day for the two Monaco fans I'd seen earlier. It made me think of trips I'd made to Hampden to see Dundee United lose in cup finals (I missed their one successful trip in 1994). I was still hoping I would be able to get a ticket for the upcoming 2010 final against Ross County, but by the time I got back the United allocation had sold out, so I had to settle for watching it on TV. Of course, they won. Then when I made it along to the 2014 final, that season held at Celtic Park, they lost again. *deep sigh*

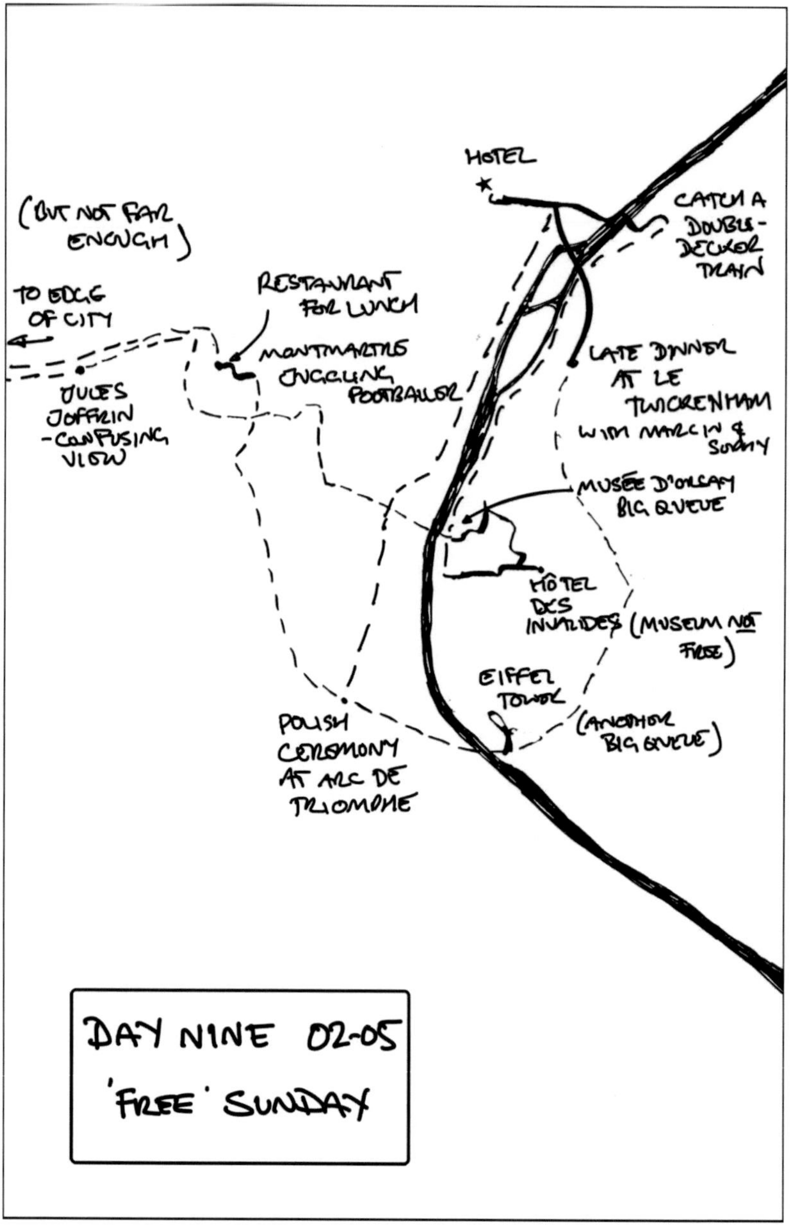
HOTEL
CATCH A DOUBLE-DECKER TRAIN
(BUT NOT FAR ENOUGH)
TO EDGE OF CITY
RESTAURANT FOR LUNCH
MONTMARTRE JUGGLING FOOTBALLER
JULES JOFFRIN - CONFUSING VIEW
LATE DINNER AT LE TWICKENHAM WITH MARCIN &
MUSÉE D'ORSAY BIG QUEUE
HÔTEL DES INVALIDES (MUSEUM NOT FREE)
EIFFEL TOWER
(ANOTHER BIG QUEUE)
POLISH CEREMONY AT ARC DE TRIOMPHE
DAY NINE 02-05
'FREE' SUNDAY

Dimanche 2 mai / 2018

Our second Sunday in Paris was when not using guidebooks came home to roost. We'd heard that on the first Sunday of the month there was free access to galleries and museums across the city. So a group of us decided to go to the museum at Les Invalides. I'm not sure if everyone was as keen as I was to visit; some people maybe thought it was only worth seeing if it was free.

We walked across the river to the Gare d'Austerlitz and got an RER train a few stops along the Seine. It was a novel experience to get on a double-decker railway carriage. Not something I'd seen in the UK, although apparently there were experiments with them up till the 1970s. The problem was, and is, the UK's ancient infrastructure, still operating under some of the same constraints that Isambard Kingdom Brunel was working with in the nineteenth century. There are theories as to why this is, and why continental Europe's railways are so much better than ours. One is that the need to transport heavy military vehicles before and during the two world wars meant there was investment in the broader track gauges needed to carry double-decker trains, but it could also be that war damage meant that repairs could include upgrades to capacity.

We got out at the Les Invalides stop and headed to the military museum complex. As we approached, I was a bit surprised that there was no big queue of people taking advantage of the free Sunday, or even any signs about it. We asked at the desk and, no, the museum wasn't free. Why would we think it was? Isn't today the day for free entry to museums? Oh no, not for this museum. We gathered at the back of the entrance hall and came up with Plan B: go to other museums and galleries that were free today and come back here another day. I could see the logic.

At the Musée d'Orsay, down by the river, the queue outside was massive, snaking its way backwards and forwards across the esplanade in front of the entrance. As we walked by we saw Ewa, one of our classmates, close to the road as she approached another turn in the queue. She had been there a while already, but it was moving fairly constantly so she was hopeful she wouldn't have to wait too long. We looked again at the queue. It was longer behind her than it was in front and we weren't going to jump it. How sensible was it going somewhere just because we didn't have to pay to get in? Would we not be better using our time more constructively? We decided to go into a café and make Plan C.

Just after the anniversary of the Paris trip in 2018 (book status: unwritten) pub talk in the Dalriada's beer garden caused me and Lorraine to put an entry into the Edinburgh 48-Hour Film Project. I think we thought it would be too late to enter, but the organisers were cool and said there was just time to get in under the wire if we were quick.

The 48HFP is a global event, with a chapter organised in Edinburgh for many years now. I'd been involved a couple of times before. The first time, in 2009, I was the stills photographer, mostly there to document what we did, however some of my images ended up in the opening credits of the film. We didn't win anything but I liked it, and there was a sense of achievement. It's a clichéd phrase, but we really were all winners. The tight deadline squashed perfectionism and we completed a film, *Starfish*, that we got to see on the big screen in the Cameo cinema and can still be found online. A couple of years later, post Paris, I was involved again as stills photographer but with a different team. This time the director decided the film wasn't ready by the time the deadline fell, so it wasn't entered into the competition.

Anyway, without really thinking about it, we'd signed up. Ideas flew around on Friday night, a script was ready for Saturday morning and a day of shooting in and around Portobello gave us plenty to work with. Sunday was a day for editing and music and a bit of extra sound effects (with me always mindful of the film that missed the deadline). As the afternoon wore on we produced a backup version that was 'good enough' and then had time to pull together one final cut, which we handed in with half an hour to spare. Yes, there were things that weren't quite right, things we would like to have done differently or redone to get a better take, but it was *made*.

And I couldn't see why we couldn't do it again. Do our own soup-to-nuts weekend movie. But almost immediately the old doubts started creeping in. Wouldn't it be better if the weekend was just for shooting and the script was written in advance? Maybe the editing could be done the following week. The simplicity of the idea had gone. And yet . . . Look, as much as I rail against perfectionism, and blame it for how long it took me to write this book, those 48HFP films are not exactly *good*. They're okay-for-what-they-are. The fact that they're still available to watch, if you know where to look, is both a plus and a minus. But isn't it time to challenge the myth of exceptionalism, the fantasy that good art somehow appears out of nowhere without any effort? And note that this narrative rarely comes from successful artists, who frequently emphasise long hours spent learning and practising and failing.

It's a pervasive belief, that art is only created by the naturally gifted. Whether it's a bluff from so-so artists who want to protect themselves from competition, or an excuse most of us use to explain why we haven't achieved our ambitions, or 'the man' being keen to keep the bulk of the population toiling away in a cycle of work-to-earn-to-spend, and then work again. In more subsistence economies where people need to work to feed themselves and to build and maintain shelter creative activity is something for everyone, done in the bits of time when people are free from the essential labour needed to stay alive. In capitalism, however, there's a disconnect between labour and survival – we call it money – and then meaning in life becomes so entwined with money that more money equates to more meaning. Time shouldn't be wasted creating art unless that too can be monetised. We downgrade the hobbyist and the amateur when we should be celebrating their achievements. They have made something.

And yet, despite the glaring example of the undoubtedly flawed but undoubtedly *finished* film we made in May 2018, by the end of July and my annual Tour de France finale Blip I was no further forward. Team Sky won. I wondered again if I would ever see the race live. The Paris book wasn't mentioned.

As we sat around the café table in Paris in 2010, someone suggested we should go and look round one of the city's flea markets – le Marché aux Puces (or just Les Puces). Some of the other students had already visited a few and the biggest was supposed to be just north of the city centre, a bit beyond Montmartre.

We headed for the nearest Métro, took the line north and got out at Jules Joffrin. For some reason I found it really disorientating. We could see a tower in the distance and Marcin said that it was the back of Sacré-Cœur. I just couldn't picture it. It felt like the wrong direction. Surely Sacré-Cœur would be the other way? The sun was hidden behind the clouds and the light was grey and flat and gave no good directional clue. I usually have a reasonably good sense of direction and felt convinced that Marcin was wrong. So much so that when he challenged me to a bet on the issue, rather than back down I took the bet. Of course, he was right and I paid my €5 debt later in the day.

Not finding anything that looked like a flea market, we decided we weren't far enough north yet and got back into the Métro to go a more few stops. We got out at the Porte de Clignancourt, crossed the busy boulevard and walked down the hill towards the big bridge under the Boulevard Périphérique. (It sounds so much better than ring road, doesn't it?) We got as far as walking through the underpass but it didn't look very promising out the other side and so we turned back.

And that was the problem of not having a guidebook, because if any of us had brought one we would have known we just needed to press on a little further and we would have found the flea market. While it seems odd that none of us used our phones to check if we were in the right place, I need to remind myself that this was still in the era of roaming charges in Europe and we were all reluctant to rack up big bills. We'd passed some market stalls on the other side of the underpass and went back to have a wander around. A few were selling antiques and odds and ends, but it was mostly cheap clothes. We shrugged. If this was the fabled flea market, we were unimpressed.

Just to rub it in, we found out later that Anita had gone to a different market that morning, the Porte de Vanves over on the opposite side of the city, and returned with a bundle of wartime letters written between a French POW in Germany and his wife back in Paris. A trader on the market had recently cleared the old woman's house after her death and most of the things he was selling that day were from the house clearance. The letters were for sale individually but after reading a couple of them Anita felt they needed to be kept together and ended up buying the whole bundle. Had we used a guidebook while we were in the café near the Musée D'Orsay we would have seen that Porte de Vanves was closer to get to than heading north.

So we missed out on the Parisian flea market experience completely and headed back towards the centre for lunch. Near Montmartre we walked up towards the top of the hill and found an okay café on a quiet street. The five of us sat round a long table eating a late-ish lunch. Afterwards we saw a man juggling with a football close to the entrance to Sacré-Cœur, the city spread out behind him, an audience of hundreds enthralled by his tricks. I wondered then just how many people around the world must have a portrait of the same man in their phones? We joined in, and he featured in another of the four photos from the trip selected for the end-of-year college catalogue.

The football juggler was Iya Traoré, who was born in Guinea in 1986 and moved to Paris as a teenager. He tried out for several Parisian teams, including a spell at PSG, but never quite made it. He started juggling for tourists in a few different places across the city, like the Eiffel Tower, the Champs-Élysées and the Trocadéro, but when we saw him in May 2010 he had a kind of a residency on the steps of Montmartre. He has gone on to travel the world and featured in the official video for the 2014 World Cup song with Shakira. There are many YouTube videos of him in action and, from what I can see online, he's still juggling his football in Montmartre.

After watching Iya reach the climax of his act, high up on one of the lampposts at the top of the stairs, the five of us moved on to the Dalí museum. That wasn't free to get in either – so confusing! – but to prevent a largely unsuccessful day, we went in. The museum didn't contain any of Dalí's famous big paintings but there were lots of sculptures, photographs and smaller works. I liked the illustrations that he'd had produced for books, in particular the set for *Alice in Wonderland*, and some intriguing anamorphic paintings. Looked at flat, one of these appeared to be of an insect but viewed as intended, by looking at a polished metal cylinder placed on the surface of the painting, a portrait magically appeared. One thing that was unintentionally funny was a piece translated into English near the start of the exhibition. 'Dalí, like his contemporaries Picasso, Chagall, Miró and Matisse, was an intellectual giant, partaking of a huge cultural pie that defined the times they lived in.'

We came out into bright sunshine and admired the views across the city, to the Eiffel Tower, the black skyscraper of the Montparnasse Tower, the roofs of the Louvre and the Musée d'Orsay, before making our way down the hill again, where we decided to split up. Two went back to the hotel and Marcin, Sophy and I headed for the Arc de Triomphe, where the usually hectic road was closed for a ceremony. People were arriving in Polish national costumes, carrying Polish flags. This was of particular interest to Marcin, who is Polish, but a colourful spectacle for everyone. A Polish dignitary, the ambassador to France perhaps, was introduced to soldiers and veterans. We were in the week leading up to 8 May, the date France celebrates Victory Day and the end of the Second World War, so it was presumably a ceremony to commemorate Franco-Polish cooperation during the war. (In this context 'end' is slightly complicated. While 8 May was the date in 1945 when Nazi Germany surrendered, the so-called Atlantic Strongholds of Dunkirk, Lorient and Saint-Nazaire didn't surrender until a day or two later.) Once the ceremony was over and the dignitaries had left, the road was cleared and the traffic started racing round the roundabout once again.

On our wedding anniversary in September 2018, Lorraine and I planned to go on a bike ride but the weather looked dodgy so we went to the pictures instead. Best of a not very inspiring choice was *Mission: Impossible – Fallout*. Aside from the joke in the title after twenty-two years of marriage, I loved the sequences in Paris, especially the bit in the Palais-Royal. It brought back memories of my different visits there in 2010. Afterwards we bought a new toilet seat at B&Q. (Twenty-two is 'toilet seats', isn't it?)

Marcin, Sophy and I made one final attempt to take advantage of free admission that day by going to the Eiffel Tower. Except, not surprisingly, when we got there the queues were massive. Not quite as long as the Musée d'Orsay queue, but enough to make us change our minds. So we set off, a little aimlessly, to find a place to eat. At Bir-Hakeim we got on the Métro and travelled a few stops east. On a very quiet Boulevard Saint-Germain we checked out a few menus and decided that Le Twickenham looked okay. By then it was late and the café-bar was very quiet. We ordered food – I went for moules marinière – and shared a bottle of red as the three of us talked about what we'd been doing. We were already past the halfway point of the trip and while I felt like I'd seen a lot already, the others' stories reminded me how much more was out there, and how I was only ever going to be able to scratch the surface before we left. Then there was a second bottle and, before we knew it, it was past midnight. Time to head back.

The streets were very quiet as the city slept, ahead of the working week. I almost felt like a resident, rather than a visitor, a total contrast with the hyper-tourism I'd experienced earlier in the day, among the crowds on the Sacré-Cœur steps watching the footballing busker. Which was the 'real' Paris: a deserted Boulevard Saint-Germain late at night or a thronged Montmartre in the middle of the afternoon? And which one should I be trying to capture?

PÈRE LACHAISE CEMETERY

OSCAR WILDE

BUT NOT THE COMMUNARDS' WALL

ÉDITH PIAF
JIM MORRISON
FRÉDÉRIC CHOPIN

MEN WITH LARGE FORMAT CAMERA

STRANGE SUPERMARKET

EVENING MEAL AT CAFÉ L'INDUSTRIE WITH SOPHY

★ HOTEL

DAY TEN 03-05
PÈRE LACHAISE

Lundi 3 mai / 2019

A day that started in the hotel with a hour or so looking over the pictures I'd taken so far. I hadn't found many with a sporting theme and was toiling to pull together anything meaningful. The weather was dull and overcast, hinting at rain, but I'd decided to visit Père Lachaise so when I finally stepped out of the hotel I just followed our street all the way to the far end, covering almost the full width of the eleventh arrondissement.

Rue de Chemin Vert is a very ordinary Paris street, although it does cross a couple of the bigger boulevards. Close to the hotel was the double-width Boulevard Richard-Lenoir, with its central space that's used by the market I had visited on Thursday morning. Underneath the boulevard is the Canal Saint-Martin in its underground stretch. Further on I crossed Boulevard Voltaire, one of the roads radiating out from the Place de la République. Part of Haussmann's redesign, the wide street connects République with Place de la Nation.

Chemin Vert ends where Avenue de la République reaches the Boulevard de Ménilmontant. At the junction that day there was a group of three young men, students perhaps, fussing around a large camera set up on a tripod on a traffic island. Maybe they were recreating a specific old photograph looking down République, using an old-school large-format camera. I never found out because, unlike the Bristol Jon of 2017, the Paris Jon of 2010 wasn't confident enough, and certainly not in French, to ask.

Instead I crossed the road and into the northwest corner entrance of Père Lachaise. No guidebook meant no definite plan, no long list of famous graves and where to find them. But I still had a few in mind. Number one was Chopin, but something felt off. Maybe I was dimly aware that I was slipping into the straitjacket of a tourist mindset – ticking names off a must-see list. Making sure that later, in any conversation about visiting Père Lachaise I could confirm that, yes, I'd seen the graves of J, O and E. And yet it also felt perverse to deliberately not visit them.

I looked at the map on the noticeboard by the gate and picked out some names, matching numbers to the little dots on the map. I found Chopin, Jim Morrison, Oscar Wilde and Édith Piaf and drew myself a rough sketch from the map. Why I didn't just take a picture of the map with my phone, I don't know. Probably the fact that I still mostly thought of my phone as a phone and my camera as a camera. Anyway, as a result my exploration of the cemetery's forty-four hectares and one million graves was guided only by a mixture of my memory of the entrance gate map and the roughest of sketches in my notebook.

I stopped first at a grave that wasn't even on my list, but had a small group already gathered around it, which piqued my curiosity. Although the name was familiar, I wasn't completely clear exactly what Colette was famous for, only that she'd been a writer of fiction, including a book that had something to do with a film that maybe starred Audrey Hepburn. (Of course the book was *Gigi* and although Hepburn had been selected by Colette herself to appear in a Broadway adaptation of the story, it was Leslie Caron who starred in the US film version. Keira Knightley had a go at playing Colette in a biopic in 2018.) Colette had an incredible life, though, moving from her early coming-of-age novels published under her first husband's name to a scandalous stage career to becoming France's 'greatest living writer'. She was also a prolific journalist and the first woman to get a state funeral in France.

This vivid life contrasts with Colette's simple black headstone and its confident, minimalist inscription – ICI REPOSE COLETTE 1873 1954. I took a picture and moved on.

Another cluster of people round a grave, close to the main entrance, brought me to the tomb of Abelard and Héloïse. I needed to look them up afterwards too, as I wasn't aware of their story. Abelard was a medieval philosopher and teacher who started an affair with the younger Héloïse in Paris in the early twelfth century. She had his child – the marvellously named Astrolabe, after the scientific instrument – and they later got married in secret. In a complicated story, they both ended up in religious institutions and published separate accounts of their relationship. They also were not originally buried in Père Lachaise but were moved there in the nineteenth century as part of an early marketing campaign by the city authorities to persuade Parisians that the newly opened cemetery was not in fact too far from the centre of the city and was actually *the* place to be in death.

I headed up the hill towards Chopin's grave. When I got there I found it decorated with flowers and red-and-white Polish flags, some maybe to commemorate Polish Constitution Day, 3 May, a national holiday in Poland that marks the Constitution of 1791. I took a few phone pictures to send to Lorraine. A ginger cat sat on a nearby grave, watching. And then a crowd arrived, with a tour guide who started giving a talk about Chopin, so I moved on again.

Next was arguably the best-known grave in Père Lachaise, at least in the English-speaking world. Jim Morrison died in Paris aged just twenty-seven, and his grave in Division 6 of the cemetery has long been a place of pilgrimage for his fans. The paying of respects here seemed less respectful. There was rubbish left behind and damage to nearby graves. Transgressive tributes to a man noted for transgressive behaviour. The cemetery authorities have tried various means to reduce the impact of visitors on Jim's grave and those around it. When I visited it was fenced off. In the past there was much more graffiti on the headstone. Considering all the attention it receives, the grave itself was rather ordinary and low-key. Another close by, with an image of a large Alsatian dog, was much more striking.

The other graves on my notional list were some distance away so I walked on, looking at memorials to less famous people. The weather was still overcast. Sombre. The weight of history seemed to be pressing down on me and I felt rather small and inconsequential, like the snail I found making its way across the top of one of the graves.

The symbols of death led me to a more introspective frame of mind, especially when I found some more monuments to the victims of the Holocaust. These were individual family graves for people who had been taken away and, towards the top of the cemetery, several large sculptures that commemorated the thousands who had died in particular camps. I took some pictures, but I found myself struggling to come to terms with the scale of it all. Impossible to capture it in single photographs. I'd discussed it earlier with one of our tutors, the way I found it hard to say what I wanted in just one image. Perhaps that was one of the reasons for embarking on this book in the first place – a way to bring together pictures and words.

Close by was Édith Piaf, in a family plot with her father, daughter and second husband. Her grave too was adorned with fresh flowers. And in the same division was the grave of Gerda Taro, a war photographer who was killed in Spain in 1937, during the civil war. She was born Gerta Pohorylle, the daughter of Jewish parents who had emigrated to Germany from Galicia, then still part of the Austro-Hungarian empire. To escape rising antisemitism in 1930s Germany, the family had to move again. Gerta moved to Paris, where she met a Hungarian photographer

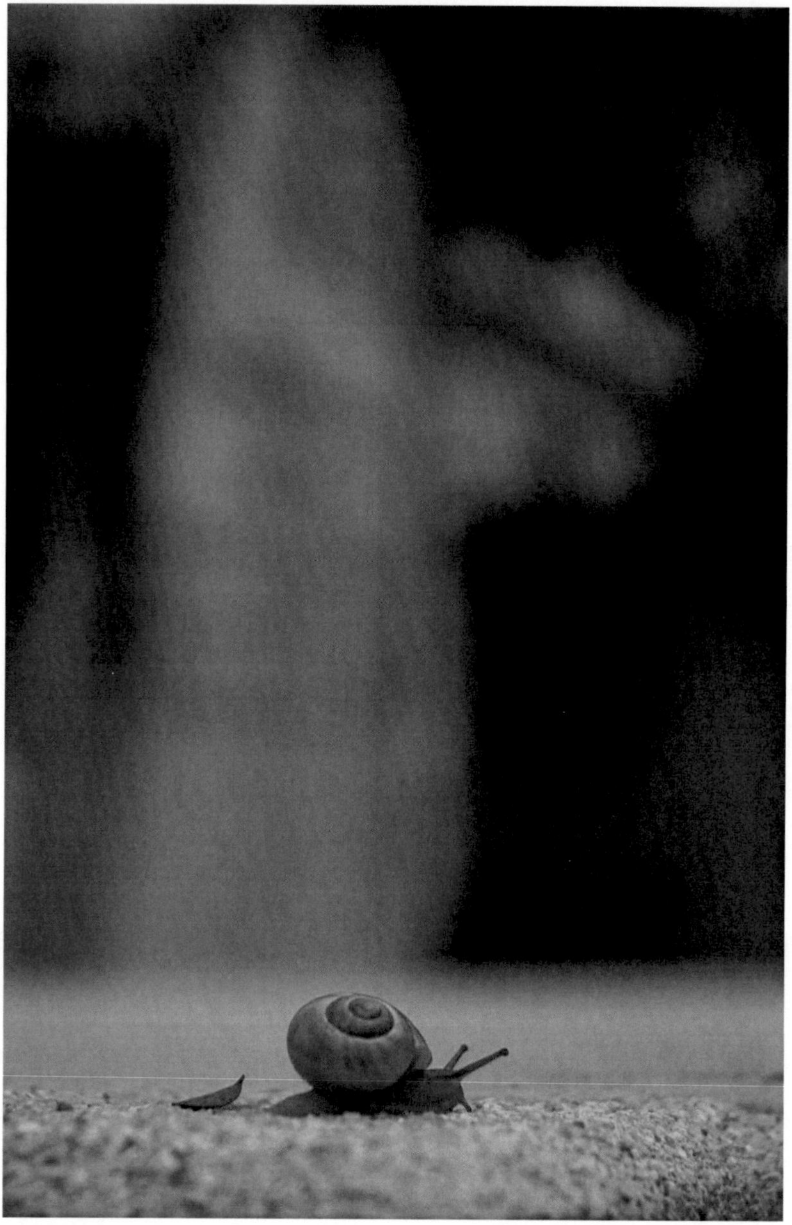

named Endre Friedmann. They became lovers and photographic partners, deciding to invent a photographer, Robert Capa, to improve their earning prospects – their fictional American was able to ask for three times the commission rate that they could get. To start with both took pictures as Capa, but later Gerta worked independently as Taro. In 2010 I was familiar with Robert Capa but I wasn't aware of Taro. I wasn't the only one as, unlike now, her grave didn't appear on the official Père Lachaise map, so I was unlikely to have found her even if I'd been looking. She only really came to my attention in 2018, when she featured on a Google Doodle 108 years after her birth. Due to the nature of her and Friedmann's early collaboration it is sometimes difficult to disentangle which of Robert Capa's photographs were actually taken by her.

Something else I didn't find in 2010 was the Communards' Wall, the place where the Paris Commune of 1871 reached its bloody climax. I was disappointed I hadn't seen it, but decided it would be something for my next visit (which it was, as you know, in 2013).

In 2019, nine years had gone by since the trip and I felt no closer to realising my vision for a book about it. It was time, then, to return to first principles and ask myself: 'What do I want to say and how do I want to say it?'

I looked for a thesis, a position or proposition to discuss, using my Paris trip as a particular example of something more general. I think I lacked confidence that simply recounting my own experiences would be enough. Too much thinking about how to interest or please hypothetical future readers and not enough time doing the hard work of writing things down.

I felt that the principal idea of the book was that travel can enrich our lives and that seeing things and places can provide a link with other stories. That everyone's life is a tapestry. This would be my story, my tapestry, and show the way my threads link to people like Margaret de Valois, Walter Benjamin, James Whistler, Ernest Hemingway and Juliette Binoche. Connections to films, books, TV, art and ideas. To *Midnight in Paris*, *Life: A User's Manual*, *A Moveable Feast*, the final stage of Le Tour, *Whistler's Mother*, Art Walk Porty, flâneurs and flâneuses.

But I wasn't sure how to write my story and bring together these ideas, whether I should start with an explanation, an introduction to the thesis. Set the scene and then use the structure of the visit, the quinze jours of a French fortnight, to bring in the ideas I wanted to explore. But was the idea to explore Paris or to explore exploring? My exploration one example of a Paris, my Paris, that could encourage other explorations, other versions of the city. Or was it an example of how to visit any place in a different way? To bring into focus the way that any visit is seen through our own lens – the things we remember, the things we already think we know. And then, having been and walked around, do the new threads we come across afterwards have greater relevance, more traction, because we have walked down that street, sat in that café, seen that view for ourselves?

I wondered if the fact that it was *Paris* made a difference. One of the world cities – New York, London, Paris, Munich . . . (if you're of a certain age, you're singing a pop song now). Did that make it more accessible or did information overload make it harder to make sense of the place? How hard should we have to work as a visitor? As a tourist? We all bring knowledge with us when we travel. Religious travellers bring more than knowledge, they bring a story, about their destination but also about their journey, the getting-there an element that's integral to the pilgrim experience. As tourists we travel to collect a story, the story of a place, but we also bring to it an ongoing story – our story – even if we aren't always aware of it.

As tourists, how much interpretation do we need given to us to make sense of things? While a city's publicity department would like to sell us one set of stories, they're not the only ones. There are other narratives, but in popular tourist destinations like Paris and Edinburgh the loudest story is about the city centre and its beautiful old buildings, ignoring the realities of life for city inhabitants. Notre-Dame rather than the banlieues, the Fringe rather than the problems of finding a place to live. Stories become political in their telling and, even more critically, in their not-telling. I think of France coming to terms with the nation's role in the Shoah, the Roundup in Paris. Politicians telling a story that previously hadn't been told.

We are what we have done, where we have been, what we have seen.

There are many ways to experience places you've never been to. Books, films, TV, photographs and websites all let us see without going. But being in the same physical space can be uniquely powerful. Events that happened long ago can still resonate: the place is the same, the time is different, and the idea that 'big things happened here' is a cornerstone of how we understand history. I explored this a bit in my battlefield photographs. Some sites were preserved close to how they would have looked at the time of the battle but at many others the landscape had changed dramatically. At Culloden, for example, although parts of the battlefield were managed by the National Trust for Scotland from the 1930s, for many years much of the wider site was obscured by twentieth-century conifer plantations. If you'd visited in the 1970s, as I did as a child, you would have found it difficult to appreciate any concept of the historic battlefield. Then, the lines of battle were marked by paths through the trees and the places where individual units lined up shown by flags in the middle of the woodland. That changed when the NTS purchased the woodland from the Forestry Commission in the 1980s and removed the trees, to return the site more closely to the way it must have looked in 1746. The last time I visited, in 2016, I felt the battlefield made much more sense and it was easier to imagine the battle as you looked across the site.

In Père Lachaise I walked around the northern side of the cemetery to Oscar Wilde's elaborate tomb, sculpted by Jacob Epstein in one of his earliest commissions. It was covered with lipstick kisses, a tradition that apparently started in the 1990s. I wondered again what impulse led people to leave their mark, to express their love, in such a damaging way. It's clearly ancient, whatever it is, as there are examples of graffiti dating back to Roman times. But while I can see the attraction of a blank wall as a potential canvas, it seems strange in the context of a cemetery. Perhaps technology will provide a less destructive way to commemorate your visit in the future. Something more imaginative and attractive than just a plastic barrier, like a digital scroll of messages you can link to from your phone or type in while you're there.

Shortly afterwards I found Proust's grave – another simple black slab – and as I walked away a woman approached me and asked me, in French, if I knew where Proust was. I was able answer in my rudimentary French and point her in the right direction. She asked if I was from Paris and was a little surprised when I said no, from Edinburgh, in Scotland. It turned out she wasn't French either, though, so it probably wasn't the linguistic compliment it first appeared.

The cloudy sky still threatened rain as I turned towards the entrance where I'd come in. My walk through the cemetery had affected me more than I'd expected. I knew that a graveyard would be a dour place but had thought that not actually knowing any of the people there while they were alive would make it more of a tourist experience, akin to visiting an old church. After all, visiting Montmartre Cemetery the previous week had felt more that way. Maybe it was just that the sun had been out in Montmartre. Maybe it wasn't just the cemetery. I was sad at time running out. Our trip to Paris already past its halfway point and on the way down towards the end. And then a deeper sadness in appreciating my own mortality. Unlike many of my classmates, still in their twenties and with much more of their lives ahead of them, I was approaching fifty. The trip had been, and was for a few more days, a brief, bright return to student life, to living on a whim, with minimal responsibilities. A time for hanging out in cafés and impromptu late-night dinners in restaurants. The freedom of not having plans. I don't know.

During the course of the afternoon I'd been in touch with Sophy – she'd also been having a quiet day, doing a bit of shopping – and texting as I walked we arranged to meet for dinner.

I visited a few more graves on my way back down the hill, including French man of letters Honoré de Balzac. But I missed seeing the tomb of Theodore Gericault, which has a bronze sculpture of the artist, brushes and palette in hand, on top of a plinth decorated with bas reliefs of some of his work, including his most famous painting, *The Raft of the Medusa*. I'm familiar with that from the doctored version on the cover of the Pogues album *Rum Sodomy & the Lash*, but it also came up in conversation with a friend only the other day as we talked about examples of great translation. In the Asterix books I was so fond of as a child, there's a scene with the pirates after another of their unfortunate encounters with the Gauls that closely resembles Gericault's painting. The pirate chief in the French edition says 'Je suis médusé', which literally translates as 'I am dumbfounded', but is a pun on the one-accent difference in the French for medusa – 'méduse'. Clearly a literal translation wouldn't preserve the joke, so instead the English version has the pirate chief say 'We've been framed, by Jericho', hinting at the same artistic allusion.

 I left the cemetery by the same entrance I had come in by and headed back towards the hotel via a supermarket. I only wanted to buy a snack, but it turned out to be a surprisingly confusing experience. There was something strange about the set-up, as it seemed there was something about paying for things that depended on chance. Random numbers flashed up on screens above the checkout and there was some unfathomable connection between them and the stuff on the conveyor belt going through. I think the cashier took pity on the obviously completely bewildered foreigner and she just asked me for the money to pay for the bread and cheese and can of juice in my basket. Try as I might, I've never been able to find any explanation for what was going on. Was it a convoluted way to avoid the laws against supermarkets above a certain size inside the city? I've no idea.

 I met up with Sophy and we went to the Café de l'Industrie, a restaurant close to the hotel and highly recommended in Sophy's guidebook. It didn't disappoint. It was full of young Parisians and there were only French voices to be heard around us. We ordered in French and talked about the things we'd seen and done so far on the trip and what we might do after college. The food – tuna steaks – seemed good to my unfussy palate, but the setting elevated it to being a more memorable meal. It felt more 'real' with so many locals eating there and everything around us in French.

Back at the hotel I dropped in on some of the others in their rooms. It felt a lot like being back at uni in Durham, even to the extent of heading out for a late drink, much like we did in the college bar in time for last orders after a night with your head stuck in a book. It's interesting, though, the way that friendships vary and the different trajectories they have over time. There were twenty-five photography students on the trip. We flew into Paris with a small group of make-up students who were going to do work experience in Parisian salons, but apart from occasionally seeing them in the hotel we didn't spend any time with them. There were large group activities, like the first few evening meals, the picnic in the Champs de Mars and the meal on the last night, but mostly we did things in smaller groups, so there were about a dozen people I spent time with on the streets of Paris.

Of those, Petr, Agni and Jo were the people I knew best in college and hung out with most on the trip. I've seen the three of them in the years since and we were in touch during lockdown. The fact that two of them were in Poland and Petr was living out in the Scottish Borders made no difference – they were all equally inaccessible in those physically restrictive times. On the other hand, Sophy seems to have slipped off my radar (Anita too, who introduced me to Blipfoto). We kept in touch for a while as Sophy finished her degree and I moved on with my freelance photography business. The last I heard she'd moved to London, but the connection's gone. Some of the others, like Trisha, Anna and Sam, I have sporadic contact with, mostly on socials. But for me, for some reason, it's always been a concern – the number of friends I have. I'm not sure if it comes from an insecurity about not fitting in, something I was very conscious of as a child, growing up

English in a Scottish city. Or is it an aspect of my neuroatypicalness? That's something I've become increasingly aware of in recent years, that my brain seems to be wired a little differently; and although it's difficult to work out why that might be – whether it was established before I was born or as the product of my early life experiences, or a mixture of both – it is what it is. As a teenager I used to keep a diary and measure my friendships by counting up how often people appeared and producing a connection league table at the end of the year. It was as if the number of mentions was some way of measuring the strength of the friendship.

Looking back, I wonder if it was an attempt to quantify something I found difficult to gauge in a qualitative sense, maybe because I found it difficult to read social cues. Social media can provide the same quantitative measures of friendship that my teenage self collated from my diary entries. Does that make things easier for me, or more difficult? By presenting the data so easily, I can see much more clearly the people I've lost touch with. It used to be that there were manageable numbers of people to keep track of – those you saw regularly in person, the ones you saw less often, the people you exchanged Christmas cards with but didn't see from one year to the next, and the names in your address book that you hadn't heard from in years and who probably didn't even live at the same address any more. Facebook, on the other hand, regularly (yet unpredictably) points out the missing, presenting photos or old status updates that remind me of people I know but no longer see or hear from.

Clearly we can't maintain meaningful connections with all the people we meet, or even with the smaller subset we get along with when our paths cross. There are various estimates for how many actual *friends* a person can have, such as the Dunbar number (150), and yet the average number of friends people have on Facebook in 2025 was 338, which, for many people, creates an artificially inflated idea of our friendship circle. At this time of writing I have 1,167 Facebook friends (not boasting, they're mostly work-related), but I meaningfully interact with a fraction of those people. It all makes sense – friendships come and go as we move through life – but why I am bothered that I seem to have lost touch with some of the people I spent time with in Paris? I've lost touch with other friends, and that bugs me a bit too if I'm honest, but given that the fortnight in Paris was such an intense experience for me I guess that heightens the sense of loss.

It helps to know it isn't entirely personal. I met another of our Paris group, Kerstin, in Glasgow a few years ago. Kerstin and Anita had gone around together in Paris a fair bit, but she'd not heard from Anita for a long time either. A slow drifting apart in which you don't realise how long has passed since you last met or last heard from someone, and then one day you do, and it's years and years. It's the thing I often find difficult. Is it ghosting or is it down to me and a misunderstanding of my relationships? Am I still that socially awkward teenager measuring friendships on some quantitative basis, mistaking 'proximity acquaintances' for friends? Without the activity that brought about the proximity, the acquaintanceship lapses. We have the main stuff going on in our life – family, work, pastimes – and then there are the 'other people', who we met at some point in the past but are now peripheral. There just isn't enough time to keep up with everyone.

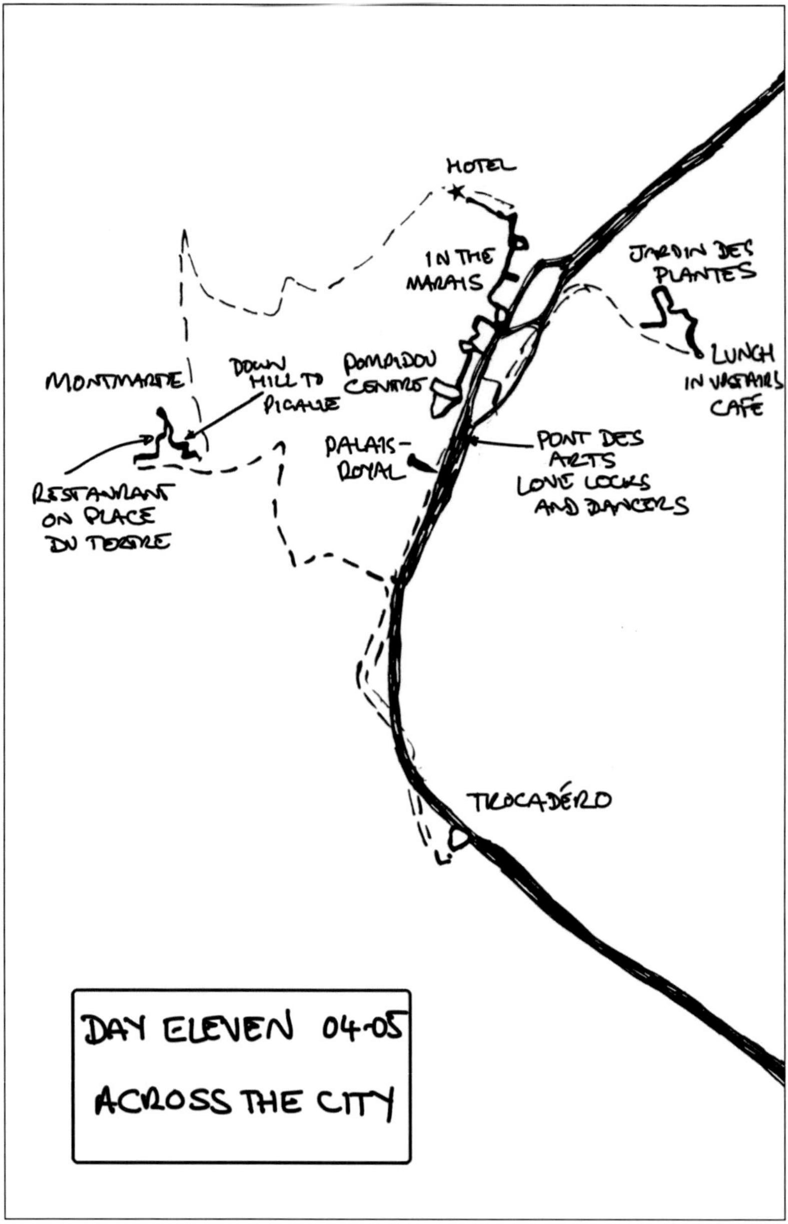
HOTEL
IN THE MARAIS
JARDIN DES PLANTES
LUNCH IN UPSTAIRS CAFE
MONTMARTRE
DOWN HILL TO PIGALLE
POMPIDOU CENTRE
PALAIS-ROYAL
PONT DES ARTS LOVE LOCKS AND DANCERS
RESTAURANT ON PLACE DU TERTRE
TROCADÉRO
DAY ELEVEN 04-05
ACROSS THE CITY

Mardi 4 mai / 2020

Tuesday was 'Star Wars Day' – May the Fourth. It was still a niche thing in 2010, but even if it wasn't it wouldn't have meant anything to me because I've never seen it. Yes, as I write this, I am one of those people. It's become a meme and there was once a radio show called *I've Never Seen Star Wars*, based on the idea of trying out things you've never done before.

During lockdown in 2020 Lorraine and I watched all the Indiana Jones movies and all the Back to the Future movies, but with *Star Wars* I only got as far as reading an article in *Vogue* written by someone else who'd never seen it and then went on to discuss the best ways to watch the entire franchise. It was hard not to see that as just marketing for the streaming premiere of the ninth film, following its release the year before.

Exploring the meme, and the idea of shared cultural experiences, led me to a discussion online about the ways in which the original film (by which I mean the fourth one of the nine) has changed over the years. Apparently there's a particular scene in which Han Solo shoots an alien bounty hunter called Greedo that was altered in subsequent versions of the film. Director George Lucas used advances in digital technology to make it clear that the alien had fired first and Solo had killed him in self-defence. Some fans were disappointed that Lucas had altered Solo's narrative and therefore who he was. The director responded by saying, 'I'm sorry you saw half a completed film and fell in love with it.'

A sub-meme grew around the controversy – 'Han shot first' – and Lucas continued to defend his decision: the movie is a work of fiction, he's its author, and he could effectively rewrite the past if he wanted to. In contrast to our get-it-finished-and-out-there 48HFP experience, he was still tinkering decades after his movie had supposedly been completed. Lucas described Solo as a cowboy in the John Wayne mould who would be honourable and give the bad guy a chance (before gunning him down). I wonder what people who saw the original version, but have never seen the revised versions think. What happens if they get into a discussion with someone who has? Each completely convinced in their view of Han Solo. And search engines are of course infected too. If you search for 'Han shot first', Google asks 'Did you mean: Greedo shot first'.

One thing the Covid lockdown provided was time, even if I recognised the pressure I felt to use it productively could be less than helpful to my mental health. Sometimes I decided that just getting through the day would have to be enough. However, on the tenth anniversary of the start of the trip I resolved to begin writing something about Paris. I'd done the NaNoWriMo writing challenge in 2018 and 2019 (50,000 words during the month of November) and set myself a target of writing between 1,500 and 2,000 words a day for the next month.

Ten years on it was sunny in Portobello, just as it had been sunny and warm on the day of our arrival in Paris. I suspected the wind off the sea was keeping the temperature down. Only 'suspected' because as I wrote we were still deep in lockdown and just popping out for a few minutes on the beach whenever we felt like it was something we'd not been able to do for several weeks.

As I began, I instantly questioned whether this was the best time to finally write this book – a book that had been in my head for a decade so far and never made it to the stage of anything like a first draft. (Spoiler alert – it wasn't.) I pondered the framework that had rattled around for years: the hard structure of the fifteen days spent in Paris. I looked back at my Blips for every anniversary of the trip as it came, and went, which brought me to 24 April 2020. Ten years for the moveable feast to be sorted and re-sorted on the shelves, ready to be taken down again when prompted by news events, a new book or a new film. There had been so many such instances in the previous decade that I was starting to realise something: that the process of not-writing, the way I was struggling, might be as much the subject matter I wanted to explore as was the original trip.

One undeniably great thing about the internet age is the way it allows anyone in the world to visit distant locations virtually. To me, in lockdown, that applied to anywhere out of reach of the government-prescribed one hour of exercise, even the other side of Edinburgh. But it also allowed me to revisit Paris from my desk. Paris, a city with exceptional photographic coverage in terms of clarity and detail.

And so, through fifteen days that exactly mirrored on the calendar the dates of the trip, I remembered in 2020 what had happened in 2010, rephrasing my memories and 'walking' down the same streets. This was the easy part of the process, which I knew because it wasn't the first time I'd done it. But it was the rest of it, the ideas that filled the second half of that month of writing in May 2020, that I found/find the most interesting and yet have wrestled the most with as I attempt to sort them into something coherent.

I'm a numbers guy, a systems guy. If I make a schedule, it's going to get followed. So no sooner had I started my ten-years-on fortnight of writing than I found there wasn't enough time to do it right. I had so much to say, I was reaching my daily word count before I was getting to the end of the Paris day's activities. But then, frustrating as that was, after a few days I started to run out of things to say before I ran out of words, and therefore began to riff on the post-visit aspect of the book, the sort of thing I'd only expected to be writing when the day-by-day catalogue of the trip was done.

I started considering the long tail of the visit, the connections I'd made since with the places visited (and not visited, too). I wrote about the Paris I'd glimpsed since 2010 and how it overlapped with the Paris I'd seen. The annual arrival of the Tour de France, coming into the city from different directions and following different routes. Some years it had been from the southwest, a bit I barely visited, completely unfamiliar. Other times it had been from the east, in past the Jardin des Plantes and the Bastille. It always joined up with the regular final circuit up and down the Champs-Élysées, across the Place de la Concorde, round by the Louvre and through the tunnel. Out again by Norwegian Corner and down the Rue de Rivoli, between the shops and the fairground in the gardens and back onto the wide space of Concorde before turning once more to start another lap.

I found myself thinking about other locations that are frequently mentioned but that I realised I was uncertain of. When the French Open tennis came round again, I wondered where exactly was Roland-Garros? Or the Parc des Princes, the home of PSG? Very close together it turned out, down in that unfamiliar southwest quadrant and just outside the Boulevard Périphérique. And like with any internet search, this led me down a winding trail . . . that European Cup final against Bayern in 1975, Jules Rimet, football club mergers, St Pauli, Livorno, Boca Juniors . . . Was that just me, lacking the focus to concentrate on words that weren't coming easily? Or was it a product, accidental or otherwise, of the constantly available, inexhaustible encyclopedia of online information?

I'm aware I need to answer questions, as well as ask them, but for the moment I want to know why these facts were of any interest to me when I was in the middle of doing something else. It was like pulling at a loose thread in a jumper. Was there a hidden sense of order to be found in these bits of history? Why, for example, did it fascinate me to discover that the 1938 World Cup, hosted in France when the Latin American nations believed it should have been their turn, was boycotted by Argentina, Uruguay and others and was only attended by three non-European nations? Maybe I'd just rather be writing about football!

Back in 2020, as well as my jack-in-the-box brain, the struggle to write was probably to do with the days I was writing about, particularly the second Sunday, with its failures to get into museums and galleries or find the flea market. But I was also starting to doubt the whole project. This was a point I'd reached before, in writing down my Parisian experiences. The first week was the most vivid, while the second felt kind of flat, as if I couldn't get any deeper. I was losing faith in what I'd thought was the guiding idea behind the book – the value of visiting a city without a guidebook. After all, how could that still stand up as a concept when I was writing an account of a day that showed its very weakness? Maybe the idea itself was dead wrong.

I started May the Fourth 2010, like I'd started several other days in Paris, by walking out of the hotel into the Marais area west of the Bastille. Past the Place des Vosges and into the Jewish quarter. I photographed some of the wall plaques commemorating Jewish residents who were taken away and killed by the Nazis. Like the one at 16 Rue des Rosiers in memory of 12-year-old Rosette and her father, Hersz Lewkowicz; Esther and Henri Merkier; Esther Ita Sokol and infant Paulette, her 2-year-old brother Victor and their mother Rywka. Terrible events described so matter-of-fact that they hit you like a heavy weight as you pause to read the words. A pendulum swinging through time from 1942 to 2010.

I couldn't capture in a photograph the way I felt seeing all those modest memorials. It brought home the distance I felt, having lived my whole life on an island that had always managed to keep some separation from the wars in Europe. Although in Britain there are many public memorials to all the soldiers that didn't come back, and reminders of the effect of bombing raids, either in formal plaques or the subsequent rebuilding to replace damaged properties, those had never had the same impact on me. Something about the ordinariness of the people and the places that contrasted with the enormity of the death camps.

In 2020 my writing schedule reached the anniversary of our return, signalling the end of the day-by-day section. I now had to work out how best to structure the remaining words. At that point I'd taken to avoiding calling it a 'book', as I wasn't sure how the words I wrote might get out into the world (other options might have been a series of essays, Insta reels, a dedicated blog or a standalone website). To start, keeping with a 'writing about the problem' approach, I came up with two different plans, both of which kept the details of the actual visit, including the streets walked and the routes taken. I could keep the fifteen-day structure and slot in the material that connected to the themes and ideas with the description of the days themselves, or I could split the project in two and keep the Paris days as part one and the other stuff as part two.

To help me decide I looked to Blipfoto for a post-Paris chronology of when and how various themes had emerged since 2010, through the years of repeatedly trying and failing to get something written. Part of the problem, I could see, had always been the very transition I was struggling with now: how to bridge the gap between memories of the days in Paris and connections to Paris that I've become aware of since. I felt there was no clear and obvious precedent that I was aware of, couldn't see how I could knit all the digressions and tangents together in a readable way. I decided I'd continue to keep them separate.

Finding indoor subjects for Blips was a bit of a struggle during lockdown, so I started setting up tableaux using one of those articulated wooden figures that you see in art shop windows, the ones that are supposed to help you learn to draw the human body in animated poses. I imagine they're mainly sold to beginners or bought as well-meaning gifts. Whether they're actually any help in drawing anything other than *Still Life Incorporating Articulated Wooden Figure* is another question.

I actually had a whole box of them that had all been painted yellow. There was an installation created as part of the 2016 Edinburgh International Festival, called *Anything That Gives Off Light*, which featured a thousand of these figures on platforms in the ponds in front of the Scottish Parliament. Each of the figures was supposedly painted by a different pupil, who also wrote a poem inspired by the idea of light. I say 'supposedly' because while that was the description for the piece at the time, and quite possibly the original intention, when I started to share my photos of them online someone commented that they'd worked for the festival that summer and one of their first jobs had been to spray large numbers of the figures yellow. Maybe they'd only been helping the school pupils in the painting process, but even so that feels a long way from the idea that 'each figurine was painted by a primary seven pupil' as described in the festival publicity.

At any rate, without the individual connection to specific school children, it's no surprise that after the installation was dismantled there were lots of unwanted figures out there and I was able to claim a small box of them from someone who was giving them away. They seemed the sort of thing that might be useful at some point, but after a few Blips early in September 2016 I'd put them in a cupboard. I took one out a year later, inspired by hearing the author Michel Faber talking about his late wife, Eva, and the photography she created. One of her last projects was a series using one of these same wooden mannequins, positioned in the landscape. I went down onto Portobello beach and staged a picture with the yellow figure as a photographer, complete with a miniature camera. I shared the image on Blip and it ended up being used as the basis for a classroom discussion led by the photographer I'd met earlier that summer in Bristol. So having started as a school project (at least officially) the figure had ended up back in the classroom.

In 2020, the first shot I set up was very similar to that one on the beach, although this time the miniature photographer, like me, was stuck inside, looking out through the window. In those lockdown days when maybe whimsy got more of a free pass, the picture seemed to amuse people, and so I set up another yellow figure sunbathing. That went okay too, so I panicked for more ideas and thought about recreating some iconic photographs. The one that immediately came to mind was 'Behind the Gare Saint-

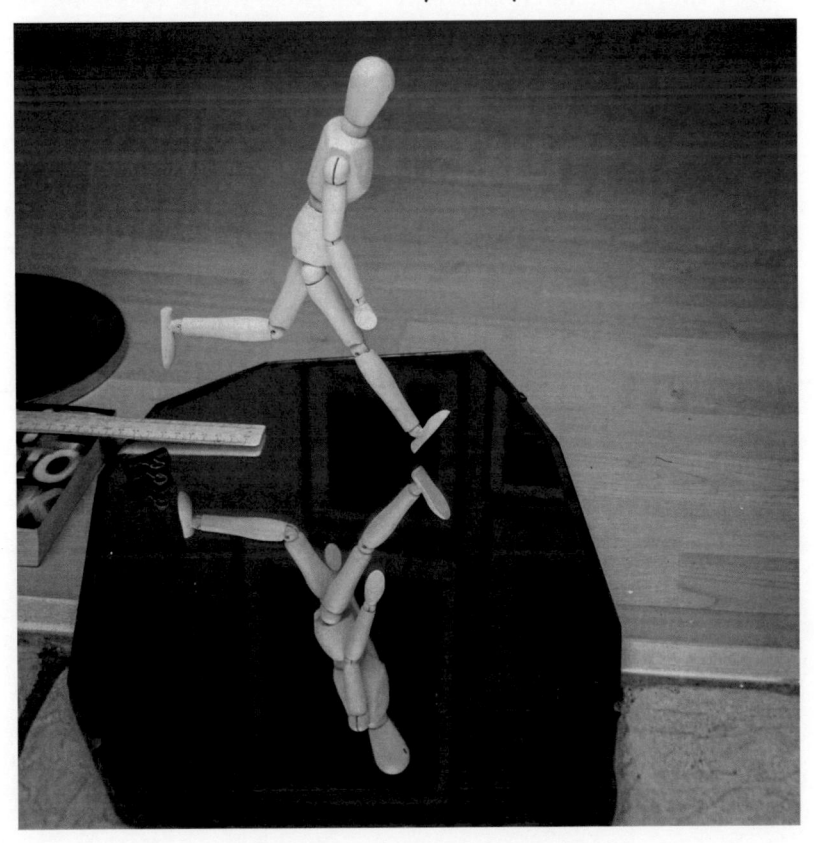

Lazare'. I carefully posed the jumping figure, using a mirror in place of the puddle, and captured the instant before his heel touches the surface. I followed that with other shots inspired by other images I remembered from my photography studies back in college, such as August Sanders' 'Bricklayer', Diane Arbus's 'Child with Toy Hand Grenade in Central Park, N.Y.C. 1962' and Arnold Newman's portrait of Igor Stravinsky. Nothing original, but as well as keeping me busy through several weeks of lockdown it forced me to work out how to put together a look using whatever materials I had available in the flat. Sometimes there were other details added into the mix that maybe only I was aware of. There's a portrait Annie Leibowitz did of Hilary Swank, for example, where she's running on a beach, background split between waves and sky, so I used our turquoise living-room wall and white skirting board to reverse the turquoise sea and white sky in the original.

Although I managed to produce a daily yellow figure Blip until the end of May 2020, I came up with next to nothing about Paris. In the middle of the month I missed a whole day's worth of writing in my self-imposed schedule, so I started the next day a full 2,000 words adrift and wrote that it would be tough to claw my way back. Tough, but not impossible. There were twelve days left in my thirty-day regime and a little less than 22,000 words to write. I kept circling back to the idea that the struggle might *not* be irrelevant, might not be, dare I say it, shameful. The trials of lockdown, the trials of writing. Trials. Mine were minor in comparison to others'. I know that.

The first bit had been easy, with plenty of remembered content from each day of the trip, but that bit was *always* easy, so did that mean I should use the fortnight as an overarching framework? It could be a form of psychogeography, using my remembered map to go and find Jon. I wondered if I needed to properly map those fifteen days, plot out every single place I went, every street I walked down. That would be comprehensive, and I'd be satisfied I'd done the experience some kind of justice, but how would a book incorporate all the other stuff? It felt really multidimensional, better suited to a website with a lattice of hyperlinks. Or maybe not. Maybe it *could* fit into a book, each day a chapter, a map, a bundle of digressions.

And while this was going on I asked myself repeatedly the biggest question of all: what would make it worth reading? If it was just an elaborate personal diary of a fortnight of my life, what's that to anyone else? Which brought me back to the struggle involved in writing it. An artistic journey that gathers bits and pieces along the way. The nature of the internet, the way that looking something up can lead to hours of reading about the Paris Commune or the Vél' d'Hiv' Roundup, following links to links to links.

I thought about the things we do with our time and the way that we're encouraged to value some things and dismiss others, like what happened with me and the photographic-technique police and selective-colour images. Investing in some kinds of invented worlds, such as soap operas or films in particular genres, is mocked but other fictional creations are not. If art, in all its forms, is just a toy then one thing is as good as any other, as long as it holds our attention. And if it isn't, if art has some greater purpose connected to our progress as a species and the accumulation of a cultural treasure chest to be enjoyed by future generations, then who knows what might resonate with those distant descendants? It's a commonplace that many great painters died penniless and unrecognised, only achieving fame after their death. Maybe that will apply to fragments of *Emily in Paris*, preserved in a computer archive and revered like Shakespeare for the way the dialogue perfectly encapsulates one aspect of the human condition. Even a stopped clock and all that. But maybe the quest for meaning is a curse. Evolutionary biology holds that our fundamental goal as individuals is to do our bit to continue our species, just keep churning out humans and leave it to genetic chance to determine who might come up with the next big idea to benefit all humankind. For those of us without biologically related children our contribution might be art. That might be how our effect extends beyond death.

My worldview currently has no role for – let's just use this word – God. I find faith difficult, even without a supernatural element, hence the nightmare I was having with this book. Thinking of Goethe's questions about making art – What did I set out to do? Did I do it? Was it worth doing? – it's clear my doubts about the last one were leading me to obsess over the other two. I needed faith, or rather belief, but didn't know where to find it. I can't see religion as anything other than a human construct, so instead of the human race having some divine purpose I see us like ants, living and dying in our colonies. Socially advanced and culturally sophisticated ants, but ants nonetheless. The logical endpoint of holding that view could be nihilism or living a completely hedonistic life, but there's also an obligation to safeguard the future, to treat the world and the people around us with care and respect, because then we get that back and civilisation can continue. I'm aware as I write this, though, and maybe I always was aware of this, that the struggle I'm in is to *write a book*. So that's called privilege. And I'm surely pretty wealthy compared to most of the world.

Writing that, in the 2020 draft, made me try and see where I fitted in the global wealth distribution curve. I then got sidetracked by social media and news websites and email and a bit more social media and finally returned to the page only to realise I didn't actually get as far as finding out the answer to the original question and by then it was time for aerobics, another part of our lockdown routine, which segued straight into lunch and then more aimless iPad futzing about before the bi-weekly trip to the shops for supplies.

When I did finally get back to it, I spent hours trying to untangle wealth from income, getting wound up by lazy reporting slash systemic bias, which I could dimly sense was going to be a pointless digression, and yet . . . How ambitious a project might I create if I didn't limit myself? Could I see my whole life through the lens that was a fortnight in Paris in 2010? It came back once again to the themes of psychogeography and the way we see things out in the world, every one of us different, the product of our personal past. Maybe there was something too in my baggage related to my neuroatypicalness. That was bound to influence the way that I wanted to tell the story.

Mardi 4 mai / 2020

Meanwhile, despite the income/wealth investigation, I still missed my daily target by 300 words. I then managed a few better days as I wrote about the way the idea for the book developed in the years after Paris, and in particular our trip to Paris for my 50th, but then I stalled again. I was now 13,000 words short of my target for the first draft. I'd got as far as the autumn of 2013, which, in 2020, was seven years ago, but I was unsure how much to bring out from those seven years and whether it would add anything significant to the story. I had the realisation, though, that the book was about multiple journeys, on different levels. One of them – the one that gives this book its title – was the one in 2010, which was largely being written about by me in 2020 without moving from the chair in the window bay of our flat in Portobello. A seat with a view boxed in by buildings on either side, looking sideways down the street to the sea, a small rectangle of blue or grey between sand and sky. To the left was the red sandstone of our tenement and to the right the off-white painted render of the modern block opposite. More than a hundred years of history on opposite sides of the street. The sea and sky reminded me of my fifty-fifty photographic project: a hundred days of split images, sea and sky. It was a distraction from my typing, as were the swallows that had recently appeared, swooping past at eye-level up on the second floor, high above the street.

(I wonder now, in 2025, about cutting the whole of that last paragraph. I know I've already introduced the three dimensions of the book back in the Introduction, but I like the way it represents me, and the way my mind works, truthfully. Starting off in one direction and then distracted by the details, with references to things right in front of me and memories of things passed. I've cut a lot of other similar passages. I'll leave that one in.)

While I was physically in the same place every day, the screen I used to type the words for the book could also transport me across time and space. Much as Zoom fused together work and social contact at that time, so the easily accessible internet made my ever-doubted writing even more fragile, assailed by constant temptations towards procrastination. A switch to check the details of a date or place would lead to hours lost in the long, hyperlinked weeds of idle curiosity. What would a map of the cyber-journey I had been on during just one lockdown morning look like, I wondered.

Well, it turned out it was possible to at least see my browser history. (I guess I should have known that.) The bigger black hole was the Facebook-based stuff – simple scrolling through actual Facebook content or reading directly linked articles. Still, even the browser history showed in stark detail the constant battle for my attention. On 17 May, for example, I drifted off course into an article about an artist moving glacier ice from Greenland to London. After that, one of my Paris Blips from the Rodin Museum led me to Camille Claudel and the film made about her in the 1980s. Then checking up on the football led me to Dundee United's Wikipedia page and from there the page on the Dundee football derbies. From there, somehow, I went to an article about the CEO of Airbnb for the letter he sent staff that were being made redundant because of the Covid shutdown, saying how good it was that he let people keep their laptops. Surfing for coronavirus updates then a jump to a financial piece about a woman in Dundee and how she spent her money last week. More coronavirus updates, a bit about the flats at the end of the street, then the historical development of Portobello, its architecture. Are you nodding (off) yet? I feel sure we are all afflicted by this to some degree now. For me, the bottom line was that the tool that put all the reference materials I could possibly ever need at my fingertips was also my biggest obstacle.

The next day, 18 May 2020, went by without any writing. I noted another tangential Paris connection as I Blipped a distant zoomed-in photograph from the day before of three women walking on Portobello beach. Mother and daughters were in traditional Norwegian costume to mark Norway's national constitution day. The holiday, simply known as 'syttende mai' (Norwegian for 17 May), commemorates the signing of the Norwegian constitution in 1814, even although Norway remained in union with Sweden until full independence in 1905. Edinburgh's Norwegian community, many of them young students, has an annual parade in the city centre. I'd been there to see it a few times with my camera and on moving to Portobello I started photographing a local group who gathered to walk along the prom in their costumes.

That wasn't possible in 2020, but three members of the same family were able to go out and I just happened to be looking out the window as they were walking along the sand. The picture reminded me of the Skagen paintings by P. S. Krøyer and others, many of which feature women walking along the beach, although usually later in the day in fabulous evening light rather than early afternoon. A Swedish friend who saw my picture online told me about the personal life of the artist, Peder, and his wife, Marie. I looked them up and it turned out, although their paths had crossed in Copenhagen, they really met in Paris, in a café close to the Palais-Royal. Nowhere I had actually been when I was in Paris – in fact it hadn't been a café for almost a hundred years – but, once again, there it was.

In the Paris of 2010 I wandered along, taking pictures of shops and people, and an old wooden synagogue. I was still looking for subjects for my documentary project. Good sporting images were hard to find, so I made a pragmatic decision to try and produce a decent set of pictures on a more generic 'on the streets of Paris' idea. I reached the Pont-Neuf and paused to look at the Henri IV statue in the middle of the bridge. Recently I've discovered that there's a claim that this might be where the first photograph of a human being was taken. Daguerre's Boulevard du Temple image, you'll remember, was taken in April or May 1838 but there is another image that was taken while he was still experimenting, perhaps as early as 1836, which shows the Henri IV statue from an upstairs window of a building across the street and includes what appears to be one or possibly two workmen lying in its shade.

I took a picture of an elderly man in one of the alcoves on the bridge, apparently surrounded by his belongings, and thought again of the film *Les Amants du Pont-Neuf*. As I stood in the middle of the northern span, looking down into the water, I imagined the moment when Michèle and Alex jump into the river and are picked up by a passing barge. For an instant I wondered what it would be like to jump in myself. Not in any serious self-harming way, just . . . What would it be like?

I shook myself out of my reverie and walked further along the river to the next bridge, the Pont des Arts, where the metal railings had a small scattering of padlocks attached to them, like the last few leaves on an autumn tree.

There are various stories about where the practice started but the strongest claim seems to belong to the Serbian town of Vrnjačka Banja. So the story goes, a school teacher met her lover, an army officer, on one of the town's bridges. He left to fight in the First World War and while away he fell in love with someone else. The school teacher never recovered and died soon afterwards. Not wanting to share her tragic fate, local couples started fixing padlocks to the bridge, as symbols of firm attachment.

The story received more attention when it inspired a poem by the Serbian poet Desanka Maksimović and the bridge became known as the Bridge of Love, but the worldwide explosion in the practice seems to originate from an Italian novel (and subsequent film) called *Ho voglia di te* (*I Want You*), written by Federico Moccia in 2006. In his story a man persuades his girlfriend that there is an old legend associated with attaching a padlock to a lamppost on the Ponte Milvio in Rome and then throwing away the key, again to symbolise unbreakable love. There was no such legend in wider culture, though, it was simply created by Moccia as a part of his novel. But soon lovers in Rome did indeed start leaving locked padlocks on the bridge and throwing the keys into the Tiber. As the number of padlocks increased, city authorities became worried about damage to the bridge and introduced additional posts and chains specifically for people to attach locks to. However, even that was not enough and in 2012 the locks were finally removed entirely.

In Paris the practice was just getting started in 2010, although a week after my visit all the locks on the bridge were removed in the middle of the night by an art student to include in an installation. It carried on, though, for several years and the railings were so full that they looked like a wall of padlocks when I went back in 2013. By 2015 there were a million of them, comprising forty-five tons of metal, and they were eventually completely removed in order to save the Pont des Arts from collapsing. The sides of the bridge were altered, replacing the railings with Plexiglass, so there was no longer any way to attach a padlock. So folk moved downstream to a different bridge – the Passerelle Léopold-Sédar-Senghor between the Tuileries and the Musée d'Orsay. That bridge of locks features in the 2023 film *Murder Mystery 2*, but location filming in Paris completed in April 2022 and before the end of that year the padlocks had been removed there too and Plexiglass installed.

The tussle between lovers and city authorities around the world continues, with padlocks appearing and being removed and reappearing on many bridges and other tourist locations. Cities are conflicted in how to respond. On one hand too many padlocks can obviously damage urban infrastructure; on the other, they're exactly the sort of viral Insta-based free publicity that tourism departments pray for. There seems to be a rise recently in criticism of the practice, though, portraying it as selfish and irresponsible, so maybe the authorities will find less resistance to removing them.

As I stood on the Pont des Arts I became aware of some sort of organised activity going on at the other end of the bridge. A well-dressed couple were being filmed dancing in the middle of the walkway, with members of the crew holding people back from crossing the bridge while they finished a take. As I watched I got a text from Jo to say that she and Agni were in the Jardin des Plantes if I wanted to join them. I'd taken all the shots I wanted on the bridge so I said yes and caught the Métro half dozen stops along Line 7 to Place Monge.

Jo and I went for a cup of tea in the café in the gardens, then went to look for Agni, who was somewhere among the plants. When we found her she was photographing a squad of gardeners working the beds and another group of men who were creating a wooden structure across a large expanse of gravel in front of one

Mardi 4 mai / 2020

of the natural history buildings. It wasn't clear what it was, maybe a platform or a stage, but there was a lot of discussion, looking at plans and wielding of theodolites. It's always interesting to photograph people engrossed in a task, though, and my brain likes patterns.

Jo went to get the Métro and we said we'd catch her up, only we spent too long taking pictures and she'd gone by the time Agni and I got to the station. We had some sandwiches in a café then took Line 7 to Palais-Royal. There, we took photos among the lines of trees then moved on again, taking the Métro to somewhere new.

Mardi 4 mai / 2020

Trocadéro was rammed with sellers of souvenir tat, hip-hop dancers and no end of tourists photographing their own versions of the iconic view of the Eiffel Tower from the terrace. We walked a circuit of the park, past the mini fairground, and on our way back took some group photos for tourists.

Sitting on the steps below the viewing area, we got into conversation with a young Korean guy. He was travelling around Europe, Paris just one city among many on his itinerary. Agni took his picture with her Kiev, and I took a picture of her taking her picture, on the steps, photographer and subject with the Eiffel Tower between them in the background. Two travellers from different continents in a city, and country, strange to them both and photographed by someone from another, fourth, country. I put the photo on Facebook and we kept in touch for a while.

In 2020 a settled structure was still tantalisingly out of reach, like staring at the letters in your Scrabble rack, feeling sure there's a seven-letter word in there if only you could see it. I also wondered whether fretting about structure was what I did when I was worried the words I was typing on the screen would never match the aspirations I had for the finished book. Doubts were everywhere. Should the photographs be more central? Was it really about the maps? What makes any of this *interesting*?

New books I'd found that seemed similar were both encouraging and dispiriting. Books like Éric Hazan's *A Walk Through Paris: A Radical Exploration*. It being published in 2018 meant there was clearly an audience for this sort of work – but also that it had been done now, by an established author, so it didn't need doing again by me. I clung, though, to the idea that there was value in delineating the writing journey in the context of the daily walks I took in Paris. Also all the other paths that I'd learned of in the decade since 2010, and even in the years before. Could the book progress before they were all plotted? As well as Hazan's walk, there are so many journeys through Paris in other books and films. Like the Parisian elements of Jean-Baptiste's travels in *Perfume*, the novel I read on the plane on my way to Paris, Pascal's wanderings in *The Red Balloon*, the riverside journeys of Michèle and Alex in *Les Amants du Pont-Neuf*, Hemingway's Paris in *A Moveable Feast*, Gil's time-hopping night-time walks in *Midnight in Paris*.

The system-driven perfectionist in me was drawn to building a database of films and novels that touch on Paris in some way and creating maps for each of them. Fortunately I recognised the procrastinating impulse lurking in that plan and decided instead to concentrate on my own journeys, starting with my Parisian day-by-day, which would then be overlaid with a decade-and-more-long journey that explored the city from a distance and through the lenses of filmmakers and the words of other writers. Still too concerned with hypothetical readers, I wondered if this might become an exemplar for the sort of city exploration anyone can do. You start with a physical visit but then complement that with the virtual visits afforded by the cinema and the bookshelf, the internet and TV. A bit like the way that distance working with colleagues based in a different city works so much better when you've met in person. Isn't it the same with visiting a city – once you've been there, isn't Street View on Google more meaningful and vivid than if you haven't?

It seemed to me that I needed both approaches. People can and do write novels set in places they've never visited, leaving readers astonished when they learn all the dynamic description and insider knowledge was based on research done at a distance. And how much is physically visible on the ground anyway? Even if you read every single word on signs and notices in public spaces you will only ever scratch the surface of the stories about the place. Where did street names come from, what architecture used to be there, why did some old buildings survive and others not? Not to mention the inhabitants, past and present, and all their stories. Someone has started telling the stories in certain Edinburgh tenement blocks – picking a tenement and then researching old newspapers and other archives for any mention of the building, following up the people he finds and piecing together narratives. The stuff of guidebooks, yes, but it can be either read in situ or caught up on later while 'walking' digitally down Google's version of the streets.

On the 20th of May 2020, five years on from when Mum died, I wrote again on Blip about the structure of the book but also about what she might have said about my ideas.

At times over the years I had felt that she was disappointed that I had given up a good job in IT for something as uncertain and low-key eccentric as trying to become a professional photographer. My grandfather, her father, had been 'different', working in a mill during the day but writing books and plays in his spare time. That might have been uncomfortable for a child and I wondered if that was why she seemed to want me to be more conventional, more like other people. Something else I can never ask her now.

I had discussed the book a little bit with Lorraine and how it might come together. She liked the structure in my original idea, or at least the idea I'd been working with once I got beyond thoughts of a simple picture book. There would be a series of essays, each starting with the story of a specific day but then taking a different direction, following themes and ideas inspired by where I went that day. That had the bonus of creating standalone pieces that might have marketability on their own. Only later would I bring them together as chapters in a book. I wasn't convinced I could pull this off, but I could see the potential especially as discrete essays could have very different subjects and therefore different readerships. And doing it that way round might be more commercially attractive because anywhere that might publish an essay wouldn't want it if it had already been published in a book, but having previously published a few chapters *would* help in pitching a book.

As I approached my self-imposed 50,000-word finishing line, it seemed like it might be just in time as the First Minister announced the route map out of lockdown.

Lockdown gave me time to write and therefore lockdown now feels like a part of my Paris, as if I'd taken out Hemingway's metaphorical hamper every day as I sat in the window of our living room. I'd walked the streets of Paris once again, which gave me space to work things through, just as I used to do on the daily walk to and from my job in IT. A commute that is all on foot feels different to one on public transport. (I don't drive or cycle, so I can't talk about those.) To begin with, when I first started at the bank in January 1998, we lived in the Old Town and I worked out at the Gyle so there was a short train journey, or a bus, involved. Generally I much preferred the train. When we moved to near Haymarket the following year it was with half an eye on the journey to work, but then our department moved back into the city centre and I was able to walk from Hampton Place to Dundas Street and back again. There were various route options, as there was no simple straight-line path, but after a while I tended to stick with going through the West End and the lower streets of the New Town, avoiding Haymarket, Shandwick Place and Princes Street.

I always think it's a pity I wasn't on Blipfoto while I was still working at the bank and doing my twice-daily walks across the city centre. But although the site's founder Joe Tree posted his first Blip in October 2004, it took a while before he opened it up to anyone beyond his close friends, so in practice there's not much of an overlap. 'Psychogeography' and 'flâneur' weren't in my

Mardi 4 mai / 2020 223

vocabulary back then, but I knew walking was a place to think – and I was thinking about leaving.

December 2006 was when I finally did it. After kind of an aimless year spinning my wheels, I started at college early in 2008. Which meant another routine journey, once again out to the Gyle. I tended to take the bus this time: it took longer, but went closer. On some days over the next three and a half years I'd take a longer walk in order to get a different bus home, still enjoying the opportunity for at least an element of a walking commute, and by the time I was Blipping regularly in my final year at college, several Blips were from that longer walk.

Walking while on the lookout for a daily photograph means seeing things that I might otherwise miss. That's why Blip is so important to my life, to my work, and to this book.

On 23 May 2020 I had one more day to complete my goal. (The numbers imp in my brain insists I point out that that day was my twenty-ninth 'chapter' but the thirtieth day of writing, after my wobble in the middle.) The book still had, or at least I thought it had, an easy bit and a hard bit, namely that while there was a natural boundary around the recollections of the Paris trip, there was an almost infinite amount of stuff that could come from following the threads that had started in Paris and continued through the decade and more since. Like two days earlier, when writing about Petr and me in the fifth and sixth arrondissements led me into an exploration of the Paris meridian and units of measurement (an account of which has *not* made the cut but suffice it to say that the measurements became standardised, official metres were installed across Paris and I saw that we must have walked right past one on the first Sunday as we moved on from the Luxembourg Gardens looking for a place to watch the cycling).

At this point it occurred to me that I should look out all the different books about and related to Paris that I'd gathered over the years. All the books about other people walking through Paris. I had such a strong feeling that my credentials were seriously lacking in comparison with people who had lived there for years. They were often incomers, granted, but that was more a product of my reading books in English, therefore mostly written by English-speakers. Then there were all the books and blogs devoted to the alt-tourist, people looking to discover the 'authentic' Paris via a tip off about some undiscovered place. I had a queasy feeling about some of that being the product of a colonial or imperialist mindset, the idea that places aren't relevant or even simply don't exist until they're 'discovered' by people like us, even although they've been there all along. There was also the tension between France and the English-speaking world, and specifically the three-way relationship between France, the USA and the UK. All three project unified identities that are not as solid as their respective centralised governments would like people to believe and so the apparent triangle is really a much more complex shape as different groups with different agendas play up or down specific differences and similarities.

In popular UK culture much is made of a supposed rivalry with France despite the countries fighting together in two world wars in the twentieth century and numerous other conflicts since. Undoubtedly this is to do with British exceptionalism and looking back fondly to the empire, the high-water mark of which was probably in the nineteenth century when the UK and France competed all over the world for colonial territories. And yet in Scotland, despite our being part of the UK for more than two hundred years and part of Great Britain for a century more, the popular idea of the Auld Alliance remains, buoyed up annually in the Six Nations rugby competition which always sees Scotland and

France (and everybody else) make common cause in wanting to see England lose.

I wondered whether that year's match in Edinburgh had contributed to the spread of Covid, with all those visiting French rugby fans in close proximity to their Scottish hosts at Murrayfield and in the city's pubs, hotels and restaurants. Did a small number of infected but asymptomatic fans provide an early jump start to the spread of the virus in Scotland? The first fatality in Scotland was a French rugby supporter. It also appeared that the football match between Atalanta and Valencia was a key event in the spread of the virus in northern Italy and Spain, and the Cheltenham Festival had been related to a cluster of cases in England.

All of which seemed further away than ever from the Paris theme of the book. Except that the overarching idea, of a series of essay pieces, one per day, based on the specific journey on each of the fifteen days of the trip, allowed for digressions in all sorts of directions. (Lorraine was also writing something at this time and was finding it possible to write thousands of words describing a single scene. Hers was fiction, so there was more scope for characters to introspect, but what's this book if not an exercise in introspection.) I asked myself how much further I should I go in my research, how many novels and films were there set in Paris. Did I need to read and watch them all? Obviously not. But I said that very quickly, 'obviously not'. Actually, I wasn't sure.

The conviction developed that I was writing a multi-dimensional description. I remembered something from primary school. We had a games cupboard and if you'd finished your tasks for the day you could take a game off the shelf to play. One of them was called Space Lines – a plastic three-dimensional noughts and crosses. It had four levels, a black one at the bottom and three clear ones above, each with sixteen upright pegs arranged in a four-by-four square. There were three sets of coloured counters and you had to try and make lines of four in any direction. We thought we were like Captain Kirk and Mr Spock, who played three-dimensional chess on *Star Trek*. Anyway, my personal map of Paris in 2010, the lines that represented each day in the city, was the middle layer. Below that was the Paris of the past before my visit; above it, the Paris I'd encountered since 2010. And not just three layers. Just as there were many historical maps of Paris, from different eras, so too were there different new ones, like the 2020 lockdown map I made as I travelled virtually across the city. Checking the details, I corrected errors I'd made in my original 2010 map, creating something new. And there were other stories, driven by my personal connections but then researched further to flesh things out. I'd need a way to limit those, though, to stop me attempting a completeness that can never be achieved.

I made a choice at this point to include overt discussion of my neuroatypicalness. It wasn't easy for me to decide to do that because I don't have a clinical diagnosis, but I do have traits and behaviours that are shown in online models and tests, and I have a feeling I'm not fully in control of how I go about gathering material and expressing my thoughts. The way that things catch my interest so often that I can't even tell I've been distracted until I've spent hours hopping from subject to subject and then it's almost like I wake up and wonder what happened. I hoped to find a way to lean into this and make it an asset if I could only find the right form, but I felt nervous and not sure I was up to it. The book *Ulverton* by Adam Thorpe came to mind. Brilliantly summed up in a Goodreads review as '*Aikenfield* meets *Cloud Atlas*', it describes in fiction centuries of change, like *Paris* by Edward Rutherford – a big volume of interconnected stories, blurring fact and fiction.

A few days after finishing my month of writing, I decided to wind up my yellow figure Blip series. After many days recreating iconic photographs, the fiftieth and final one would instead be a very personal favourite of my own – the May Day picture from Palais-Royal (see p. 165). It was slightly prompted by the suits I'd pencilled on for the previous day's recreation of the *The Specials* album cover, but it also provided something a bit different.

A few weeks later my annual Blipday rolled around once more. I now had ten years' worth of Blips, which had all started with that conversation in Paris with Anita. As I approached the anniversary I'd been wondering what to do to mark it. Should it be numbers, like years eight and nine? Probably not numbers on the beach, drawn in the sand, which seems more appropriate for the round-number days that Blip marks but aren't 'real' Blipdays. (At least not in my very literal head, where Blipdays should only mark another year's worth of Blips.) Ten years seemed worthy of something a bit special and Lorraine suggested I do a self-portrait – not entirely unknown on my Blip, but something that would stand out amid all the pictures of other people, birds, sea, sky, street views and the rest. I was open to the idea, and then a football result helped me decide for sure.

In 2020 my 'English team' – Leeds United – had been out of the top division in English football for sixteen years. They even spent a few seasons in the third tier (confusingly known as League 1 now but always the Third Division to me). But now they'd won promotion! So I posed in my Leeds top, a replica of the one worn in the 1972 FA Cup final by the scorer of the winning goal, Allan 'Sniffer' Clarke.

My support of Leeds has always been a distant one, as I wrote about in an article for the Scottish football magazine *Nutmeg*. I've only seen them live fourteen times. But following Leeds has been a part of me for more than fifty years. It's different from supporting United (that's Dundee United), though just as significant in moulding my personality – all that childhood disappointment as the team lost out on trophies.

Growing up in Dundee with English parents, it's perhaps inevitable that my football attention was initially focused south of the border. My Mum still followed her local team, Huddersfield Town, so when 6-year-old me picked a team I chose another Yorkshire side. I remember it was impressed on me how important the decision was: once I'd picked a team, that was it, no chopping and changing every season. I think my choice also had to do with Leeds' Scottish contingent, which included a player from Dundee, but the fact they'd just won the league probably didn't hurt. If only I'd known what I was letting myself in for.

It wasn't unusual to support two teams, so around 1974 I started to follow Dundee United as well. With my English accent, I didn't always feel like I fitted in at school but one thing that helped was to support a Scottish team as well as an English one. I still didn't go to matches but if anyone asked I was a Tangerine rather than a Dark Blue.

Back in Paris in 2010 the sun was beginning to appear between the clouds. Agni and I decided it might be worth going up to Montmartre to look at the view. When we got there the panorama across the city from Sacré-Cœur was beautiful, with constantly moving clouds creating shafts of light that picked out distant buildings amongst the wash of evening blues and greys. There was the Tour Saint-Jacques and the west front of Notre-Dame and, further over, the St Paul's-like dome of the Panthéon.

We walked to the square at Place du Tertre and watched the pavement artists, busy providing tourists with creative souvenirs. We went into a café on the edge of the square. Almost certainly a real tourist trap sort of a place, and it felt much less 'authentic' than where I'd been the night before with Sophy, but still there was something about it. It was dusk by the time we'd finished eating so we started down the steps of the Rue du Calvaire towards Pigalle, past extravagant blooms of wisteria that filled the air with scent.

Mardi 4 mai / 2020

Down narrow, steeply sloping streets to the bright neon lights of the Boulevard de Clichy, where we made one last stop in a pastry shop for a cake to eat on the street, before catching the Métro back to the Bastille.

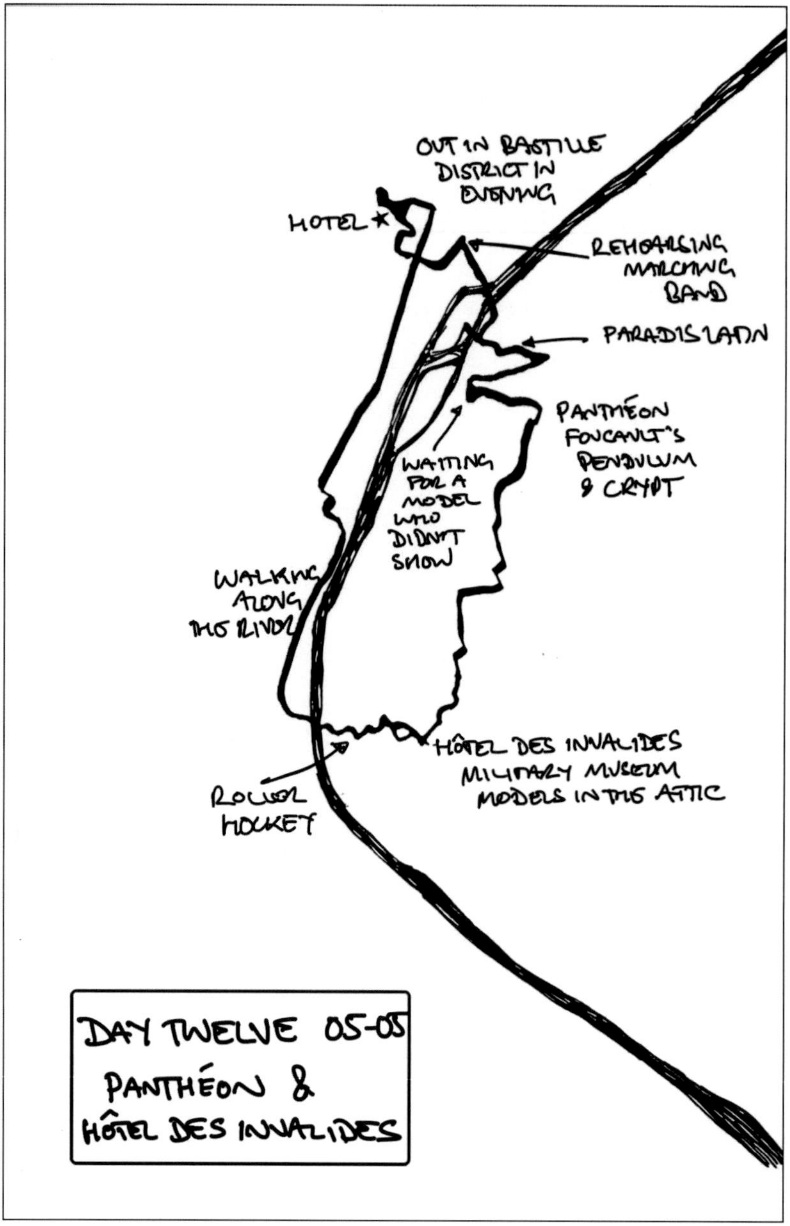
OUT IN BASTILLE DISTRICT IN EVENING
HOTEL ★
REHEARSING MARCHING BAND
PARADIS LATIN
PANTHÉON FOUCAULT'S PENDULUM & CRYPT
WAITING FOR A MODEL WHO DIDN'T SHOW
WALKING ALONG THE RIVER
HÔTEL DES INVALIDES MILITARY MUSEUM MODELS IN THE ATTIC
ROLLER HOCKEY
DAY TWELVE 05-05
PANTHÉON &
HÔTEL DES INVALIDES

Mercredi 5 mai / 2021

The day was sunny and there was a plan for a photoshoot over on the Left Bank. On Tuesday Agni had got chatting with a woman leaning out of her flat window who was, or at least claimed to be, a model, and the two of them had arranged to meet up. Having seen several little groups taking photographs and filming in different locations over the previous week and a half, I was pleased to be asked if I wanted to go along.

The rendezvous point was on the Boulevard Saint-Germain and as I was walking down the Boulevard Henri IV, I heard the sound of trumpets. I looked through a gap between two buildings and saw a wide open space and a group of men on horseback, in formation, all playing trumpets. I found out later that they were members of the Mounted Fanfare Band, part of the French Republican Guard Band who perform on special occasions, including Bastille Day. I watched a bit of behind-the-scenes ceremonial activity before crossing the river on the Pont de Sully. On the Rue du Cardinal-Lemoine I passed the Tour d'Argent restaurant – mentioned by Proust and Hemingway, and the inspiration for Gusteau's in Pixar's film *Ratatouille* – and, further down, the entrance to the Paradis Latin theatre.

Without a guidebook all I could see was that it was a cabaret theatre but when I checked out its history I discovered the Latin Theatre, named for its location in the Latin Quarter, was established by Napoleon himself in 1803. It was a highlight of

Parisian society for decades before being destroyed by fire during the Franco-Prussian War in 1870. The theatre was resurrected some years later by Gustave Eiffel (he of the tower) and reopened as the Paradis Latin in 1889. The foundations used to support the new building's metal framework included portions of the old Philippe Auguste wall, tying the building into the historic fabric of the city. It closed in the early 1900s, when the centre of gravity of Parisian nightlife moved across the river to Montmartre. The building was then used as a factory and warehouse by a glass manufacturer and then lay empty for years until a property developer bought it in the 1970s, looking to convert it into apartments. Removing false walls and ceilings, he discovered the framework of Eiffel's building and decided to renovate it as it once was. The Paradis Latin as it is today reopened in November 1977 and has been hosting cabaret events ever since.

I took more photographs on the streets, like the classic traiteur window – an old-style takeaway with many traditional French dishes on display. It resembled the contents page of a French cookery book. I recognised a couple of dishes but had to look most of them up later. Dishes like Parmentier de Boeuf – a version of shepherd's pie; Dos de Cabillaud au Pistou – cod in a basil-based sauce from Provence; Souris d'Agneau à la Tomate – lamb shanks in tomato sauce.

The planned meeting time with Agni came and went and there was still no sign of our model. Agni contacted her and she was still getting ready so we killed time in a café. We waited and waited, but I started to feel like this wasn't the best use of my day so I decided to cut my losses and go and do something else. It was a short walk up the hill to the Panthéon and, having arrived just as it was closing the previous week, now seemed a good time to visit it properly.

It's an interesting building: a church that isn't a church, reminiscent of Hagia Sophia in Istanbul, or at least the Hagia Sophia I visited in 1992, which was built as a Christian cathedral in the sixth century, then changed to an Ottoman mosque after nine hundred years, and then, almost five hundred years after that, became a museum in a secular Turkey (though in 2020 the Turkish president oversaw its re-designation as a mosque).

The Panthéon was built in the late eighteenth century, originally as a grand replacement for the church of the Abbey of Saint Genevieve, which had become rundown and was no longer seen as a fit resting place for the remains of Paris's patron saint. Neither King Louis XV, who commissioned the project, nor his architect Jacques-Germain Soufflot, lived to see the completion of their building in 1790, by which time revolution had converted France into a secular republic which saw no need for cathedrals. It was decreed that it should instead become a mausoleum for the remains of illustrious French citizens, much like the Pantheon in Rome (even though that remained a Catholic church). Through the nineteenth century the French Panthéon flipped between secular temple and Christian church, reflecting the turbulence in wider French society as emperors and revolutionaries in turn took control of the state. In the 1880s it became the secular national mausoleum once again and has remained so.

The main body of the building is decorated with nineteenth-century murals and in the centre, beneath the dome, a replica of Foucault's pendulum swings across the space. Léon Foucault dropped out of medical school in 1839, when he realised he couldn't cope with the sight of blood, and in September of that year he and his former schoolfriend Hippolyte Fizeau went to see Daguerre demonstrate his new photographic method. The process had only recently been bought by the French government and then given to the world, on 19 August 1839. Foucault and Fizeau wanted to improve on Daguerre's thirty-minute exposure time and began experimenting with alternative chemicals to speed things up. Foucault also started to work as an assistant for his former medical professor, Alfred Donné, in ways that didn't require him

Mercredi 5 mai / 2021

to deal with patients. Soon Foucault began using photography in his medical research with Donné, and found a way to take photographs through a microscope. The two men published a book of microscopic images in 1845. Around this time Foucault and Fizeau were asked by François Arago, he of the pavement medallions and at that time the director of the Paris Observatory, if they could take a photograph of the sun. The resulting image is the earliest surviving picture of the sun.

Foucault went on to conduct other experiments for the Academy of Sciences, including one he devised to demonstrate the rotation of the Earth. The first experiments were done at Foucault's home, on the corner of Rue d'Arras and Rue de Vaugirard, using a 2-metre-long pendulum. There's a plaque and a stone representation of a pendulum on the side of the building (though I never saw it in 2010). Foucault's twentieth-century namesake, the philosopher Michel, lived for many years in a flat at the other end of Rue de Vaugirard.

Foucault first conducted his experiment in public at the Paris Observatory in February 1851 using an 11-metre pendulum and a few weeks later installed another one using a 67-metre-long cable from the top of the dome of the Panthéon. The installation moved to the Conservatoire National des Arts et Métiers and then went back and forth a bit (sorry) between the two buildings. The one in the Panthéon now is a replica. As it happened, and unbeknownst to me at the time, the original ball hanging in the Musée des Arts et Métiers had been damaged only a few weeks before our visit in 2010, when the cable snapped, sending it crashing onto the marble floor.

At the time, I think I was mainly trying to remember Umberto Eco's book named after the pendulum, which satirised the world of conspiracy theories, but the science is actually fascinating. As I understand it, the pendulum keeps swinging in the same plane but because of the rotation of the Earth it appears to slowly rotate relative to the ground. In fact, it is the ground that is rotating beneath the pendulum. In practice it isn't as straightforward as that unless you are at one of the poles. A hanging pendulum above the north or south pole can be considered to be attached to a fixed point on the Earth's axis of rotation and therefore the hanging ball at the bottom of the pendulum will appear to take one day to return to the same position relative to the ground as the Earth completes one rotation below it. At other latitudes the 'fixed point' from which the pendulum is hanging isn't fixed at all, because it is also rotating around the Earth's axis, meaning that it will take longer for the ball to return to the same place, relative to the ground. Mathematics provides a formula whereby one full rotation will take one day divided by the sine of the degree of latitude. The sine of 90° is 1, so at the poles (latitude 90°) that works out at one day; but as latitude decreases so the sine decreases towards zero. Dividing by a smaller and smaller fraction means the period of rotation increases. At Paris's latitude (close to

49° N), it is about thirty-two hours. In Cairo (around 30° N) it is two days. In Goa, southern India (around 15° N), it is almost four days and at the equator it doesn't appear to move at all (sine of 0° is 0 and division by zero is infinity). Sometimes the neatness with which mathematics describes the world blows my mind.

After standing and watching the swinging ball for a while, I went to look around the crypt downstairs, where famous people's remains were to be found in a series of small rooms. There were just two women, out of more than seventy people, and one of those was only there because she was laid to rest beside her husband. The only woman there in her own right was Marie Curie, also with her husband, as it happened, but both there on merit, being Nobel Prize winners for their scientific work. Marie was a double honoree, one of only four people to receive two Nobels and the only person to win prizes in two different fields. Since my visit there's been a halfhearted attempt to correct the imbalance between the sexes, with three of the seven new inductees being women and one of the four men only there to accompany his wife. Several of the people recently commemorated in the crypt are there symbolically, as they remain buried elsewhere. The memorials to two women of the resistance, Germaine Tillion and Geneviève de Gaulle-Anthonioz, recognised in 2015, contain soil from their grave sites, as both families didn't want the bodies to be disturbed. And the one for Josephine Baker, also recognised for her work with the resistance, contains soil from several places significant to her life, including her birthplace in Missouri and her final resting place in Monaco.

From earlier drafts of this book I can see how information about the crypt has evolved over time. During lockdown, for example, it was near impossible for me to find out exactly how all the different tombs and memorials were arranged in the crypt's many rooms. I could find a list of all the people interred there, and the ones who had been removed when they fell out of favour with the authorities or at the request of their families, but no detailed list showing who shared a room with whom. Since then, though, someone more diligent or dedicated to public service than I am must have discovered the information was missing because now you can easily find it all on Wikipedia.

Back upstairs I took some photographs of the murals before setting off across the Left Bank towards Les Invalides. I had in mind that it would be fun to go back to the Musée de l'Armée and try and get a look, more than thirty years later, at those fortification models, which had all been set out up in the attic space of the building, a little neglected but fascinatingly intricate. I wrote a short piece about it years later.

Initially, I could find signs only for the Musée des Plans-Reliefs but pleasingly they pointed upwards and, after climbing a single staircase up to the top floor, there they were. The collection had obviously undergone some restoration since the 1970s (in the 1990s, I found out later) and it didn't have quite the same magic of having being left to gather dust. The glass cases containing the dioramas were spread out across the gallery, divided by geographic region. The smarter presentation obviously reflected the care that had been taken but the modern lighting also made it more difficult to imagine the models being used by trainee artillery officers two centuries before.

The models were still not popular. While the lower floors of the museum had been busy with crowds slowly moving between the display cases, up on the top floor there were just a handful of people. The three-dimensional models-cum-maps were detailed representations of fortified towns, both the layout inside the walls and features of the surrounding countryside, which could be used to simulate sieges and counter perceived defensive weaknesses. The earliest dated from the late seventeenth century and the collection grew with the territorial conquests of the French kings through the eighteenth century. What became a royal collection was kept first in the Tuileries and then in the Louvre, before moving to the attics of Les Invalides in 1777.

Seeing the models again took me back to playing war games with model soldiers, recreating Napoleonic skirmishes on my bedroom floor, and to wondering: did a diminutive young Corsican, training at the nearby École Militaire, visit this collection with his classmates? One of Napoleon's important early successes was in the siege of Toulon and one of the larger models shows the port of Toulon and its surrounding fortifications. I had imagined, as a boy, Napoleon remembering the model from his training when coming up with his proposed plan to retake the fort from the combined royalist, British and allied forces. Unfortunately the dates don't quite match. The model in the museum was made between 1796 and 1800, whereas the siege took place three years earlier in 1793. So the ambitious young artillery officer couldn't have seen the model now on display.

Ah, well. Back downstairs I rejoined the crowds and briefly watched an artist painting their own copy of a portrait of Napoleon. I then went to see the tomb of the man himself. This edifice, the centrepiece of the entire building, is a polished red sarcophagus with a gently curved lid ending with scrolls at each end, like the ornamentation at the top of a Palladian column. All on a massive scale and in a circular gallery beneath a golden dome.

He's complicated, this man who conquered Europe with a revolutionary army and then declared himself an emperor. The traditional British perspective on history is that Napoleonic France was the enemy and that the tide of events followed a similar pattern to the Second World War: territorial expansion by a European power was stopped by a disastrous attempt at Russian conquest and then defeated by British force of arms, with some foreign assistance. But, not surprisingly, there seems to be a different perspective in France. Here, he's the man who made France great, albeit only for a decade or so.

Although 2021 started with another period of lockdown, as the year went on Covid restrictions gradually eased and vaccines became widely available. We had our first doses in March at the drive-in along at Queen Margaret University and were impressed by how slick and yet friendly the process was. Even when the regulations allowed wider contact there was still social distancing in a lot of contexts: for a while the choir I go to met outdoors, with everyone singing two metres apart. It all meant plenty of time spent indoors and, like most people, I found things to binge watch. The French series *Dix pour* cent (*Call My Agent!*), set in a talent agency, got me a good dose of Paris and once I'd finished with Andréa, Mathias, Gabriel et al. I might have moved on to the higher-profile, love-it-or-loathe-it escapism of *Emily in Paris*, but I didn't, because everyone said it was crap.

In November 2021 I didn't do NaNoWriMo but Lorraine and I still went to Wigtown for a week, where I looked again at what I'd written during lockdown in 2020. Doing this – reviewing drafts of chapters – felt like progress, but was it? I've recently come across James Clear's book *Atomic Habits* and am really struck by the distinction he makes between 'being in motion' and 'taking action'. The latter is behaviour that produces an outcome; the former is fine and good and often necessary, but it doesn't produce a tangible result. (Example: making a list of places to go and take photos is motion, whereas taking photos in one of those places is action.) Looking back at me in Wigtown in 2021, I see someone in motion. I was going over old ground (again), finding the content tailing off towards the end of the book (again). Another year ended with the book seemingly stalled.

In 2010, after a few hours in the military museum, I went outside into the daylight and walked down to the river, retracing what had become familiar steps. On the way I stopped to photograph some young people playing roller-hockey. I liked the shot and if nothing else it was sport-related and would fit, however tangentially, with my sports documentary thing.

And then I walked back along the riverbank, through the heart of the city, to our hotel. That night, after bread and cheese with Jo and Agni in their room, I went out later with a group to celebrate Sam's 21st. We stopped at a few different places, all pretty dead on a Wednesday night, before ending up in a curious little disco on the ground floor of what looked like an office building. Like those pubs you see at the bottom of a modern office block that presumably replaced an old pub that had been demolished. It was almost as if someone had hired the space for the night and was using it in an unorthodox, even clandestine sort of way, like an illegal pop-up. Still, whatever it was, I liked it and didn't get back to the hotel until 4 a.m.

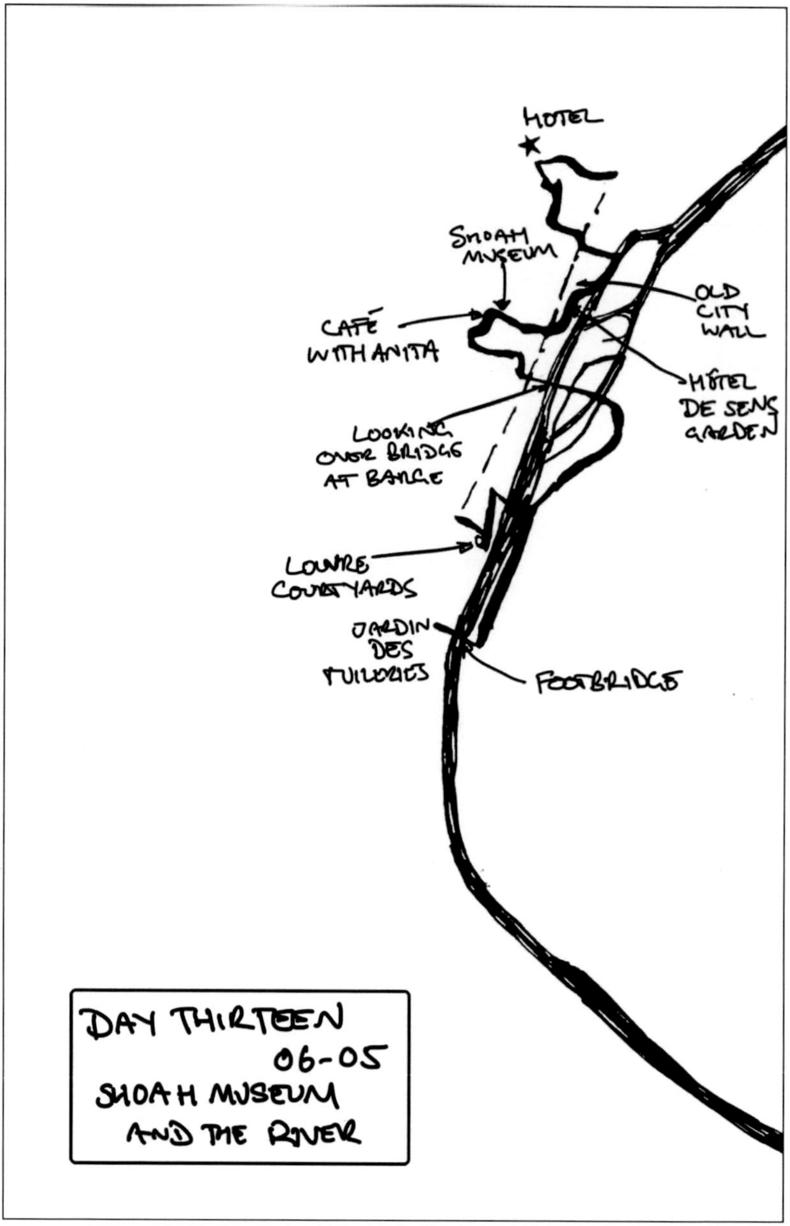
HOTEL
SHOAH MUSEUM
CAFÉ WITH ANITA
OLD CITY WALL
HÔTEL DE SENS GARDEN
LOOKING OVER BRIDGE AT BARGE
LOUVRE COURTYARDS
JARDIN DES TUILERIES
FOOTBRIDGE
DAY THIRTEEN
06-05
SHOAH MUSEUM
AND THE RIVER

Jeudi 6 mai / 2022

The thirteenth day started with a catch-up in the hotel with Petr, Anita, our tutor Matthew and several others. People discussed how they were getting on with taking photos for their documentary projects and how they were finding the trip in general. I talked about finding it hard distilling what I wanted to say into a single image. I wasn't sure whether the difficulty was that expressing things in a single image got in the way of working out what I wanted to say or did I know what I wanted to say but a single image that could convey that was near impossible to find. In many ways this was a key dilemma throughout my time studying photography and has remained a source of confusion and uncertainty ever since.

The type of course I was doing taught the technical competencies of photography and the practical aspects of making a living as a photographer. As a result the focus (sorry again) was very much on the nuts and bolts of taking a picture to satisfy a client. Our tutors did introduce us to the history of photography and the work of famous photographers, but it was nothing like an art college photography course in which ideas are much more important – something that mystified me when I'd visit the art college degree shows and see more than a few pictures that seemed poorly exposed or out of focus, images that would have been rejected for our college assignments. In fact one of our classmates who had a degree from studying photography at art college had enrolled on our HND – in theory a lesser qualification – specifically to learn how to consistently take the photographs she wanted to express her ideas.

That photographic training, emphasising practicalities, has meant that while I know *how* to take a picture I am much less clear on *why*. There's no difficulty taking photos of speakers and delegates at a conference to tell the story of someone else's event, but left to my own devices I struggle to find a story to tell with images of my own devising.

During the discussion that morning in Paris one suggested solution to my difficulty in capturing everything in a single image was to consider film-making. I'm not sure that's the way to go, though, and still feel more drawn to putting still images and writing together.

At breakfast I'd also mentioned in passing something I'd failed to find the day before – the Shoah museum in the Marais. I'd tried to follow some street signs but the building they seemed to lead to, an old synagogue, had looked all closed up. Maybe the museum was only open on certain days, and my lack of a guidebook had come back and bit me again. Anita said she was going to visit the museum herself and it didn't sound like I'd been to the right place. It should be open every day except Saturday, the Jewish Sabbath. So, after we all dispersed, I headed off into the Marais.

I made what had become my favourite start to the day: a walk across Boulevard Beaumarchais and through the Place des Vosges. I crossed Rue Saint-Antoine and went down Rue Saint-Paul, past the magic museum and almost to the river, before turning right onto Rue de l'Ave-Maria. This took me past a schoolyard, with children playing football on the tarmac. Later I learned that one edge of this playground was made up in part by the longest surviving section of the oldest city wall in Paris, the Wall of Philippe Auguste, built in the late twelfth and early thirteenth centuries. This wall enclosed a small area at the heart of the city

Jeudi 6 mai / 2022

and the few surviving stretches have been incorporated into more modern buildings, including an office block and a multi-storey car park. In some places, while the actual wall has gone there are ghost reminders of it in strangely shaped buildings, like an ultra-thin apartment block close to the start of Boulevard Saint-Germain.

I had spent almost two weeks in Paris not really aware of the former city walls and yet they'd been visible all around me. Maybe it's because I live in Edinburgh, a city where it's also possible to read very old history in the built environment, but I find it interesting how boundaries evolve. As Paris's population increased in the Middle Ages, the walls could no longer contain it and in the fourteenth century Charles V ordered the construction of a new set of fortifications. On the Left Bank this was merely an enhancement of the existing walls, but on the Right Bank a completely new wall was built further out. This wall was later extended by Louis XIII and then, starting in 1670, Louis XIV had it removed it completely. At this point the line of the old fortifications was replaced by wide, tree-lined boulevards – the grand boulevards which remain as features of modern Paris and which I was very familiar with. The word boulevard itself originally came from the Dutch word 'bolwerc' and at first described the flat top of the city walls. When the walls were replaced by promenades, they too were called boulevards and the word came to describe all similar avenues, whether or not they had originally been on the course of the city fortifications.

The next boundary was administrative rather than defensive. The Mur des Fermiers généraux (Wall of the Farmers General) was created, further out still, in the late eighteenth century to enforce the collection of taxes on food brought into Paris. The taxes were bitterly opposed and were briefly abolished after the 1789 revolution, only to be reinstated as a source of city revenue. This wall remained until the 1860s, when it too was replaced by another ring of boulevards after the administrative boundary of

Jeudi 6 mai / 2022

the city moved out to the Thiers Wall. This was a nineteenth-century defensive fortification soon called upon during the Prussian invasion of France in 1871. It held the invaders at bay for a few months but, with no prospect of the siege being lifted and the capital starving, France surrendered. Paris, however, had other ideas and established its own revolutionary form of government – the ill-fated Commune. At that point the Thiers Wall became a defensive line in a civil war, but the Commune was soon defeated and the wall ceased to have a military purpose. It remained the boundary between the city and the shanty towns of 'the Zone' beyond and was finally removed in the 1920s. Now it's marked by a line of boulevards just inside the course of the old fortifications and the Boulevard Périphérique just outside them.

The narrow street that runs down the opposite side of the school playground to the old walls – the Rue des Jardins-Saint-Paul – features in the film *Before Sunset*, when Céline and Jesse walk through Paris after meeting at the Shakespeare & Co. bookshop. As is often the way in films, their linear fictional route jumps between real-life locations, although in this case the jumps could just about make sense.

Around the corner I stopped to photograph the neat box-hedge pattern garden in front of the Hôtel de Sens – where Marguerite de Valois stayed briefly at the beginning of the seventeenth century, many years after the gruesome events of her post-wedding feast.

I thought again of *La Reine Margot*, which also brought to mind a two-hander play I'd seen in the Edinburgh Festival the year after the film was released. The play starred Pascal Greggory, one of the leading actors from the film, and Patrice Chéreau, its director. *Dans la solitude des champs de coton* was staged in the old drill hall that was out the back of our flat on Forrest Road and was one of those pieces of theatre that transcended language, at least for me. It was performed in French and the audience, seated down two sides of the hall, were given an English translation of the text.

I found I preferred to watch the action without it as the mysterious Dealer and Client sparred with each other. Along with Yuri Lyubimov's Russian production of Pushkin's *Boris Godunov* in Leith Theatre and Syberberg's German production of *Ein Traum, was sonst?* at the King's, it was a piece of non-English theatre that has stuck with me despite not understanding the text.

Moving on, I again found the signs pointing to the Shoah museum and sure enough there was one I'd missed before. It led me further on, down an alley with a list of names on one of its walls. This was le Mur des Justes – the Wall of the Righteous – and the names those of several thousand French people who had done what they could to help Jews during the Second World War. Around the corner was the entrance to the museum and memorial, a modern building amidst old streets. I had a sense of bringing together strands I'd been gathering over the previous two weeks – the little plaques on tenement buildings, the graves to individuals in the two cemeteries, the much larger memorials to the thousands in the camps. The whole thing so embedded in the fabric of the city.

There was strict, airport-style security to get in, probably the tightest security I went through on the entire trip, including the airports, much more the norm to access places these days but it was striking back then. At ground level there was a bronze column embossed with the names of the different camps and the Warsaw ghetto. Underground was an eternal flame and the museum. As I walked round I took in information about the antisemitism that existed in France and the rest of Europe long before the Nazis came to power, as well as many stories of deportations and of the camps. And a wall of photographs of children. So many children, in a seemingly endless set of images, wall after wall.

The Shoah museum was where I was introduced to la Rafle, the Roundup. As you've already seen, after my return home I'd come across other tellings of the story through films and books, and I'd learn about things I hadn't discovered for myself during my stay, like the Vél' d'Hiv' memorial close to the Eiffel Tower. They all weighed more because of that room of pictures at the end; all those ordinary faces on the walls, the Jews of Paris, taken from the city. The othering of people that seems once again on the rise.

I left the museum and then caught up with Anita, who had also just finished looking round, although we'd somehow managed to miss each other. We found a café, and I'd love to tell you which one but I haven't been able to track down exactly where it was. I did wonder if it might have been Au Petit Versailles du Marais, but it looks too grand. Perhaps it was the one across the road, at the end of the street leading from the museum. Anyway, wherever it was, we got a table and talked about what we'd just seen, and about our time in Paris and our experiences of the whole photography course. In a way it was a continuation of the earlier thing, as I talked about my interest in stories and how I felt like I couldn't capture them in my pictures. I told her about a school athletics event I'd photographed back in Edinburgh. There had been a small group of girls waiting for one of the last boys in the race. They were all from the same school and they were cheering him on. One girl in particular seemed so genuinely excited. Maybe the boy was her brother, but it didn't feel like that. I tried to capture her spirit in a picture but I'm not sure I managed it. I saw her again at the finishing line in the next race, still cheering on her friends. She struck me as embodying the essence of what sport is all about. I told Anita that I wished I could have taken a picture that could do her story justice. Even now, writing this, I wonder where she is and whether she's still as passionate about her friends and about sport.

Anita and I were among the older people in the class and seemed to have a bit more in common. And as we talked that late morning over tea and pastries she told me about a website she shared pictures on called Blipfoto. A guy in Edinburgh had created it, she said, and it was very simple. You shared one picture a day, for the day on which the picture was taken, and you could add words if you wanted or leave it as just an image. And that was it. She'd been posting images for more than three years and they were already building up into a fascinating record of her life. It sounded like something that might have been designed just for me and I said I'd get signed up when I got home.

The day was passing and we decided we both needed to get back out there and see more of the city. We said goodbye outside the café and I walked on, taking pictures of shops and people and the river. I took photos from the Pont d'Arcole over to Île de la Cité, capturing the barge *Foujiyama* as it passed beneath my feet. I was intrigued by the platform at the back with a rowing boat and a small car side by side.

In 2022 I was still 'in motion' rather than writing my book. I bought Elaine Sciolino's book *The Seine: The River That Made*

Paris. Although it tells the story of the river, from its source to where it reaches the sea, there's a lot about Paris and its connection with the river. The book mixes history and geography, but once again my relief and excitement at discovering that someone else saw the value of such a synthesis soon turned to disillusionment. This author had just done so much more, read more, seen more, spoken to more people. And her credentials. Lived in Paris for two decades. Awarded the Legion d'Honneur for her contribution to the friendship between France and the United States. Jesus Christ.

In 2010, having crossed the north channel of the river onto Île de la Cité, I stopped in front of Notre-Dame, photographing people and pigeons again before heading over to the Left Bank and walking downstream for a bit. After passing several bridges I crossed the Passerelle Léopold-Sédar-Senghor, taking several pictures of its interesting design. From a distance it looks relatively conventional, with the gentle curve of the main walkway supported by a more pronounced curved metal framework underneath. When you get up close you discover that those curves are actually steps leading up from the riverbank on each side of the bridge to the upper walkway. At that time, coming from the Jardin des Tuileries the best route was to take the underpass beneath what was then a very busy road and walk up the lower steps onto the middle of the bridge. Once you were there, the choice was to keep on the upper level across to the Quai Anatole-France (now renamed the Quai Valéry-Giscard-d'Estaing) and the Thomas Jefferson statue or go down the other flight of steps to the Port de Solférino (now the Promenade Édouard-Glissant). In these less car-friendly times the busy road alongside the Tuileries has been tamed and there's a pedestrian crossing from the garden gates that leads straight onto the upper level of the bridge.

Standing in the underpass, I saw the pattern of people walking up the steps in front of me, the horizontal lines, the vertical shapes of their bodies. I took a few photographs, not sure what I was trying to capture but that's often the way it is.

Jeudi 6 mai / 2022

A little while later I got a message from Agni to say that she and Jo were going for something to eat if I wanted to join. We met up on Boulevard Saint-Germain and had pizza in a workaday little restaurant. Afterwards Jo went back to the hotel and Agni and I walked back down to the river, where she saw a poster for an exhibition that interested her and went into a museum but I walked on, crossing the Pont des Arts once again.
    I took several pictures on the bridge, including an artist at work painting the Pont-Neuf, which was busy with people heading home from work. I had the idea somehow that the Louvre was

open late on a Thursday, but when I got there it seemed not so I walked around the courtyards before making my way back to the hotel.

In 2022 I had just about persuaded myself that, despite other books being out there, however good they were and however more qualified their authors, I could still produce something that was mine. When I read Andrew Gallix's almost 600-page collection *We'll Never Have Paris*, which includes works from seventy-nine different authors exploring the myth of Paris in the English-speaking world, I wondered if what I was doing was more of the same – or worse, an unexamined view of the city that fell into all the stereotypical traps – but come November I resolved to use NaNoWriMo to write a first draft.

I'd arrived at the decision the way I often do: by putting it off until an external deadline caused me to panic. I'd been feeling an itch to write something new from scratch, a novel probably, but the more I thought about it, the more I could see that this was the lure of a shiny new thing and that the writing I really wanted to get done was my Paris book.

On Blip I posted the map of Paris that had been up on the wall in my office for some time. I wrote that, having been thinking about it for more than twelve years, it was time to get something finished. I told myself that it was okay that it wouldn't be perfect, I just needed to get it done, not least to make space in my head. This was when Lorraine said I should try thinking of it as my *first* Paris book, if that would lift some of the anxiety I felt about getting it wrong or leaving something out.

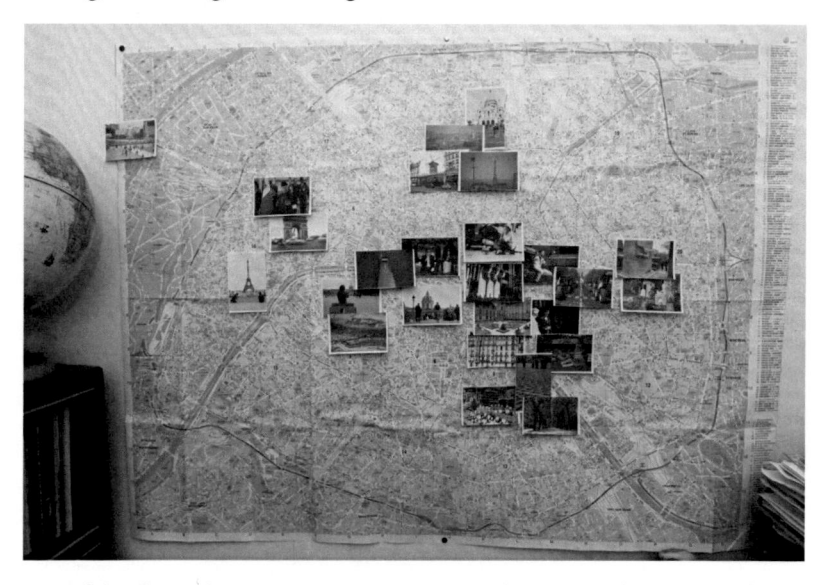

I felt clear that I was writing something psychogeographical about my stay in Paris but despite that clarity I still couldn't get it onto the page. The 'geographical' bit, the description of where I'd been and what I'd seen, was okay; but the 'psycho' bit, what I thought and felt about it, wouldn't come. My difficulties with the latter then made me doubt the former. If I wasn't writing a guidebook, then what were all these streets and buildings doing in there? Worrying about the kind of book I *wasn't* writing was creating red lines and forbidden zones that left me with nowhere to go. November ended and the first draft still wasn't complete.

Thursday night in Paris, Petr and I went out for a late dinner (or 'late' to my Edinburgh way of thinking; given how busy all the restaurants were, it seemed it was many people's perfectly ordinary teatime). We went back to Café Hugo. The place was busy, as usual, but it had become my favourite because the staff were always friendly and the food was good. Stone walls and dark-wood furniture made it feel like we were eating in a restaurant outside time. Looking back now, I can imagine it as a setting for some *Midnight in Paris* time travel – you go in in the twenty-first century and come out in the 1920s, or the 1820s. This time I ordered the filet de bar and Petr had the steak tartare. I had the Sancerre that I'd enjoyed the previous week. A woman singer walked between the tables, accompanied by a guitarist sitting in a corner.

As we sat drinking second glasses of wine and listening to the music we saw Anita, Kerstin and Matthew outside, coming back from an evening in the Marais. In that moment I felt a flash of belonging. Here I was, in my regular restaurant, seeing people I knew pass by on the street outside. I don't think I fully understood in 2010 how much that was missing in my life, but when we moved to Portobello a few years after the trip I began to see what being truly rooted in a place could feel like. I'm thinking in particular of Sunday nights when we used to play mahjong with our friends in the Skylark, before Covid blew so much away. Sitting at the prime window table and seeing familiar faces go by on the High Street.

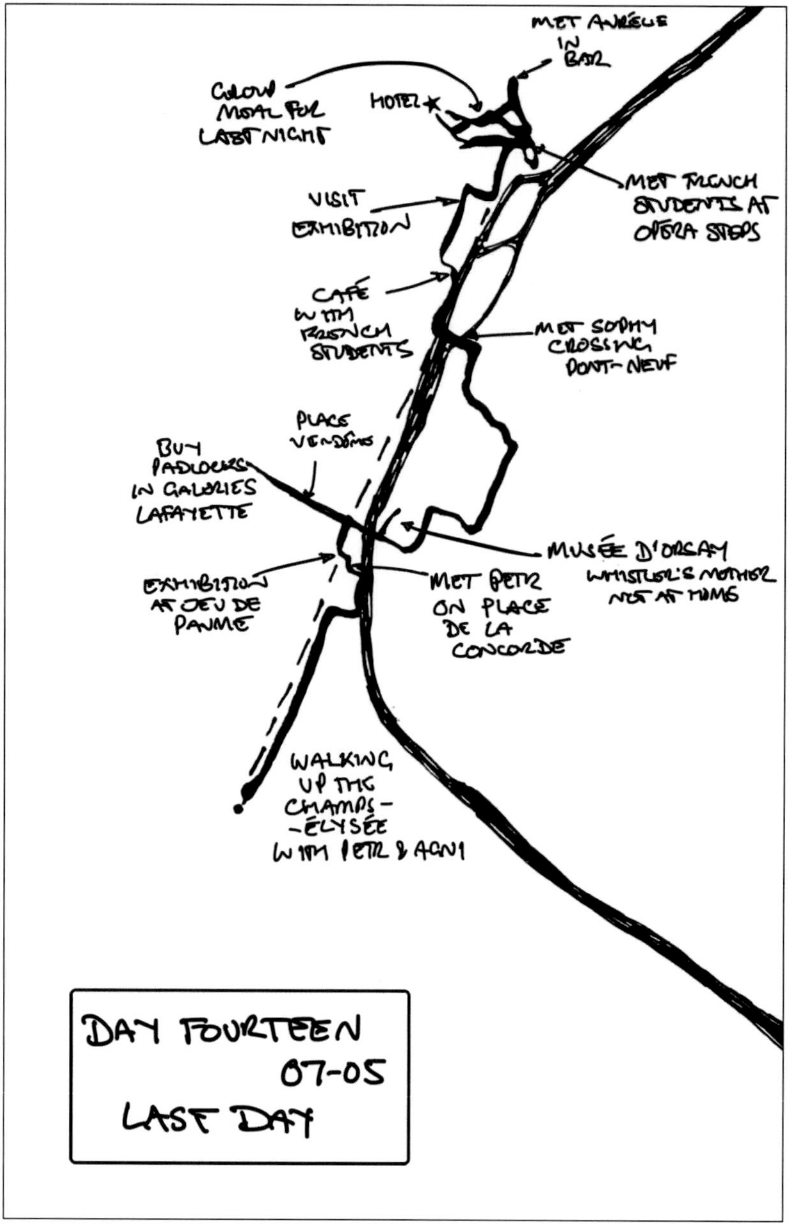

Vendredi 7 mai / 2023

On our last full day in Paris we'd arranged to meet the students from the exchange college. We all gathered at the Bastille and when everyone was finally in place someone took a group photo on the wide steps of the Opéra building. It's funny how often when photographers gather together that a group photo is an afterthought or even forgotten entirely.

As in Edinburgh, there was no plan about what to do. A few groups of people drifted away immediately but a number of us felt we should make some sort of effort to hang out. It was a shame it was so ad hoc, really. If we'd met in the first few days of our stay, with a definite shared project, connections could have been made and built on through the fortnight. I might have not wanted to use a guidebook, but local knowledge is something else, and maybe I'd have been able to bring to a Parisian the fresh eye of the visitor. I don't know, maybe I was just being too optimistic and our two groups simply didn't have enough in common.

Someone suggested going to a photography exhibition at a nearby gallery and it seemed it was that or head our separate ways. Coming out of the exhibition there was an attempt to meet up with one of the splinter groups that had scattered from the Opéra steps. It became clear at that point that the Edinburgh students had a better grasp of the local streets than our Parisian counterparts, although they were in an unfamiliar part of the city for them and we'd been getting to know it for a fortnight.

After a bit of faffing we gave up trying to organise and a few of us just went into a café on the Rue de Rivoli, close to the Hôtel de Ville. Sitting at pavement tables, Petr and I talked with the French students in a mixture of broken French and broken English. It was a conversation in which the shared effort was more important than what was said. I've kept in touch with a few of the people I met that day, albeit in a sporadic and tenuous way, notably Aurélie but also to a lesser extent Ally and Alex, who's become a paramedic. Aurélie continued with photography after college and a couple of years later shared some interesting memento mori still-life photographs, as well as pictures of Saint-Valery-Sur-Somme on the Picardy coast. Saint-Val is familiar to me as somewhere my parents loved to go on holiday, and I've seen many of their photographs of the town. The intersections of life criss-crossing.

On the Rue de Rivoli we said our goodbyes in front of the café. Aurélie and her friends were taking advantage of an afternoon in the city centre to visit the shops; me and Petr were headed out to do some final sightseeing in different parts of the city.

I crossed the river, passing Notre-Dame one more time, and then over the Pont-Neuf, where I bumped into Sophy heading the other way. Both hurrying to fit things in and feeling the pressure of time running out, we didn't stop for long and pinged off in opposite directions.

In 2023 my Blips in April and May (anniversary of the trip), and on Bastille Day in July, made no mention of my book. I was clearly beyond making public statements of intent that repeatedly came to nothing. However, as we got into the summer I set a target of completing a full draft by the time my 60th birthday came round in September. It wasn't the first time I'd tried to hang a deadline on another peg, but this time it worked. I had a settled structure – fifteen chapters, each a blend of one day in Paris in 2010 and one year of progress, or not, from the subsequent years – and, for whatever reason, it worked. I finished the draft, 78,000 words, three days before my birthday. I then put it aside for a few months, thinking I could come back to it fresh for first revision when we went to Wigtown. It still felt too recent come November, though, so for NaNoWriMo I wrote fiction, playing with ideas of a alternative Portobello which still had a pier. My main character lived in a tenement on the promenade, round the corner from our flat, which in this version of reality hadn't been demolished in the 1960s, creating a space where the boat club is now. I've always really loved counterfactuals, so this was that and sort of playing with a *Life: A User's Manual* too.

In 2010 I decided that if I wasn't going to have time for the Louvre, I could at least pay a visit to the Musée d'Orsay. There was a short queue, nothing like the one we'd seen the previous Sunday, and I was soon inside.

It was just as everyone said: a spectacular, repurposed building with some very impressive art, but not so vast as to overwhelm. And for me it was a chance to see again one of a handful of paintings I'd been familiar with practically my whole life.

I think I first saw a photo of *Whistler's Mother* in the children's magazine *Look and Learn*. Once I was aware of the image, I got the joke in numerous visual parodies of the painting, such as Ward Kimball's 1964 picture that shows the sitter watching a small TV, but I didn't see the original until I went to a major Whistler show at the Tate Gallery in London in the 1990s. It didn't make a great impact. Several rooms into the exhibition, it certainly had the biggest crowd of people gathered around it, but not so many that you couldn't get a good look. And it was a decent size, so it wasn't that it just seemed much smaller than I'd expected. No, I just think that years of familiarity had bred, if not contempt, then at least indifference. Other paintings I saw that day, such as the infamous painting of fireworks that led to Whistler's libel case against

Ruskin, and the series of nocturnes of the River Thames, blew me away. But Ma was meh.

Later again, I read Walter Benjamin's essay 'The Work of Art in the Age of Mechanical Reproduction' and understood that reproduction, whether it's parodic or faithful, a cartoon, a canvas or a keyring, 'substitutes a plurality of copies for a unique existence . . . [and] leads to a tremendous shattering of tradition'. Which perhaps applies more to Whistler than most because he was an accomplished self-publicist and the painting of his mother was exhibited *a lot* in the years following its completion. Almost equally important were the numerous reproductions of the image that began to appear, for, as Benjamin says, 'man-made artefacts could always be imitated by man. Replicas were made by pupils in practise of their craft, by masters for diffusing their works, and, finally by third parties in pursuit of gain.'

To begin with, these copies involved considerable effort, such as the wood engraving that appeared in the *Illustrated London News* in 1872, or the many hundreds of copies that were handmade by amateur painters. These manual reproductions spread awareness of the original without having much impact on public perception, but after the painting went on display at the Museum of Modern Art in New York in the early 1930s, the image (as an *image*) entered into popular consciousness. Everyone 'knew' what the picture looked like. *Arrangement in Grey and Black No. 1* became *Whistler's Mother* and part of the vocabulary of visual reference. It was used in song lyrics and even became the nickname of a US warplane in the Second World War. As Benjamin describes it, the image had moved from having a nineteenth-century 'cult value' to a twentieth-century 'exhibition value'. Today, with apps and all that, anyone can produce or even be their own 'mother'. In fact I know of a group on the Flickr photo-sharing website devoted to new interpretations of the image. But there is a vestige of something exclusive and mysterious that attaches to the original and I was looking forward to seeing the painting again, to giving art another chance to sock it to me on my last day in Paris.

Only, it wasn't there. In the space where *Arrangement in Grey and Black No. 1* should have been was a card saying it was currently away on loan. I checked out where it had gone and it turned out that maybe if I'd just joined Eva in the queue the previous week I would've been able to see it before it went.

It was a downer, but softened by seeing many other works by famous Impressionists that are now part of wider popular culture, such as Manet's *Le Déjeuner sur l'herbe*. Although the gallery was busy, there weren't any really big crowds around specific paintings except for another of Manet's works – *Olympia*. And standing with the others crowded around the painting, I felt an aura. Perhaps the setting, the almost church-like atmosphere of reverence there is in museums, was part of it. Curiously, Benjamin saw the development of patronage away from the Church and towards private individuals as the 'democratisation' of art, whereas today I think we'd argue the opposite: that art moving from public religious spaces to private collections is elitist.

While I wasn't able to test Walter Benjamin's thesis on that visit, I did and do wonder whether we have now moved from mechanical reproduction into an era of digital reproduction. Art galleries are still places of reverence, though, and to me original works of art do have a sense of significance, a weight, that is hard to shake off. Is that feeling a product of my age? What do much younger people think? A digital display can't reproduce the physical texture of an original painting but, given that we aren't allowed to touch the paintings on the museum wall anyway, maybe it doesn't matter if what we look at is 'only' an image.

Is there an opportunity to learn about a painting more effectively *without* seeing the original? Since I was in Paris in 2010 galleries have been finding new ways for people to experience the art they hold. The Musée d'Orsay has been working with digital artists, notably Sébastien Devaud, known as Agoria, who created the exhibition AGORIA {Le Code d'Orsay} in 2024, linking immersive, participatory digital art with the museum's historic collection.

There's been something of an explosion of immersive art in general, quite a lot of it commercial exploitation of the works of long-dead artists such as Van Gogh and Monet. Various competing Van Gogh exhibitions have taken projection-based exhibitions to cities around the world. One featured in an episode of *Emily in Paris* in 2020 and another visited Edinburgh in 2022 (though I didn't go to see it). In 2025, a virtual reality experience in New York titled Tonight with the Impressionists, Paris 1874 offers the opportunity to travel in time back to Wednesday, 15 April 1874 when a group of artists including Monet, Renoir and Degas met in the photographic studio of Félix Nadar. They were members of the Société anonyme des artistes peintres, sculpteurs, graveurs, etc. (Anonymous Society of Painters, Sculptors, Printmakers, etc.) and they'd gathered on this night to show their work as a challenge to the salon curated by the Académie des Beaux-Arts. The meeting is now widely considered to have been the first Impressionist exhibition.

While the commercial companies involved in these sorts of attractions claim they provide new ways for people to connect with art and encourage new audiences towards learning about art history, the art establishment remains sniffy. It thinks these exhibitions are primarily about making money and do little more than provide Insta backdrops, but the original remains the source for all derivative works, and licensing, which means legitimate use of the image feeds revenue back to the owning/exhibiting institution. Having said that, I'd imagine museum shops don't sell as many postcards as they used to. At the time of writing there's rules against using flash, tripods or selfie sticks at the Musée d'Orsay, but that means that, as when I visited in 2010, you can take a snap with your phone, post it to your socials, and then what? Most of us have thousands of photos we don't look at but it's a rare person who wouldn't get their phone out when standing in front of one of the most famous canvases ever painted. If you really like a painting, you wouldn't print your own photo of it anyway, you'd buy a print – *Whistler's Mother* (A4) will set you back £9.99 on Amazon, but it's also very cool that a first printed edition aquatint could be had at auction for about $1,000 only last year. I wonder how many copies of the painting are hanging somewhere on a wall right now. Must be tens of thousands worldwide.

    I don't think the queues at the Musée d'Orsay are just feeding their socials, I think they're also feeding a need for connection. I was disappointed not to see *Whistler's Mother* that day because I'd wanted to stand in front of it for the second time in my life and see what I felt when I told myself that *this* is the canvas he worked on. It's like the uncanny feeling you get holding a Roman coin or a Stone Age tool, touching things that were touched by another person in another, very distant, era. A form of time travel: this object here, now, was also an object there, then. It would make my hair stand on end, if I had any.

After a few hours in the gallery I headed back outside. I'd been thinking about the padlocks on the Pont des Arts and thought I'd try and find a pair to take home and then bring back with Lorraine if we visited Paris together sometime in the future. (When we did visit for my 50th, I forgot to bring them. But by then then the padlocks were controversial, so maybe it was just as well we didn't add to the problem.)

    Not entirely sure where might be the best place to buy such things, I headed for the world-famous Galeries Lafayette – why not go big? It was almost a direct line from the Musée d'Orsay, over

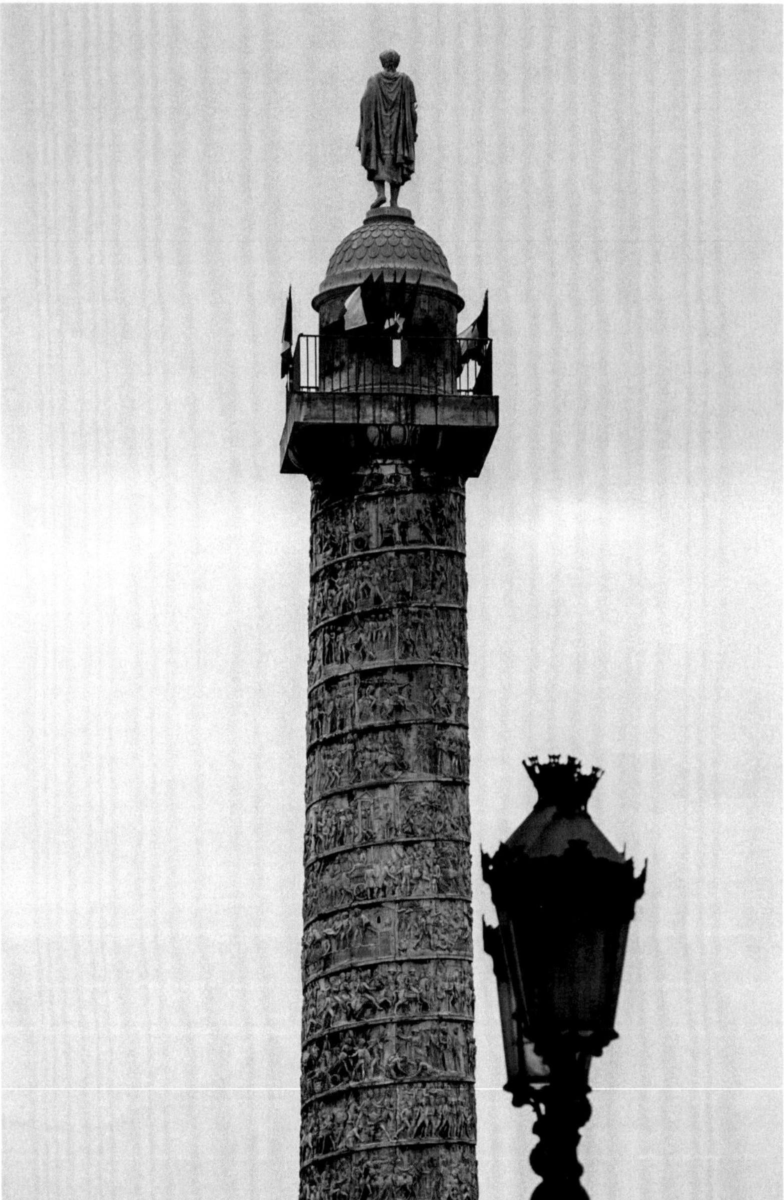

the elaborate footbridge, straight across the Jardin des Tuileries and through the decidedly upmarket Place Vendôme. With its grand shops and central column, topped with its statue of Napoleon, this is a place I've recognised since in a perfume ad with Kiera Knightley riding a motorbike through deserted Parisian streets. It was filmed very early in the morning, before the traffic.

After the Place Vendôme it was round the Palais Garnier and onto the Boulevard Haussmann. This bit of Paris, the Haussmann-redesigned Paris, was something I hadn't really seen much of in my two-week stay. The interior of Galeries Lafayette was grand – to my Edinburgh-centric mind, it was like an upscaled Jenners. I found the hardware department and bought a pair of small, blue padlocks and was on my way out again when a message from Agni suggested meeting at the Place de la Concorde to look round a photography exhibition.

The exhibition was on at the Jeu de Paume, a gallery on the edge of the Tuileries, overlooking Concorde. It was a collection of street photography by the Austrian-born American photographer Lisette Model. As we walked round, I wished I was seeing these photos on the first day of my visit rather than on the last. Seeing how another photographer had seen Paris might have guided my own reactions and given me some reference points, maybe even some shots to emulate on the same streets. Although, given how intimidated I'd felt on that first day, maybe comparison would have inhibited me and made it even more difficult to take my own pictures of the city.

And it was difficult, taking pictures in Paris, far more difficult than I ever would have imagined. Looking back, I can see how the odd status of the visit – not a holiday, but also not really work; not a long stay, but longer than the weekend that people often spend; you're with people you know, but not your closest people – put things in tension. The impulse to take a photo in the early days was always at risk of being blunted because time wasn't against us and you could always come back to it. I didn't want to follow a tourist itinerary, but having a documentary project to work on switched me sometimes into a mode where I was deliberately hunting for certain images, which led to a feeling that I was consciously not open to seeing what was there. And now, writing about what it was like coming to the end of the trip, I find myself torn as to whether photography needs an idea to explore and a plan to achieve it, or you can just leave it to serendipity and see what you make of it afterwards, when a post hoc interpretation can provide some semblance of structure. If I were to discover that one of my Paris photos was an accidental homage (even if, strictly speaking, it couldn't *be* an homage without awareness of the original), would that be exciting or embarrassing?

Moving on from Model's pictures of Paris, we looked round the other exhibitions in the galleries, including an installation of two film screens, set up facing each other, showing a woman interviewing herself, answering questions about her life in Sweden. Another form of autobiography.

Outside onto the Place de la Concorde, and were standing on the pavement wondering if there was time to go anywhere else when Petr walked by. I laughed at the coincidence, still tickled by meeting people I knew on these famous streets. The three of us went down to the river and took a few pictures there before walking on, between the Grand and Petit Palais.

Back at the Champs-Élysées we looked up the hill to the Arc de Triomphe and, seeing a big French flag in the centre of the arch, we decided we'd walk up there.

Heading up the wide street was a vivid reminder of the final laps the peloton does around the central Paris circuit in the well-established conclusion to the Tour. We walked briskly, so briskly at times that Agni said it was hard to keep up with me and Petr. The slope became more obvious, certainly steeper than it looks on the TV. At some point during the final stage, most often when there is a breakaway rider on their own, tucked into the kerb, avoiding the cobbles and heading for the Arc, the commentators will make

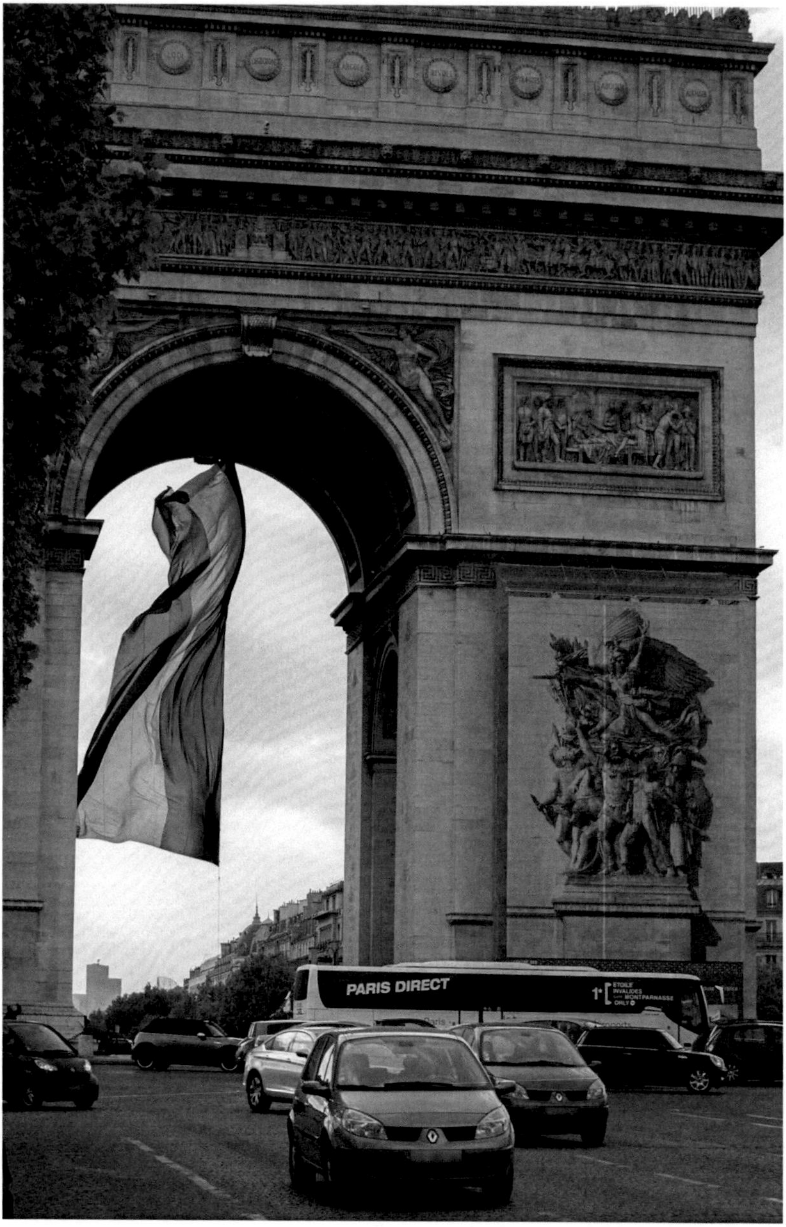
PARIS DIRECT

some remark about the deceptive climb. I don't think Petr and I were consciously hurrying, though – just quick walkers, I guess.

The massive tricolore was flying in preparation for the May 8th celebrations the next day, to mark the anniversary of the end of the Second World War. I took a last few pictures of it, and of the traffic circling the monument, before we all caught the Métro back to Bastille in time for one last group dinner.

Someone had booked us in at the Café de l'Industrie, but in the extension across the street rather than the place where Sophy and I had gone on Monday night. Around the table we shared stories of our last day and afterwards I went with Jo, Agni, Marcin and Sophy for a drink. We all felt we'd enjoyed quite enough of the chaos of Tape and ended up at a vibey place further along Rue de la Roquette. The bar's name – Les Furieux – had seemed vaguely familiar when we went in and when I bumped into Aurélie waiting to be served I realised why. She'd told us earlier that she was going to be out in the Bastille area that evening, as her boyfriend's band had a gig. They were the ones playing through the back, but it was too loud to talk over, so she went back to the music and I rejoined our group in the quieter front of the bar.

Getting back to the hotel, we were a bit subdued. The fortnight in Paris was all but over and tomorrow we'd be flying back to reality in Edinburgh.

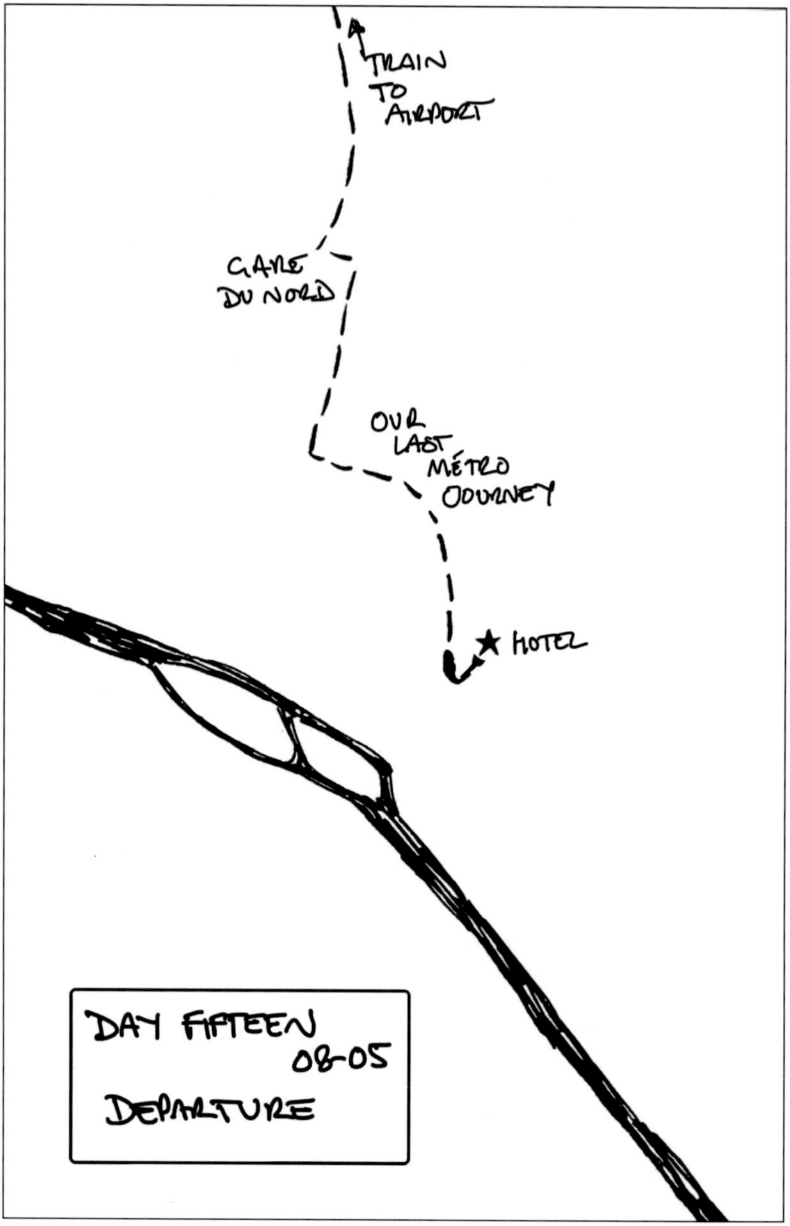
TRAIN TO AIRPORT
GARE DU NORD
OUR LAST MÉTRO JOURNEY
HOTEL
DAY FIFTEEN
08-05
DEPARTURE

Samedi 8 mai / 2024

It started cloudy on our last day. Day fifteen, like the French term for fortnight, 'quinze jours' – fifteen days. Apparently this is a feature of other Romance languages, such as Italian and Spanish: they make the first and last days inclusive, unlike English and German, which consider a fortnight to be fourteen days/nights, hence the clue in the name.

We checked out and took the Métro to the Gare du Nord by a peculiar route, changing once, to avoid an 'incident' on the direct line to the station. Back above ground the train to Charles de Gaulle rattled through the northern edge of the city. I could see the towers of Sacré-Cœur that had so confused me the weekend before.

The carriage was busy and a busker was playing to a trapped audience. I wondered if the journey out to the airport was more lucrative than the one into the city. On the way home, back then, tourists might have loose change to get rid of but equally they might be tired of buskers and beggars asking for money. Now, and especially since the pandemic accelerated contactless payments, has the situation changed? Do the buskers on the train in 2025 operate with contactless devices, making currency exchange automatic? It's easy to do, and people are astonishingly trusting about where they tap their cards.

At the airport terminus I really liked the modern architecture: a completely integrated transport hub that blends the railway

274 · *Fifteen Days in Paris*

Samedi 8 mai / 2024

station seamlessly into the airport. We checked in and then waited for our flight. It usually takes longer going through departures than arrivals, so there was more time to notice things, but maybe I was also paying more attention to my surroundings than I had when we'd arrived two weeks earlier, when I was itching to get into Paris proper. In the lounge people were still taking pictures, sharing photos on our phones, talking in small groups.

Early in 2024 I decided I would watch *Emily in Paris*. You'll remember I'd been put off it by the near universal panning it received, but it gave me what I wanted: lots of dynamic, well-shot footage of familiar streets. I found it fun to watch, an obvious but joyful fantasy of Parisian life. It creates a world that looks like the real one but is just as fictional as the more clearly signposted fantasy worlds we also consume, with their wizards and goblins and whatever. As Philippine Leroy-Beaulieu, who plays Emily's French boss Sylvie, says, 'I tell people there's enough space in my brain for [Ingmar] Bergman and *Emily in Paris*, and I'm always sad when people say they're so selective, because life is so rich. There's so many different things to taste, so why not?'. One of Leroy-Beaulieu's early roles was in the film *Trois hommes et un couffin* (*Three Men and a Cradle*), which I saw at Filmhouse. It was nominated for an Oscar as Best Foreign Language Film and then remade in Hollywood as *Three Men and a Baby*. It was the highest-grossing film of 1987 and I was always irritated in an 'I preferred their early stuff' kind of way at the lack of any mention of the French original.

So I enjoyed watching Emily as she discovered Paris for herself, seeing the landmarks and working out where some of the less well-known locations actually were. For example, her apartment block close to the Panthéon, and the nearby bakery where she buys her morning pastry, and Gabriel's restaurant. Did I walk down that street on the first Wednesday afternoon as I explored the Latin Quarter at teatime? Some might say it was a guilty pleasure but I think we're over that, aren't we?

After we arrived back in Edinburgh our group scattered almost immediately. Some people were picked up by family or friends in cars while the rest of us caught an airport bus back into the city. (Still no trams in 2010, as the construction work was less than half finished.) Waving goodbye to the others, I got off just after Roseburn, crossed the road and walked the hundred yards or so to my house. It seemed such a mundane end to the fortnight: getting off a bus at the top of the street like I did so often coming home from college.

For days afterwards it was odd not to be checking in all the time. Not arranging to meet in Chinatown, on the Left Bank, or in the Marais. The experience had been a cross between a holiday, living in a student hall of residence and being in a Fringe show. The way that sharing meals, especially breakfast at the start of every day, heightens friendships. We're used to meeting friends for lunch or dinner, but breakfast is usually only shared with the people we live with, and that's what it had felt like: an extended family, two dozen of us, in Paris.

In June 2024 Éric Hazan died. He was a leading intellectual on the Left. In his forties he took over the family publishing house – Éditions Hazan – and then when that was subsequently taken over by Hachette Éric left to form a new company, La Fabrique, which concentrated on political writing and critical theory. As well as publishing the work of others, he started writing himself, particularly exploring Paris.

The Invention of Paris had been an important book for me, back in the early days after the trip, as I developed the post-Paris aspects of what was to become this book. That, and his *A Walk Through Paris*, was both encouraging and dispiriting to my progress, depending on my mood. If I felt good about the idea, they showed that my subject matter was of interest to a wider readership; but when I had doubts, they seemed to be the books I wanted to write, already written and on the shelf. I admired his easy writing style and the apparently effortless way he brought together history and geography to tell a story that spanned hundreds of years, all from an unashamedly leftwing perspective.

Later in the summer Paris was at the centre of the world's attention with the staging of the Olympics and Paralympics. Rather than the usual stadium event, it was the wider city and in particular the River Seine that was to be the focus of an innovative opening ceremony. Sitting in my living room in Portobello, I was transported back to locations I knew and locations I'd missed. Me being me, I couldn't ignore how a-geographical was the route the story took, but I loved all the references, big and small, to French cultural life.

Like the moment when the Pont d'Austerlitz exploded with a tricolore of fireworks to mark the start of the six-and-a-half-kilometre river procession. The first boat, carrying the Greek team, came through the smoke beneath the arches of a bridge I remembered walking over on my way to the Jardin des Plantes on the second Tuesday. As the other national teams followed on (in alphabetical order as usual, but in French, which I took a moment to realise when the German team appeared earlier than expected from my Anglocentric viewpoint), the attention switched to the first of the twelve 'scènes' – 'stages' but also a pleasing homophone for the river itself. The first was called 'Enchanté', and while it started on a temporary set of golden steps leading down from the Square Barye at the upstream tip of the Île Saint-Louis, after Lady Gaga had finished her number it moved down the channel between the island and the Left Bank. There, eighty dancers from the Moulin Rouge performed a can-can in the rain across from where Lorraine and I sat eating pastries in 2013. Then, as the camera panned round, there was the apartment block that features in my first Blip. Overhead, the masked flame-carrier sped between the two islands on a zip-wire above the bridge where Petr and I had stopped to listen to the band playing that first Sunday.

The second scène began, and as its name came up on screen I clapped my hands with delight. The title was 'Synchronicité' – a close cousin of serendipity, a concept that had been such a feature of my time in Paris. My reading of the two is that much of the difference between them depends on how we think about the meaningful coincidences they each describe. Serendipity celebrates the unexpected and unplanned, ascribing instances to the randomness of chance. Synchronicity, on the other hand,

Samedi 8 mai / 2024

believes a mystical or spiritual force to be at work, somehow guiding us along a particular path. The sceptic in me favours the former.

'Synchronicité' focused on the workers restoring Notre-Dame, and the dancers on the scaffold reminded me of something I'd seen when I was studying in London in the mid 1980s. There was a spectacular outdoor concert at London's County Hall, back in the last months of the Greater London Council. The sixty-plus saxophone players who arrived on forklift trucks and mobile cranes in the car park behind the council building were all members of the French avant-garde group Urban Sax. And there was Notre-Dame itself, where more than once I'd watched pigeons and tourists in front of the west facade.

The masked figure who linked the scènes together moved on to the Monnaie de Paris and the making of the Olympic medals, each one incorporating a piece of the Eiffel Tower. The medals were supposedly transferred into elaborate carrying cases, which were used in a dance number on the Pont-Neuf. Looking down onto the bridge, I remembered gazing over the parapet, wondering what it would be like to jump in like Michèle and Alex, and meeting Sophy there as we hurried around, fitting in our last bits of sightseeing.

The Pont-Neuf was also used in 'Liberté' and then 'Egalitié' was on the Pont des Artes. I thought back to watching the dancers being filmed there, and to taking photographs in the early evening as people crossed the bridge on the way home from work, and the artist who was painting the view upstream. The padlocks we saw in 2013 long gone.

The fifth scène – 'Fraternité' – moved inside the Louvre and featured a video sequence of paintings emptied of people, including Gericault's *Raft of the Medusa*. As referenced in the Asterix joke, the grave in Père Lachaise. I never made it inside the Louvre in 2010, or 2013, but then the action shifted to the Musée d'Orsay across the river. Seeing Eva in the queue outside on free-entry Sunday. Me later looking for, but not finding, *Whistler's Mother*.

Through all this the flotilla of athletes continued to pass by, now through an avenue of golden statues commemorating great French women – 'Sororité' – and past a singer atop the Grand Palais, where Petr, Agni and I stopped on our last afternoon. The athletes glided past 'Sportive', a set of barges on which people demonstrated different sports, reminding me of watching roller-hockey games in the park leading down from Les Invalides to the Pont Alexandre III.

The procession was approaching the venue for the culmination of the ceremony but not before the truly spectacular 'Solidarité', in which a spotlit silver horse and rider made their way along the river. The horse was mechanical, the rider real, representing the goddess Sequana, the spirit of the River Seine itself. I knew about this myth after reading Sciolino's book, but there continues to be debate over who the rider was meant to represent. Anglocentric sources describe her as Joan of Arc (Jeanne d'Arc), the patron saint of France, but most French sources only mention Sequana. So perhaps the reference to Joan was so obvious in France that it didn't need stating, or maybe one observation in English that the rider looked like Joan of Arc got repeated and amplified and has become internet-true.

Watching the silver horse galloping up the river in the dark, past all those familiar locations, brought a lump to my throat. The fact that it was tipping it down helped. All the flags of the competing nations, all the people on the riverbank, drenched, taking pictures with their phones. The horsewoman, now on a real horse after a creative sleight of hand, joined the parade across the Pont d'Iéna and into the arena on top of the Trocadéro fountains. The fountains that Agni and I had walked around on May the Fourth.

Samedi 8 mai / 2024

At the Louvre the flame was handed over to a series of French athletes and then carried into the Jardin des Tuileries, where the balloon-like Olympic cauldron was lit above the Grand Bassin Rond. This was where Lorraine and I ate clafoutis, and Petr, Sophy, Graeme and I walked on the first Tuesday afternoon. It had been a long ceremony, four hours, but to me it was a deep refresh of the moveable feast. A long, leisurely, and sweetly nostalgic view, of the city I'd once got to know for fifteen days.

Fifteen Years of Paris

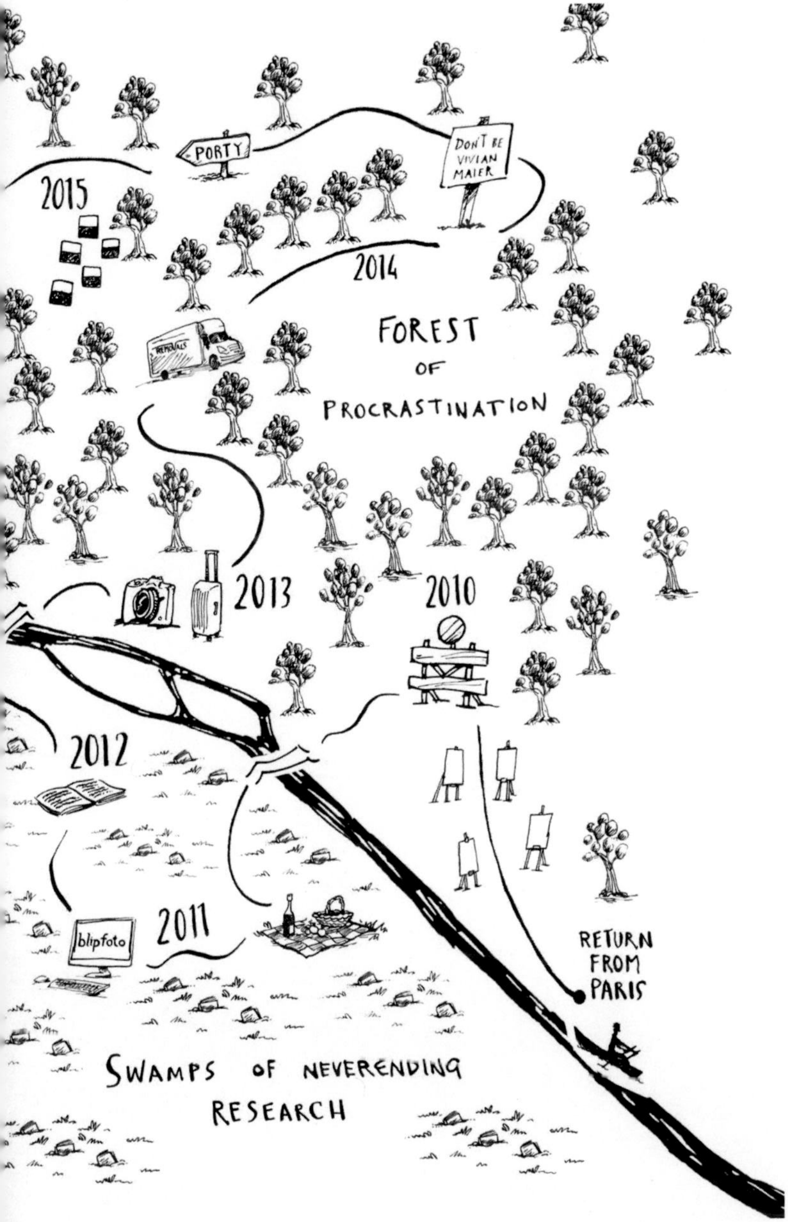

PORTY
DON'T BE VIVIAN MAIER
2015
2014
REMOVALS
FOREST OF PROCRASTINATION
2013
2010
2012
blipfoto
2011
RETURN FROM PARIS
SWAMPS OF NEVERENDING RESEARCH

Acknowledgements

There are lots of people to thank in the creation of this book. I should start with the people I was in Paris with in 2010: my twenty-four fellow students and in particular my room-mate Petr and the other friends I spent most time with – Agni, Jo and Sophy. Special thanks to Anita for telling me about Blipfoto in that café close to the Shoah museum. And Trish, Anna, Sam, Marcin, Graeme, Iza, Diane, Sara and Scott, who I spent time with exploring Paris at some point in the two weeks. Thanks also to the two college lecturers who came with us – Graham and Matthew – and the friends I made from the partner college, notably Aurélie and Alex.

Thanks to my parents, who brought me and my sister up to have enquiring minds and who took us to Paris, the first time, back in 1976.

Since Paris a lot of people, too numerous to mention all by name, have listened and encouraged as I have discussed my ideas for the book: my wider family, friends, and people on Blipfoto.

Thanks to Eugenia for leading our group through the Artist's Way course in Tribe and for the rest of the group that helped and encouraged, especially Philippa, who hosted our group that continued to meet after the end of the course.

Coming to the book itself, I must thank Tom for his wonderful illustrations that capture the fifteen days in Paris and the fifteen years of the book-writing project.

Acknowledgements

Thanks to Paul for writing the Foreword – he is an inspirational figure to me for his work in establishing the Big Beach Busk and for his regular writing on his Substack.

Thanks to Morag and Stuart for their help in scanning the slides I took in Paris in 1976.

Finally, thanks to Lorraine. Without her I suspect I'd still be working in IT, clock-watching towards retirement. She has encouraged and supported my creativity as long as we've been together. More specifically, I'm very grateful beyond words for her editorial and design expertise. By coming out of retirement to work on this book, she has made it better in so many ways.

List of photographs

All photographs © Jon Davey

1. (p. 16) Eiffel Tower and Pont de Bir-Hakeim, 1976.
2. (p. 17) Toy yachts in front of Luxembourg Palace, 1976.
3. (p. 29) Flats on the Quai aux Fleurs, 2010.
4. (p. 33) Middle Meadow Walk, 2011.
5. (p. 36) Houseboat at Pont-Neuf, 2010.
6. (p. 38) Vélib bikes, 2010.
7. (p. 41) Edinburgh phototrail, 2011.
8. (p. 45) Rue du Petit-Musc, 2010.
9. (p. 49) Festival Square, 2011.
10. (p. 58) Galerie Vivienne, 2010.
11. (p. 60) Le plan, 2012.
12. (p. 65) Palais-Royal, 2010.
13. (p. 69) Eiffel Tower cake, 2012.
14. (p. 71) Bastille Day planning, 2012.
15. (p. 80) Farmers' protest on Boulevard Voltaire, 2010.
16. (p. 83) Flowering wisteria, 2013.
17. (p. 86) Quartermile from Bruntsfield Links, 2013.
18. (p. 91) Flats on the Quai aux Fleurs from Left Bank, 2013.
19. (p. 93) Communards' Wall, Père Lachaise, 2013.
20. (p. 94) Tape Bar, 2013.
21. (p. 95) Love padlocks on Pont des Arts, 2013.
22. (p. 97) Eiffel Tower, 2010.

23. (p. 101) Hôtel des Invalides from Musée Rodin
24. (p. 103) Where we went, 2013.
25. (p. 108) Jardin des Plantes, 2010.
26. (p. 113) Eiffel Tower, 2010.
27. (p. 115) Stall on Rue Mouffetard, 2010.
28. (p. 117) Fishmonger on Rue Mouffetard, 2010.
29. (p. 120) Lost dog poster on Avenue des Gobelins, 2010.
30. (p. 124) Setting up on Boulevard Richard-Lenoir, 2010.
31. (p. 125) Market stall on Boulevard Richard-Lenoir, 2010.
32. (p. 127) Sacré-Cœur, 2010.
33. (p. 131) Mum's funeral, 2015.
34. (p. 134) Montmartre Cemetery, 2010.
35. (p. 135) Truffaut's grave, 2010.
36. (p. 136) Montmartre Cemetery cat, 2010.
37. (p. 141) Moulin Rouge, 2010.
38. (p. 142) Agni and Jo, 2010.
39. (p. 148) Arc de Triomphe, 2010.
40. (p. 149) Buildings at La Défense, 2010
41. (p. 155) Reflections at La Défense, 2010.
42. (p. 156) Arc de Triomphe from La Défense, 2010.
43. (p. 161) Flowers for Raymond, 2010.
44. (p. 162) Muguet box on street, 2010.
45. (p. 165) Yellow men in Paris, 2020.
46. (p. 179) Eiffel Tower, 2010.
47. (p. 180) Polish soldiers at Arc de Triomphe, 2010.
48. (p. 185) Colette's grave, Père Lachaise, 2010.
49. (p. 186) Chopin's grave, Père Lachaise, 2010.
50. (p. 188) Snail, Père Lachaise, 2010.
51. (p. 192) Oscar Wilde's grave, Père Lachaise, 2010.
52. (p. 204) À la memoire, Rue des Rosiers, 2010.
53. (p. 207) Decisive yellow man, 2020.
54. (p. 215) Love padlocks on Pont des Arts, 2010.
55. (p. 217) Jardin des Plantes platform, 2010.

List of Photographs

56. (p. 218) Palais-Royal, 2010.
57. (p. 229) Panthéon from Sacré-Cœur, 2010
58. (p. 232) Paradis Latin, 2010.
59. (p. 233) Traiteur window, 2010.
60. (p. 235) Foucault's pendulum, Panthéon, 2010.
61. (p. 241) Roller hockey, 2010.
62. (p. 245) City walls, 2010.
63. (p. 248) Hôtel de Sens, 2010.
64. (p. 251) Foujiyama stern, 2010.
65. (p. 251) Foujiyama bow, 2010.
66. (p. 253) Pigeons at Notre-Dame, 2010.
67. (p. 254) People on the steps, 2010.
68. (p. 255) Painter on Pont des Arts, 2010.
69. (p. 256) Work in progress map, 2022.
70. (p. 266) Vendôme Column, 2010.
71. (p. 268) Agni and Petr, 2010.
72. (p. 269) Champs-Élysées and Arc de Triomphe, 2010.
73. (p. 270) Flag at Arc de Triomphe, 2010.
74. (p. 274) Airport platforms, 2010.
75. (p. 275) Airport architecture, 2010.

Sources

Books

Arthus-Bertrand, Yann and Gérard Gefen. *Paris: Vu du Ciel*. Paris: Éditions du Chêne, 2002.
Baxter, John. *The Most Beautiful Walk in the World: A Pedestrian in Paris*. London: Short Books, 2012.
Bayles, David and Ted Orland. *Art and Fear: Observations on the Perils (and Rewards) of Artmaking*. Santa Cruz: Image Continuum Press, 2009.
Benjamin, Walter. 'The Work of Art in the Age of Mechanical Reproduction'. In: Hannah Arendt (ed.), *Illuminations*. New York: Schocken Books, 1969.
Benjamin, Walter. *Charles Baudelaire: A Lyric Poet in the Era of High Capitalism*. Translated by Harr Zohn. London: Verso, 1997.
Benjamin, Walter. *The Arcades Project*. Translated by Howard Eiland and Kevin McLaughlin. Cambridge: Harvard University Press, 2002.
Cameron, Julia. *The Artist's Way*. London: Pan, 1995.
Carhart, T. E. *The Piano Shop on the Left Bank*. London: Vintage, 2001.
Castigliano, Federico. *Flâneur: The Art of Wandering the Streets of Paris*. Self-published, 2017.
Chéroux, Clément. *Henri Cartier-Bresson*. Translated by David H. Wilson. London: Thames and Hudson, 2013.
Clear, James. *Atomic Habits*. London: Random House, 2018.
Conrad, Winston. *Hemingway's France*. Emeryville, California: Woodford Press, 2000.
Constantine, Helen (ed. and translator). *Paris Tales*. Oxford: Oxford University Press, 2004.
Couperie, Pierre. *Paris through the ages*. Translated by Marilyn Low. London: Barrie and Jenkins, 1970
De Waal, Edmund. *The Hare With Amber Eyes*. London: Vintage: 2011.
Dorment, Richard and Margaret F. MacDonald. *Whistler*. London: Tate Gallery, 1994.

Dyer, Geoff. *Paris Trance*. Edinburgh: Canongate, 1998.
Eco, Umberto. *Foucault's Pendulum*. London: Picador, 1990.
Elkin, Lauren. *Flâneuse: Women Walk the City in Paris, New York, Tokyo, Venice and London*. London: Vintage, 2016.
Falloux, Count de. *The Writings of Madame Swetchine*. Translated by H.W. Preston. Boston: Roberts Brothers, 1869.
Gallant, Mavis. *Paris Stories*. New York: New York Review of Books, 2002.
Gallix, Andrew. *We'll Never Have Paris*. London: Repeater Books, 2019.
Goldsworthy, Andy. *Midsummer Snowballs*. London: Thames and Hudson, 2001.
Hazan, Éric. *The Invention of Paris: A History in Footsteps*. Translated by David Fernbach. London: Verso, 2011.
Hazan, Éric. *A Walk Through Paris: A Radical Exploration*. Translated by David Fernbach. London: Verso, 2019.
Hemingway, Ernest. *A Moveable Feast*. New York: Scribner, 2003.
Hemingway, Ernest. *A Moveable Feast: The Restored Edition*. London: Arrow, 2011.
Hemingway, Ernest. *On Paris*. London: Hesperus Press, 2013.
James, William. *The Principles of Psychology*. New York: Henry Holt and Company, 1890.
Jones, Colin. *Paris: Biography of a City*. London: Penguin, 2006.
Loridan-Ivens, Marceline. *But You Did Not Come Back*. Translated by Sandra Smith. London: Faber and Faber, 2017.
McAuliffe, Mary. *When Paris Sizzled*. Lanham: Roman and Littlefield, 2016.
McAuliffe, Mary. *Paris on the Brink*. Lanham: Roman and Littlefield, 2018.
McLain, Paula. *The Paris Wife*. London: Virago, 2012.
Miller, Andrew. *Pure*. London: Sceptre, 2012.
Miller, Henry. 'The Eye of Paris'. In Henry Miller, *The Wisdom of the Heart*. New York: New Directions, 2016.
Perec, Georges. *Life: A User's Manual*. Translated by David Bellos. London: Collins Harvill, 1988.
Perec, Georges. *An Attempt at Exhausting a Place in Paris*. Translated by Marc Lowenthal. Cambridge: Wakefield Press, 2010.
Phillips, Andrew and Ginette Vincendeau. *Paris in the Cinema: Beyond the Flâneur*. London: Palgrave, 2018.
Rosnay, Tatiana de. *Sarah's Key*. London: John Murray, 2008.
Rutherford, Edward. *Paris*. London: Hodder and Stoughton, 2013.
Sciolino, Elaine. *The Seine: The River That Made Paris*. New York: W. W. Norton and Company, 2020.
Sinclair, Iain. *Lights Out for the Territory*. London: Penguin, 2003.
Süskind, Patrick. *Perfume: The Story of a Murderer*. Translated by John E. Woods. London: Penguin, 1987.
Thorpe, Adam. *Ulverton*. London: Vintage, 1988.

Tuffley, David. *The Artful Traveller: The Flâneur's Guidebook*. Altiora Publications, 2013.
White, Edmund. *The Flâneur: A Stroll Through the Paradoxes of Paris*. London: Bloomsbury, 2001.

Articles

'2010: 45th Amstel Gold Race', *Pro Cycling Stats*.
'7 bis Boulevard Saint-Germain', *Wikimedia Commons*.
'8 May 1945: day of victory' (English), *Chemins de Mémoire*.
'A Stroll Down the History of "Boulevard"', *Merriam-Webster*.
'About the Project', *The Jane Stirling Project*.
Aggas, J. E. 'Paris Meridian … Geometry', *Decoding Satan*, 27 May 2016.
'AGORIA { Le Code d'Orsay } · Digital Art', *Musée d'Orsay*.
Ali, Tariq. 'Eric Hazan: Friend, Comrade, Publisher', *Verso: Blog*, 7 June 2024.
'Art: Marie Krøyer', *The Arts Intel Report*.
Associated Press. '"France organised this": Macron denounces state role in Holocaust atrocity', *Guardian*, 17 July 2017.
Auster, Paul. 'Auggie Wren's Christmas Story', *New York Times*, 25 December 1990.
Avedon, Richard. 'Dovima with Elephants, Evening Dress by Dior, Cirque d'Hiver, Paris', *Harper's Bazaar*, September 1955.
Beack, Stephanie. 'Clafoutis, Flaugnarde? Both? Neither?', *Scrumptious Street Blog: A Place At My Table*, 10 November 2009.
'Biography', *Iya Traore*.
'Bridge of Love', *Vrnjačka Banja*.
Burchett-Vass, G. M. E. 'Asterix in translation: the genius of Anthea Bell and Derek Hockridge', *Aunty Muriel's Blog*, 23 December 2012.
Callow, James. 'Alejandro Valverde given two-year doping ban', *Guardian*, 1 June 2010.
'Camille Caudel', *Musée Rodin*.
Carlo, Anne-Lise. 'The story of a street: Oberkampf, from working-class area to lively bric-a-brac', *Le Monde*, 2 March 2024.
Cazes, Séverine. 'La manifestation des agriculteurs a fait le plein', *Le Parisien*, 28 Avril 2010.
'César-François Cassini de Thury: Biography', *MacTutor*.
'Closing of the Centre Pompidou: the museum will not reopen until 2030', *Sortir à Paris*.
'Colonnes de Buren – Palais-Royal', *Travel France Online*.
'Coupe de France: Horeau the hero for PSG', *ESPN*, 2 May 2010.
Critchley, Mark. '"A biological bomb": The story of the Champions League game which sparked Italy's coronavirus crisis'. *Independent*, 6 April 2020.

Cuddy, Alice and Bruno Boelpaep. 'Notre-Dame fire: Has too much money been given to rebuild it?', *BBC News*, 25 April 2019.
'Cycling 101: The Monuments', *EF Pro Cycling*, 6 October 2023.
Darcy-Roquencourt, Jacques. 'Boulevard du Temple', *L'Invention de la Photographie*, 15 December 2007.
Davey, Jon. 'Life: A User's Manual', *Blipfoto*, 25 April 2010.
Davey, Jon. 'The Inauthentic Fan', *Nutmeg*, Issue 14 (December 2019).
Debord, Guy. 'Theory of the Dérive', translated by Ken Knabb. *Internationale Situationnist* #2, 1958.
Dhaliwal, Ranjit. 'The birth of the daguerreotype – picture of the day', *Guardian*, 9 January 2013.
'Diana Tixier Herald: Quotes', *Goodreads*.
'Did You Know? A Tomb in the Montparnasse Cemetery Is Covered with Metro Tickets', *Sortir à Paris*.
'DK B91', *The Fragments of Heraclitus*.
'Domestic Box Office For 1987', *Box Office Mojo by IMDP Pro*.
'Dominique François Jean Arago: Biography', *MacTutor*.
'Dundee derby', *Wikipedia*.
'Dunkeld', *Undiscovered Scotland*.
Easby, Rebecca Jeffrey. 'Louis-Jacques-Mandé Daguerre, Paris Boulevard or View of the Boulevard du Temple', *Smarthistory*.
Edemariam, Aida. 'Wild, controversial and free: Colette, a life too big for film', *Guardian*, 7 January 2019.
Eliasson, Olafur. 'Ice Watch', *Olafur Eliasson*.
Elisa, 'Statue Henri IV, Pont Neuf – History and Legends', *World in Paris*.
'En Avant! Un Jour, un objet: Avant le selfie sur le Pont Neuf . . . la première photo en plein air !', *Musée des arts et métiers*.
'Film: Beaumarchais', *TV Tropes*.
'Fortnight', *An enthusiast's lexicon*, 11 March 2011.
Fotheringham, William. 'Alberto Contador gets two-year ban and stripped of 2010 Tour de France', *Guardian*, 6 February 2012.
'Free Your Love. Save Our Bridges', *No Love Locks*.
Frost, Rosie. 'Will cars be banned in Paris after lockdown', *euro news*, 15 May 2020.
Galliot, Lorena and Perrine Mouterde. 'These tractors belong to banks not farmers', *France 24*, 27 April 2010.
Garcia, Patricia. 'How to Watch *Star Wars* If You've Never Seen It Before', *Vogue*, 28 April 2020.
Gee, Oliver. 'The Paris wall: How to find remnants of the 1190 Philippe Auguste Wall', *The Earful Tower*, 4 June 2018.
Godfrey, Mark. 'Red Star: the oldest, hippest and most political football club in Paris', *Guardian*, 20 January 2018.

Sources

Goldberg, Alexander. 'France faces up to its Holocaust role', *Guardian*, 15 March 2010.
'Greyfriars Bobby's nose jobs [sic] fails two days after restoration', *BBC News*, 3 October 2013.
'Greyfriars Bobby's nose rubbing plea by Edinburgh Officials', *BBC News*, 31 October 2014.
Guerin, Orla. 'Hagia Sophia: Turkey turns iconic Istanbul museum into mosque', *BBC News*, 17 July 2020.
'Han shot first', *Fandom: Wookieepedia*.
Hawtree, Christopher. 'Raymond Mason obituary', *Guardian*, 25 February 2010.
'Henry IV', *Biography*.
'Heraclitus', *Stanford Encyclopedia of Philosophy*.
'Historic England Research Records: Abberwick', *Heritage Gateway*.
'History of the Panthéon', *Panthéon*.
Ihl, Olivier. 'In the Eye of The Daguerreotype. On the Rue du Faubourg-du-Temple in June 1848', *Research Gate*, August 2018.
'Jardin des Grands Explorateurs Marco Polo et Cavelier de la Salle', *EU Touring*.
Jerome, 'A visit to the Café de la Régence', *Paul Morphy Historical Research on 19th century Chess*, 10 November 2023.
Jordan, Stuart. 'British Doubledeckers', *Gaugemasters*.
'June Days uprising', *Wikipedia*.
'June Days: Paris 1848', *libcom*.
Kastner, Julia. 'Teaser Tuesdays: *This Is Where You Belong* by Melody Warnick', *Pages of Julia*, 7 June 2016.
Kington, Tom. 'The novel that has got young lovers declaring their passion with padlocks', *Guardian*, 24 August 2011.
Lawrence, Katrina. 'In Search of the Paris of Pierre Beaumarchais, Playwright of the Marriage of Figaro', *Paris for Dreamers*, 30 November 2022.
Lawrence, Katrina. 'The Marvellous Tale of the Merry-go-Round', *Paris for Dreamers*, 11 March 2019.
Leah, Vicky. 'Origins of the Fête du Muguet', *French Style*.
'L'été s'invite au coeur du printemps', *Le Parisien*, 26 Avril 2010.
'Liège – Bastogne – Liège 2010', *Cycling News*, 25 April 2010.
'Ligue1: 2007–08', *Transfermarkt*.
Liu, Rebecca. '"I never understood the hate": behind the scenes on Emily in Paris, TV's guiltiest pleasure', *Guardian*, 10 August 2024.
Lombardi, Esther. 'Abelard and Heloise', *ThoughtCo*, 30 May 2019.
'Lucas talks as "Star Wars" trilogy returns', *Today*, 15 September 2004.
'Metro line 2: a line and its history', *RATP*.
'National Workshops', *Wikipedia*.
'Œuvres d'art', *Paris La Défense*.

O'Hagan, Sean. 'Robert Capa and Gerda Taro: love in a time of war', *Guardian*, 13 May 2012.
Overgaard, Thorsten. '85 years later: Behind Gare St. Lazare', *Thorsten von Overgaard's Photography Website*, 25 June 2017.
'Paris "love locks" removed from bridges', *BBC News*, 1 June 2015.
'Paris Sacre-Coeur granted historic status despite bloody history', *France 24*, 13 October 2022.
'Paris Saint-Germain: Overview', *Planet Sport*.
'Paris', *Space Invaders*.
Park-Froud, Victoria. 'My Money: "No expenditure at all today!"', *BBC News*, 17 May 2020.
Patowary, Kaushik. 'Foucault Pendulum And The Pantheon', *Amusing Planet*, 31 October 2018.
'Pierre-Augustin Caron de Beaumarchais', *Britannica*.
'Portobello', *City of Edinburgh Council*.
Rathbone, Ellen. 'How Fast Does Spring Move Northward?', *An Adirondack Naturalist in Central New York*, 18 April 2009.
'Raymond Mason, sculptures and drawings', *OpenBibArt History of Art Bibliography*.
Reid, Carlton. 'Parisian Boulevards Built Wide Not For Cars But To Better Quell Street Protests', *Forbes*, 20 December 2018.
Reid, Lauren. 'The Flodden Wall', *Atlas Obscura*.
Renaud, Eric. 'Pont-Neuf', *Come To Paris*.
Russell, Michael (writing as 'Feorlean'). 'Anything that gives off light', *Blipfoto*, 18 August 2016.
Sabes, Sylvia. 'Ghostly Paris: Eerie Itineraries in the City of Light', *Hip Paris*, 1 November 2023.
Schofield, Hugh. 'Why I shun the crass, expensive, naff Champs Elysees', *BBC News*, 13 October 2013.
'Seinfeld: Quotes', *IMDb*.
Simon, Scott. 'Opinion: In Paris, heroes carry espresso', *New Orleans Public Radio*, 9 July 2022.
Smith, Khalil. 'What Airbnb Got Right About Announcing Layoffs', *Forbes*, 6 May 2020.
'Speech by the President of the Republic Emmanuel Macron at the Vel d'Hiv commemoration' (English), *Élysée: Official website of the President of France*, 18 July 2017.
Spencer, Luke. 'Montmartre Cemetery', *Atlas Obscura*.
Spindel, Carol. 'A Line Through the Heart of Paris', *Guernica*, 16 November 2016.
'Spring phenology analysis 2015', *Woodland Trust*.
'Stalingrad name to be revived for anniversaries', *BBC News*, 1 February 2013.

Stephen, Phyllis, 'Five things you need to know today Edinburgh!', *Edinburgh Reporter*, 6 August 2016.
Stimmler, Heather. 'Vintage Toy Boats in Luxembourg Gardens', *Secrets of Paris*, 11 June 2015.
Story, Henry. 'Code, Models and Covid-19', *Medium*, 13 May 2020.
Sturgeon, Nicola. 'Coronavirus (COVID-19) update: First Minister's speech 21 May 2020', *Scottish Government*, 21 May 2020.
Taylor, Brian. 'Coronavirus: A route map out of crisis is revealed', *BBC News*, 21 May 2020.
'The 48 Hour Film Project Experience', *The 48 Hour Film Project*.
'The Dome (Tomb of Napoleon)', *Musée de l'Armée*.
'The Lifeboat "MONA" Disaster 8th December 1959', *Friends of Dundee City Archives*.
'The Mona Lifeboat Disaster', *Dundee Maritime Project*.
'The Relief Map Museum' (English), *Musée des Plans-Reliefs*.
'The Vélodrome d'Hiver (Vél d'Hiv) Roundup', *Holocaust Encyclopedia*.
Thibault, Charles-François, 'La Barricade de la rue Saint-Maur-Popincourt', *L'Illustration*, 279–280 (8 July 1848), p. 276.
'Tombs in the Panthéon de Paris', *Wikimedia Commons*.
'Tonight with the Impressionists, Paris 1874', *Fever*.
'Translation closest to original Heraclitus quote "no man steps in the same river twice, for it is not the same river and he is not the same man"', *Stack Exchange: Latin Language*, 26 July 2024.
Tremlett, Giles. 'Gerda Taro: "deathbed photo" of one of the world's first war photographers found', *Guardian*, 19 January 2018.
'Venice Revealed', *Grand Palais Immersif*.
Walker, David L. 'Balta Sound and the Figure of the Earth', *Sheetlines*, 99 (April 2014).
'Where do I find Edmund Wilson's quote "No two persons ever read the same book"?', *Stack Exchange: Literature*, 10 May 2017.
Willsher, Kim. 'François Hollande sorry for wartime deportation of Jews', *Guardian*, 22 July 2012.
Willsher, Kim. 'Oh l'amour: Paris bridge rail collapses under weight of too much love', *Guardian*, 9 June 2014.
Willsher, Kim. 'Story of cities #12: Haussmann rips up Paris – and divides France to this day', *Guardian*, 31 March 2016.
Wood, Greg and Rory Carrol. 'Cheltenham faces criticism after racegoers suffer Covid-19 symptoms', *Guardian*, 2 April 2020.
Wood, Zoe. 'Supermarket expansion means trouble in store for France's local shopkeepers', *Guardian*, 21 March 2011.
'World Cup 1938', *Planet World Cup*.

Yoo, Alice. 'Hundreds of Tourist Photos Weaved into One (18 total)', *My Modern Met*, 16 February 2011.
Zhang, Michael. 'A Glimpse Behind the Gare St. Lazare in Google Street View', *Peta Pixel*, 19 March 2012.

TV, Radio, Films and Theatre
Allen, Woody (dir.). *Midnight in Paris*, 2011.
Assayas, Olivier, Frédéric Auburtin and Gurinder Chadha (dirs.). *Paris, Je T'aime*, 2006.
Bird, Brad and Jan Pinkava (dirs.). *Ratatouille*, 2007.
Carax, Leos (dir.). *Les Amants du Pont-Neuf*, 1991.
Dare, Bill (prod.). *I've Never Seen Star Wars*, BBC Radio 4 / BBC Radio 4 Extra, 2008–2015.
Danby, Emma. *Starfish*, YouTube.
Dunnachie, Iain (dir.). *Robin's Saturday*, 1958.
Fincher, David (dir.). *Fight Club*, 1999.
Full Opening Ceremony: Full Replays: Paris Replays, Olympics YouTube, 12 August 2024.
Garelick, Jeremy (dir.). *Murder Mystery 2*, 2023.
Haze, Hulltoon. *Her Last Words*, YouTube.
Herrero, Fanny (creator). *Call My Agent!* (French: *Dix pour cent*), France 2, 2015–2020.
Jeunet, Jean-Pierre (dir.). *Amelie*, 2001.
Koltès, Bernard-Marie. *Dans la solitude des champs de coton*, 1986.
Lamorisse, Albert (dir.). *The Red Balloon*, 1956.
Linklater, Richard (dir.). *Before Sunset*, 2004.
Maloof, John and Charlie Siskel (dirs.). *Finding Vivian Maier*, 2013.
McCann, Lorraine. *A Rose for Chopin*, BBC Radio 4, 2003.
McQuarrie, Christopher (dir.). *Mission: Impossible – Fallout*, 2018.
Nuytten, Bruno (dir.). *Camille Claudel*, 1988.
Pushkin, Alexander. *Boris Godunov*, 1870.
Raw, Helen. *Mental*, Facebook.
Sansone, Leslie. *One Mile Happy Walk*, YouTube, 2015.
Sansone, Leslie. *Two Mile Walk*, YouTube, 2018.
Spielberg, Stephen (dir.). *Schindler's List*, 1993.
Stanley Donen (dir.). *Funny Face*, 1957.
Star, Darren (creator). *Emily in Paris*, Netflix, 2020–2024.
Syberberg, Hans-Jürgen. *Ein Traum, was sonst?*, 1990.
Wang, Wayne (dir.). *Smoke*, 1995.
Wright, Joe (dir.). *Coco Mademoiselle: The Film*, Chanel, 2011.